Quality in Crime Prevention

Erich Marks, Anja Meyer
and Ruth Linssen (Eds.):

Quality in Crime Prevention

December 2005
© 2005 by Landespräventionsrat Niedersachsen, Hanover
Setting and Design: Buch&media GmbH, Munich
Cover design: Kay Fretwurst, Freienbrink
Printed and published by Books on Demand GmbH, Norderstedt
Printed in Germany · ISBN: 3-8334-4194-1

Contents

Preface 7

Erich Marks, Anja Meyer, Ruth Linssen
The Beccaria-Project: Quality Management in Crime Prevention . 9

Lawrence W. Sherman
Enlightened Justice: Consequentialism and Empiricism
from Beccaria to Braithwaite 41

Paul Ekblom
The 5Is Framework: Sharing Good Practice in Crime Prevention .. 55

Ronald V. Clarke
Seven Principles of Quality Crime Prevention 85

Britta Bannenberg
Strategies for Effect-Oriented Crime Prevention –
The »Düsseldorfer Gutachten« 98

Lars Rand Jensen
Perspectives on Crime Prevention and Quality Management 113

Michel Marcus
Evaluation : For what Purpose? 130

Gorazd Meško, Mahesh Nalla, Andrej Sotlar
Cooperation of Police and Private Security Officers
in Crime Prevention in Slovenia 133

Harold K. Becker
Impact Analysis for Crime Evaluation 144

Jim Hilborn, Anu Leps
Crime Prevention Policy in Estonia 156

Radim Bureš
Crime Prevention System and Activities in the Czech Republic ... 179

Jörg Bässmann
Evaluation as an Element of Systematic
Crime Prevention in Germany 196

Anja Meyer, Volkhard Schindler, Jörg Bässmann,
Erich Marks and Ruth Linssen
The Beccaria Standards for Ensuring Quality in
Crime Prevention Projects. 201

Appendix 210
Vitae of Authors 211

Preface

The manifold aspects of ›quality‹ still only play a minor part in crime prevention. However, a positive aspect is the continual increase in corresponding debates in the field of practical crime prevention, sciences and politics. These focus on increasing the efficiency of crime prevention and are embedded in a framework of so-called evidence-based crime prevention. This publication covers important aspects of these debates. Furthermore, a perspective on how to integrate theoretical concepts and knowledge into practical crime prevention is developed.

This publication is based on lectures and discussions held at the First European Beccaria Conference on ›Visions of a better quality in crime prevention‹ which took place in Hanover (Germany) on 20th–22nd January 2005. The book as well as the conference are part of the ›Beccaria Project: Quality Management in Crime Prevention‹ at the Lower Saxony Crime Prevention Council (Lower Saxony Ministry of Justice). The Beccaria Project was realised from December 2003 to November 2005 and was supported by the European Commission's AGIS Programme – General Direction Justice and Home Affairs. Further information can be obtained from the Beccaria website at www.beccaria.de.

The editors wish to thank all those who have contributed to the realisation of this book: First of all, the editors are grateful for the financial support of the Beccaria Project by the European Commission – General Direction Justice and Finance as well as by the German state of Lower Saxony, who have made the publication of this book possible.

Many thanks go to the Beccaria Project's five EU partner organisations and their representatives, namely the Catholic University of Leuven (Belgium), the Crime Prevention Council (Denmark), the Ministry of

Preface

Justice (Estonia), the European Forum for Urban Safety (EFUS) (France) and the Association for Probation and Mediation in Justice (Czech Republic) for a successful and friendly cooperation.

The editors are especially indebted to the authors Lawrence W. Sherman, Paul Ekblom, Ronald Clarke, Britta Bannenberg, Lars Rand Jensen, Michel Marcus, Gorazd Meško, Mahesh Nalla, Andrej Sotlar, Harold Becker, Jim Hillborn, Anu Leps, Radim Bures, Jörg Bässmann and Volkhard Schindler for the contribution of their important work. Further details about the authors and their biographies can be found in the ›Authors‹ chapter.

Finally we would like to thank all those who have contributed to this project for their support and commitment. By name we would like to mention Giles Ekblom and Vivien-Marie Drews for their competent assistance with the translation of various parts of this publication.

Although the approaches and titles of the contributions in this publication differ from each other, they all focus on one aspect: the call for more quality in crime prevention (based on evaluation). In the future – even more than during previous times – any crime prevention activity will be judged according to the things we do, whether we do them right and whether they have a good result.

For the time being, the challenge will continue to be to sensitise people for the need for quality in crime prevention, to encourage the development of a consciousness for this issue, to convince crime prevention practitioners of the urgent need for quality in crime prevention and to inform – just as Cesare Beccaria did. At the beginning of his work he also had a vision in mind. On the front cover of his most famous work, it says »In rebus quibuscumque difficilioribus non expectandum, ut quis simul, et serat, et metat, sed praeparatione opus est, ut per gradus maturescant.«

Erich Marks, Anja Meyer and Ruth Linssen

Erich Marks/Anja Meyer/Ruth Linssen
Crime Prevention Council of Lower Saxony, Germany

The Beccaria-Project:
Quality Management in Crime Prevention

The discussion about increased quality is taking place in times of massive financial restrictions. Particularly in the field of crime prevention, the matter of discussion should not be how to reduce but rather how to systematically develop quality further. Terms such as »quality management« have been borrowed from the field of business management. Although they may give the impression that management jargon is increasingly entering into crime prevention, the intent of the project is not to apply economic principles to this field. The further development of quality should instead be understood as a future-oriented task. With the Beccaria Project, the State Prevention Council of Lower Saxony signals the prelude to a qualification campaign.

Initial Situation

Notwithstanding all the previous success in crime prevention, the question remains how to increase the quality of crime prevention in the future. The systematic evaluation of crime prevention projects or programmes is still a scarce commodity nationally and internationally. Crime prevention is quite often a »black box«. We often do not know why changes result from a certain project. Does a particular measure achieve the expected effect at all? How can the quality of crime prevention work be measured?

Realising high-quality crime prevention projects requires the definition of goals and target groups at the beginning of a project. The examination of goal achievement should no longer be an exception but a normal part of a project. What is needed in the future is the development of an *evaluation culture!*

Independent methods of quality measurement have not yet been developed in crime prevention. It therefore seems obvious to fill this gap, amongst others, via evaluation research, since there are points of contact between the approaches of evaluation research and quality assurance. One aim of evaluation is to use the results to improve the examined programmes. Evaluation research therefore means immediate and direct improvement of programmes. In quality assurance, this goal is equivalent to the concept of »continuous improvement« of work procedures as a basic principle of quality management.

On a long-term basis, the evaluation and further development of quality in European crime prevention requires a professionally and scientifically sound qualification of the people who work in prevention. Basic and further training in the area of crime prevention has not kept pace so far with the increase in importance which crime prevention has experienced over the last years. Thus crime prevention has not found its way into related professional training yet. However, the impression that »anyone can do prevention« is misleading. Prevention, like every other qualitatively demanding activity, requires professionalisation or sound basic and further training. Only in this way can quality be assured in the process of prevention. In addition, terms are not used homogeneously by those involved in crime prevention. If we want to exchange information on prevention and evaluation or compare projects across Europe, we first have to come to an agreement on key terms of crime prevention. A homogeneous set of (conceptual) differentiation and description possibilities is lacking. So far, the search for a common »prevention language« or terminology in Europe has been in vain. A synopsis of the most important specialised terms (for example in the form of a glossary) could be a crucial contribution towards overcoming language barriers in this connection.

The Beccaria Project

Within the scope of the AGIS[1] programme of the EU, the State Prevention Council of Lower Saxony (in the state Ministry of Justice) is implementing the »Beccaria Project: Quality Management in Crime Prevention« in cooperation with institutions from European partner countries

---

[1] http://europa.eu.int/comm/justice_home/funding/agis/funding_agis_en.htm

such as Belgium, France, Denmark, the Czech Republic and Estonia. The Beccaria Project, which was authorised by AGIS in December 2003, lasts until November 2005.

The EU framework programme AGIS supports cooperation among police and courts in criminal cases. AGIS promotes projects in the areas of cooperation, the fight against organised crime, crime prevention and victim protection. Since 2003, this EU programme has replaced five previous EU programmes (Hippocrates, Grotius, OISIN, Falcone, and STOP). The goal of AGIS is to contribute towards a better cooperation among the member states and the acceding countries in preventing and fighting crime as well as in victim protection. Promoted projects serve the above-stated goals dealing with the promotion of cooperation among prosecution services, the basic and further training of people involved in combating crime or contain scientific research.

The »Beccaria Project: Quality Management in Crime Prevention« is named after the crime prevention theorist Cesare Beccaria (1738–1794). He is regarded as a pioneer of modern criminology and influenced the primacy of prevention in law enforcement policy. The objective of the project is to give Beccaria's ideas a firm basis by constantly improving the quality of prevention implementation. In summary, the following targets are being pursued:

The *main goal* is to further develop quality in crime prevention.

Sub-goals[2] of the project are:

1. *Sensitisation* to the topic of quality in crime prevention
2. Development of *(minimum) standards* for quality and evaluation
3. Improvement of *actions*
4. Promotion and establishment of *further training*

The general target group of the Beccaria Project consists of all interested participants and people responsible for crime prevention in Europe. After all, only a concerted effort by the numerous people involved can make quality and quality assurance a matter of course in crime prevention.

---

[2] The four (sub-)goals are understood to be of equal importance.

Step by Step to the Top: Quality

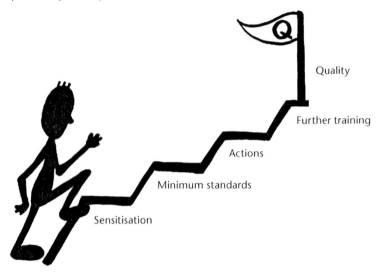

Beccaria Measures

The aims of the Beccaria Project have been laid down on a long-term basis and cannot be achieved overnight. For this reason, an action plan has been developed within the project to help further develop and improve crime prevention in all of Europe step by step. This catalogue of measures considers the needs and requirements which have to be satisfied on a short-term as well as on a long-term basis. It includes, among others:

- an *evaluation agency*
- an international *Beccaria Conference* to exchange information and establish a network of European participants in crime prevention
- minimum and minimal *standards for quality* and evaluation
- a fundamental course of studies or, in the long term, an academy for the *professional training of prevention specialists*.

In the following, the chosen measures are briefly described and explained. While this is not the entire programme of the Beccaria Project, it effectively illustrates the realisation of the whole project.

First Beccaria Conference: Quality in Crime Prevention

»Visions of higher quality standards in crime prevention« was the topic of the first Beccaria Conference, which took place on 20th–22nd January 2005 in Hanover/Germany[3].

The promotion of an international information exchange among European crime prevention experts with special regard to issues concerning »quality in crime prevention« was the defined objective of the conference, as well as benchmarking to learn from each other on a Europe-wide level. After all, an enhanced performance in crime prevention depends on the cooperation among European countries. The organisers of the conference were very happy to welcome renowned lecturers from the United States and Europe to support the conference and its call for quality standards in crime prevention. Although the approaches and titles of the different lectures at the Beccaria Conference were rather various, they still had something in common:

All the speakers focused on the issue of »quality in crime prevention« and there was great approval for the need to ask ourselves one crucial question: »What actually works in crime prevention?«, which yielded the following answers:
- We need an appropriate knowledge, for example about risk factors and relevant measures of protection.
- So far, only insufficient scientific context can be found in crime prevention.
- Scientific research on the impact of implemented measures has to be intensified.

---

[3] The Beccaria Conference is one of several initiatives of the Beccaria Project, which is realised by the Crime Prevention Council of Lower Saxony and financially supported by the EU Commission's AGIS Programme.

- From the very beginning, projects have to be designed in a way that makes evaluation possible.
- Crime prevention projects have to be based on regional analyses.
- The transfer of knowledge from science to practice has to be managed in an optimal fashion.
- Internationally available empirical data has to be considered more strongly than before.
- Crime prevention has to be organised according to a long-term perspective.
- The effectiveness of crime prevention has to be proven by appropriate empirical data or as Sherman puts it:

»Do not just believe in crime prevention, prove crime prevention through evaluation«.

The following abstracts give an impression of the lectures held on the first day of the conference[4].

Prof. Paul Ekblom[5] spoke about »The ›5 I's‹ framework: Sharing good practice in crime reduction«. Paul Ekblom is a professor at the University of Arts in London and is also engaged as a researcher for H.M. Home Office/London. He has been and is still engaged in activities with the EU, Europol, ICPC and the UN and is a scientific referee for an initiative of the Council of Europe concerned with co-operational matters in crime prevention. He strongly argues for »knowledge management« in crime prevention. At the Beccaria Conference he focused on a number of central issues to be considered when managing daily project work:

What effect is this project supposed to have? How can efficiency be achieved? How can work be conducted systematically? How can we be sure that we are actually doing the right thing? Knowledge in terms of evidence is most essential for the improvement of crime prevention activities. The sort of knowledge and information that is helpful to crime prevention practitioners was illustrated by Ekblom with the »*Five*

---

[4] The presentations are also available for downloading at www.beccaria.de.
[5] Ekblom's 5 I's and 5 K's also play a vital role at the EUCPN (European Crime Prevention Network). The application of the Five K's is intended to identify, judge, organise and transform good-practice projects in various European regions. For further information please visit www.crimereduction.gov.uk/learningzone/5isintro.htm

I's« – *Inclusion of »Best Practice«* in the reduction of crime. The »Five I's« symbolise a number of key points important for »best practice«
1. *Intelligence:* gathering and analysing information on crime problems, their causes and consequences such as risk and safety factors.
2. *Intervention:* undertaking action in order to block, disrupt or weaken those causes and risk factors, in ways which are evidence-based and appropriate to the crime problem and the context wherever possible.
3. *Implementation:* making the practical methods happen – putting them into action on the ground (according to regional/local needs).
4. *Involvement:* mobilising other agencies, companies and individuals in the community to play their part in implementing the intervention.
5. *Impact:* evaluating the impact of the action undertaken as well as its cost-effectiveness (assessment, feedback and adaptation).

The »Five I's« presuppose a certain knowledge about crime, which again can be summarized with the »Five K's«:
1. Know about crime problems such as crime types and patterns.
2. Know what works in preventing which crime problem in which context.
3. Know how to put into practice.
4. Know who to involve.
5. Know why.

Ekblom demands a sophisticated system to meet the difficulties and challenges of crime prevention and finds that the »Five I's« offer an appropriate orientation for this. He holds that it is necessary to invest in training and qualification as well as to further develop crime prevention to become an independent scientific discipline.

Britta Bannenberg is a professor at the University of Bielefeld/Germany. At the Beccaria Conference she spoke about the consequences of the Düsseldorfer Gutachten[6]. Prof. Bannenberg showed concern about the

---

[6] Please see: Düsseldorfer Gutachten: Empirisch gesicherte Erkenntnisse über

lack of scientific foundation of many communal crime prevention activities. She highlights the problems of the various activities in crime prevention and concludes that regional analyses are necessary in order to find answers for why problems accumulate in certain areas and how they can be contained by crime prevention. For Prof. Bannenberg, effective crime prevention depends on an area-wide early intervention and networking strategy of all the players involved. It is further dependent on an early and intensive support of families and children who already show signs of risk. In order to counteract any negative developments, it is necessary to have an appropriate knowledge about preventative factors and, after all, intervention will always have to take place on multiple levels[7].

Prof. Ron Clarke spoke about »Principles of Quality Crime Prevention« focusing on the conditions for high-quality crime prevention. Ron Clarke is a professor at the School of Criminal Justice at the Rutgers University/New Jersey and visiting professor at the Jill Dando Institute of Crime Science at the University College London[8]. His book »Become a Problem Solving Crime Analyst«[9], which he wrote with John Eck in 2003, covers the principles and practices of crime analysis.

This problem-, or rather problem-solving-oriented approach, represents less reactive but more foresighted policing work including the identification of crime patterns. Clarke named the following 7 principles of quality crime prevention:

> kriminalpräventive Wirkungen. Eine Sekundäranalyse der kriminalpräventiven Wirkungsforschung. Gutachten für die Landeshauptstadt Düsseldorf vom Institut für Kriminalwissenschaften und Fachbereich Psychologie – Sozialpsychologie – der Philipps-Universität Marburg. (Hrsg.) Landeshauptstadt Düsseldorf Arbeitskreis Vorbeugung und Sicherheit, 2002.
> [7] Britta Bannenberg finds there is a lack of comprehensive measures, as are found in the Olweus school programmes for example.
> [8] Ron Clarke also worked for the Home Office Research and Planning Unit for 15 years.
> [9] See also Ronald V Clarke and John Eck (2003) Become a Problem Solving Crime Analyst. Cullompton, UK: Willian Publishing; Derek B. Cornish and Ronald V. Clarke (2003) »Opportunities, Precipitators and Criminal Decisions. In Theory for Practice in Situational Crime Prevention, Crime Prevention Studies, Vol. 16 Monsey, NY: Criminal Justice Press: Website: www.popcenter.org.

1. Be clear about your objectives
2. Focus on very specific problems
3. Understand your problem
4. Be sceptical about displacement
5. Consider a variety of solutions
6. Anticipate implementation difficulties
7. Evaluate your results.

Clarke understands crime to be an interaction of the offender's motivation on the one side and the opportunity to conduct a crime on the other side.

It is crucial to put oneself into the offender's mind and to adopt the offender's perspective – to put it shortly: »Think thief«. Furthermore Clarke, being an exponent of situational crime prevention, argues for a reduction of crime opportunities by various technical appliances and therefore to:

1. increase the necessary effort to conduct a certain crime,
2. increase the risk of being detected, and
3. decrease the offender's profit.

The aim is to systematically make offending more difficult, more risky and – in the context of a cost-benefit calculation – less attractive. The aim is to ›manage‹ situations in order to reduce criminal activity by increasing surveillance, reducing opportunities and minimizing possible output. As the central tool of this approach, Clarke introduces the »Problem Analysis Triangle« [10]. The idea of the triangle is based on the assumption that three crucial elements to criminal activity exist, namely the offender, the victim and the site of a crime.

Per-Olof Wikström is a professor at the Institute of Criminology at the University of Cambridge. »Towards a Knowledge-based Crime Prevention« was his topic at the Beccaria Conference. Being the former Director of Research at the Swedish National Crime Prevention Council, Prof. Wikström is an expert when it comes to local partnerships for crime prevention. Wikström presents an approach to crime prevention which concentrates on developmental factors in terms of the offender. He stresses the importance of protective factors and the strengthening of parents' competences in bringing up their children to achieve a pro-social development and to

---

[10] The Problem Analysis Triangle: www.popcenter.org

overcome criminogenic patterns of behaviour in the first place. After all, structural problems have to be met by structural solutions.

Furthermore, Wikström is convinced that effective crime prevention can only evolve from scientific knowledge and evidence. Successful crime prevention has to be based on a long-term approach and is dependent on appropriate financial resources. However, instead of spending money on many small-scale projects, it seems much more effective to Wikström to concentrate on a few activities which are knowledge-based and therefore likely to produce a sustainable outcome. One has to know about the motivations which cause people to become offenders. Only then will it be possible to influence the factors which cause people to offend. The most efficient way to prevent offences is to keep people from considering a deviant action. Therefore, Wikström considers self-control and morals to be the most protective factors.

However, according to Hirschi and Gottfredson[11], whether Wikström understands self-control as the ability to discipline oneself remains open. Gottfredson and Hirschi differentiate between criminality (the tendency towards offending) and crime. The less one is able to stay self-controlled, the more criminality is likely to result in offending and criminal activity.

According to this assumption, Wikström differentiates between three groups:
1. the so-called protective group, which is able to resist criminal action.
2. the balanced group, in which criminal action is dependent on lifestyle.
3. the risk group, which is likely to offend.

Prof Lawrence Sherman[12] from Pennsylvania spoke about »Enlightened Justice: Empiricism and Consequentialism from Beccaria to Braithwaite«. The referee, who has acquired a global reputation with his »Sherman Report«, turned out to be a great philosophy expert. His contribution to the first Beccaria Conference was an expedition through the epochs, begin-

---

[11] About this concept of self-control please see: Gottfredson/Hirschi: A General Theory of Crime, Stanford, California, 1990.
[12] Please see: Sherman and others, Preventing Crime: What works, what doesn't, what's promising? 1997, www.preventingcrime.org

ning with the time of prosperity during the European Enlightenment in the second half of the 18th century, which brought to criminal justice the secularisation, rationalisation, liberalisation and humanisation of criminal law. Sherman looked at Beccaria's life and work – especially at his probably most famous work »Of crimes and Punishments«. Beccaria is renowned as a founder of the European and penologic Enlightenment as well as a pioneer of modern criminal justice policy.

According to Sherman, it is the Australian criminologist John Braithwaite who offers an enlightened perspective on criminal justice matters at the present time. Sherman characterises Braithwaite as a consequentialist without being a pure utilitarian. In his theory of »re-integrative shaming« (1989), Braithwaite tells us to disapprove and punish deviant behaviour while reintegrating the offender at the same time. Whereas the mischief of the deed has to be clearly pointed out to the offender, the offender himself must not be excluded from society nor must any other damaging intervention occur. The criminal action itself has to be isolated and excluded, but not the individual person, i.e. the offender. With this responsible regulation, the »sin« i.e. the offence will be condemned but not the »sinner«.

Prof. Pfeiffer spoke about »Scientific Research and Prevention – a Plea for Strict Evaluation«. The former Minister of Justice of Lower-Saxony and director of the KfN – Kriminologisches Forschungsinstitut Niedersachsen (Criminological Research Institute of Lower Saxony) highlighted three important steps:
1. The central precondition for the development of concepts for crime prevention is to prove a correlation of impact. Bivariate correlations are not sufficient: if A occurs and B can be witnessed, this does not prove any correlation of those two yet.
2. If a correlation of impact can be proven, ›Step 2‹, namely the planning of intervention, has to follow.
3. An evaluation of the intervention has to be conducted during a third phase.

Pfeiffer recommends that a project's participants be separated into an experimental and a control group. The evaluation of one's own project will also cause a certain blindness in terms of insufficient objectivity.

Furthermore, a well-planned evaluation has to start early during a project. Especially important for any preventative measure is the early detection of domestic violence. Possible signals have to be taken seriously as early as in nursery and primary school and appropriate intervention has to be planned and undertaken. The »Perry Preschool Study« from 1962 is probably the most famous longitudinal analysis of pre-school influences. It looked at 123 Afro-American families from Michigan whose children suffered from poverty and showed high risk factors and therefore were also at risk to fail in school. The children aged 3–4 (1962–1967) were divided into an experimental group and a control group. The children from the experimental group joined a nursery-school programme whereas the participants of the control group did not. Since then, both groups have been tested for certain characteristics such as general abilities and opinions on an annual basis. Finally 97% of the participants were interviewed again at the age of 40. It showed that those who had taken part in the education programme had achieved a higher level of education, enjoyed a better income and also led a more law-abiding life.[13]

The general result of the pre-school study was that prevention programmes which start at an early point, i.e. during childhood, do show a long-term effect.

Pfeiffer concludes that longitudinal analysis and a control group design are the best way to conduct this sort of research. However, in this context Pfeiffer sees Germany as still being a developing country. He demands the further development of scientific research as well as interdisciplinary prevention approaches, namely in cooperation with medical sciences, neurology, psychology, sociology, criminology as well as preschool and school research. He makes an innovative contribution by suggesting that economists be included in prevention research, in order to produce the often required cost-benefit analysis. »We have to show and prove that prevention is profitable. Only if we manage to win the minister of finance for crime prevention will prevention stand a chance. Because well-implemented prevention produces greater benefits compared to what was originally invested«.

Dr. Lars Rand Jensen spoke about »Perspectives on Crime Prevention and Quality Management«. Dr. Jensen is the President of Police

---

[13] Please see: http://www.tyc.state.tx.us/prevention/hiscope.html; http://www.highscope.org/Research/PerryProject/perrymain.htm.

in Odense/Denmark and chairman of the central SSP working group of Denmark's crime prevention council. He takes a corresponding perspective to look at the issue of quality in crime prevention.

At the same time, he is one of the founders of Denmark's crime prevention council. In fact, the Nordic countries lead the way in crime prevention; the first crime prevention councils and offices already came into existence there during the 1970s. Their work has since resulted in various recommendations concerning social and law policy. The structures of the councils in Demark are comparable to those in Finland and Island. In his lecture, Jensen focused on the questions »What do we actually do?« and »What do we want to do?«. Issues concerning quality in crime prevention correspond to Denmark's »neighbourhood policing« programme, which is a sort of joint policing work. Denmark's crime prevention network SSP has been built up during the last 30 years. The SSP working group was founded in 1975 and is subordinate to the Danish crime prevention council.

SSP stands for a comprehensive cooperation of schools, social services, health services and police. The aim of the programme is to support the communities by setting up local networks. Twelve well documented projects with a main focus on »safer cities« are combined in one guiding project in Denmark. It needs to be reviewed how far projects can be transferred, in order to formulate recommendations and guidelines in a second step. A positive effect could be noticed for projects which were well embedded in the complete system. The President of Police criticises the lack of comparison in crime prevention and complains about a lack of methods for comparing in individual countries. One possibility to overcome this situation would be the awarding of a quality mark. This applies to the quality of projects as well as to the general developments in European crime prevention. A strategy based on knowledge, comparative research and scientific evaluation as well as common standards for evaluation and corresponding quality criteria are needed to overcome this deficit.

Although the European Crime Prevention Network (EUCPN) does undertake some effort to achieve comparability between the projects and initiatives of the individual European countries, there is still a lack of methodological correspondence. For example: What exactly defines Good Practice? The European Commission's aim to develop a standardised methodology is a very ambitious undertaking.

According to Jensen, it makes perfect sense to bundle/group different methodologies and to establish basic rules. A good starting point would be to guarantee the comparability of general project descriptions as well as to develop improved statistics for comparison.

A crucial contribution to the concept of quality management in crime prevention would be the standardization of the report concerning the description and analysis of a project.

A further important step would be the development of an institutional framework, which Jensen calls a »unit«.

Under such an institutional umbrella,
a.) standards for quality marking and further development could be negotiated and decided on, and
b.) comparable research could be furthered.

The advantage is obvious: all the efforts concerning the development of quality management would be combined. However, this idea is not that new after all.

An international working group to which Jensen also belonged called »Cranfied Konfrenzen« already had these ambitions during the 1970s. And even then, the aim was to build up a central organisation on the university level (at the time at Cambridge University/UK). This institution was supposed to rest on various pillars: conferences and seminars as well as research and evaluation studies and publications. Jensen returned to this idea more than forty years later at the first Beccaria Conference. The »Unit«, which optimally would be part of an independent and well-known university, would act as an interdisciplinary and international forum. Such a network/unit would have to be connected to various programmes, European organisations, the Council of Europe, EUCPN and other relevant institutions within the EU. It would act as a service provider with permanent personnel who inform and offer support.

Although the necessity of an international forum for political decision-makers, practitioners, scientists and social services has been realised for quite some time, no corresponding action has been undertaken so far. As a cooperating partner in the Beccaria Project, Jensen welcomes and supports the reintroduction of this concept in the context of the planned Beccaria Center (AGIS Application 2005).

Michel Marcus spoke about »Better Quality in Safety Policies in Europe from a local perspective«. The general manager of the European Forum for Urban Safety – EFUS in Paris took a close look at the European evaluation landscape. Beginning with the tools and instruments which are available on the European level, he went on to speak about the tendencies in European evaluation policy and evaluation strategy as well as the barriers to evaluation.

The framework for crime prevention strategies comprises:
1. The development of a European crime prevention policy, including the development of a European network (EUCPN). However, according to Marcus, the available resources are not sufficient.
2. The foundation of a European Observatory for organised crime (including a collection of data-crime prevention strategies in Europe). It would be necessary to open up to crime prevention and develop common evaluation standards.
3. The development of co-operations on a local and national level, as for example the community safety programmes in the UK and a »Safety Protocol« as a support mechanism for evaluation.

Marcus puts forward the following questions for discussion:
- How can the economic advantage of crime prevention be measured in terms of a cost-benefit analysis?
- How can the transfer of knowledge relevant to prevention between science and practice be assured (How can the dividing line between theory and practice in evaluation be overcome)?
- How can a culture of evaluation be developed in crime prevention?
- What evaluation results are consulted in order to analyse decision-making?
- How can it be made sure that evaluation results are taken into account when developing new prevention programmes?
- How can a critical synthesis of evaluation studies be conducted?
- How do global strategies have to be evaluated?
- What does an integrated evaluation strategy comprise?
- What mechanisms can guarantee the objectivity of an evaluation?
- What is the aim and objective of evaluation studies?
- What is after all the function of evaluation?

There is one thing for sure: public policy needs evaluation.

- Knowledge has to be used in order to develop and modify different approaches to crime prevention policy. The aim is to utilise knowledge.
- Decision makers/policymakers have to use evaluation more, in order to obtain evaluation results, which they can implement in corresponding action plans.
- Scientific results have to be integrated into an overall vision.
- The results of evaluated programmes have to be passed on and have to be made available to the public.

The university of Dijon/France, in co-operation with EFUS as well as Spain, the Czech Republic and Italy, is planning to develop a network among universities in Barcelona, Prague and Florence[14] with the aim to establish a European Master's course in »Urban Safety«. This initiative would surely contribute to the further development of a culture of prevention and evaluation.

After all it is about:
- support mechanisms and
- the influence on political decision-making and available financial resources.

For Marcus, the only opportunity to receive money for evaluation research on a European level is to convince decision-makers of the benefits of evaluation and to put pressure on the EU Parliament. Currently Europe lacks an evaluation policy.

Future Prospects:

The ambitious aim will continue to be to sensitize to quality in crime prevention, to achieve a general consciousness for this topic and to raise awareness just as Cesare Beccaria did. After all, at the beginning of his career he only had a vision in mind too.

---

[14] fesu@urbansecurity.org; www.fesu.org

The Beccaria 7-Step-Concept: How to Realize a Successful Crime Prevention Project

Initial position: Project management is not a self-evident truth for local crime prevention initiatives yet. Local crime prevention projects in Germany or elsewhere in Europe do a very important job. However, it often remains unclear whether and why the initiated projects actually have a preventative effect on crime. A comprehensive definition of the targets and the target group are just as seldom as a detailed problem analysis. However, if these indicators are not strictly defined at the beginning of a project, it becomes rather difficult to measure if and how a change occurs during the course of a crime prevention project.

Unfortunately, many crime prevention projects in Germany and elsewhere are not systematically drawn up, planned and implemented. Furthermore, »nationally and internationally the evaluation of crime prevention projects and programs is still a scarce commodity«[15]. Local crime prevention on a broad scale is still far away from an assured quality standard[16]. Scientists and politicians who criticize this lack of quality awareness often overlook the lack of corresponding support in terms of transferring scientific methods and knowledge to local crime prevention initiatives. Apart from the problems around the issue of evaluation, a general lack of practical project management tools can also be witnessed in practical crime prevention.

According to this background, the Beccaria Project has the central objective of improving practical work in crime prevention and developing corresponding support mechanisms for project management and evaluation. These support mechanisms are designed to meet the needs of practical crime prevention work. Generally, support for crime prevention projects should be provided in Germany as well as in other Euro-

---
[15] Please see: Meyer, Linssen, Marks 2004
[16] Please see: Meyer, Linssen, Marks 2004

pean countries. This article does not want to repeat or summarize the international debate on evaluation in crime prevention. The objective is to use the German example in order to underline the importance of developing practical support mechanisms for local crime prevention initiatives. The Beccaria Project has developed as well as implemented various pilot schemes focusing on appropriate support mechanisms in crime prevention. At some point these will be available on a European level.

Originally, the aim at the beginning of the Beccaria Project was to produce a handbook for practical advice on project planning. A »Project Planning Reference Guide« was planned which was meant to support all sorts of players in the field of crime prevention. The central aim of this reference guide was to improve the planning, implementation and evaluation of local crime prevention projects. The idea was to achieve this by providing information on relevant methods and procedures in a comprehensive fashion.

Any crime prevention initiative should be able to conduct its own quality management. After all, local crime prevention projects most often lack financial resources to engage external experts for professional evaluation.

At the beginning of the Beccaria Project in 2003, only one leaflet »Practical Support for Evaluation« from ProPK (*Programm Polizeiliche Kriminalprävention*: Germany's Central Police Crime Prevention Unit) existed. This gives instructions on how to measure the success and effect of a crime prevention project and is now also available in English. By dividing a project into several independent steps and illustrating the function of each step with individual case studies, the leaflet has been deliberately designed to achieve a good level of understanding among crime prevention practitioners. Unfortunately, the contents of the leaflet concentrate very much on the context and organisational structures of the police. Therefore, it does not provide much help to local crime prevention initiatives in terms of »community partnerships«. At the beginning of 2004, a guide for local crime prevention initiatives was published by the Crime Prevention Council of North-Rhine Westphalia, Germany's most populous state. The guide intends to meet the needs of voluntary partnerships for crime prevention and focuses on the issues of project planning, implementation and evaluation.

The guide offers information quite similar to what had been published before by the Central Police Crime Prevention Unit. However, the North-Rhine Westphalia Crime Prevention Council worked in close cooperation with the Central Association for German Communities when developing the guide, in order to meet the needs of local community crime prevention initiatives. Apart from providing information on project management, the aim of the guide is also to show how decisions on funding can be influenced by deliberately pointing out central quality features of a crime prevention project. After all and especially in Germany, local crime prevention projects will remain heavily dependent on funding by various institutions.

The need for additional support apart from currently provided help mechanisms.

Therefore, at the beginning of the Beccaria Project, two guides were unexpectedly already available, both offering support and both meeting a high standard of quality.

At the beginning of the Beccaria Project, a survey was carried out to determine the most crucial needs of local crime prevention initiatives. Its analysis showed that the majority of participants felt a lack of support on issues such as project planning, outlining, implementation and evaluation. Obviously, support in form of a guide was not sufficient in order to effectively help local crime prevention initiatives. Especially in terms of evaluation, basic scientific methods and theories, it became apparent that there was a need for further training, external support and advice, and easy to understand working instructions. It has also been mentioned that the already existing support materials were too complicated. Also, a general mental reservation towards issues such as project management or evaluation could be noticed, which resulted in the provided working guides remaining unread. Generally, the analysis of the questionnaire and interviews revealed a latent prejudice towards quality and project management.

Reasons for this are the fear of an increased workload, the lack of methodological knowledge or the worry that project evaluation might lead in the end to an increased control of involved personnel or even a cut in financial resources. The interest in the rather abstract issue of »quality« also turned out to be very limited. It was either seen as being too complicated or just raising the issue was understood as a criticism of previous work. These aspects all added to the reasons for not integrating the suggestions made by provided guides into daily local crime prevention work. Taking into account this background, the Beccaria Project sought to provide alternative access and ways of communication in order to reach the target group and to increase interest in the issue of quality in crime prevention as well as to decrease erroneous prejudice. The project therefore does not focus on anything new. After all, the need to convince local crime prevention initiatives to apply basic project management tools is relatively uncontested. However, new ways of formulating this advice were needed in order to make these issues appear less complex and more approachable.

The 7-Step Concept of the Beccaria Project

The Beccaria Project has therefore developed the »7-step« guidelines: »7 Steps to a successful crime prevention project«. The idea was to develop various principles for more quality in crime prevention, which are deliberately designed to meet the target group's needs: »pocket-sized project management«. For this reason, detailed information had to be transferred to an easy-to-use formula in order to produce a quality outcome. The Lower Saxony Crime Prevention Councils' 7-step concept includes a mobile-phone-sized leaflet which summarizes the most important factors of successful project planning, implementation and evaluation in seven steps. Each step is represented by one crucial question.

The Beccaria Project has also developed seven worksheets, each complementing one of the 7-steps. The working materials are available for German crime prevention initiatives as well as for initiatives all over Europe or elsewhere. Accordingly, their content is kept rather general. Since October 2004 the 7-step leaflet and the corresponding worksheets can be downloaded in German as well as English at www.beccaria.de. The 7-step leaflet is regularly distributed at relevant congresses in both languages. The Lower Saxony Crime Prevention Council is also very happy to send leaflets on request. Eventually the leaflet will be translated into other languages when this practical support becomes more and more accepted all over Europe.

It was a conscious decision to use the Internet as an alternative platform for access. The internet makes it possible to provide a fast, free-of-charge, global and convenient access to the information. One can also expect that almost every local crime prevention initiative will have access to the World Wide Web these days. Last but not least, the Internet is probably the best and most uncomplicated way to distribute and provide information on an international scale. The content of the 7-step leaflet is kept very short and one needs little time to grasp its meaning. There is no need to read dozens of books anymore.

The 7-Step Leaflet: The pocket-sized manual guide and the 7-step worksheets as its useful complement

Neither the 7-step leaflets nor the complementing worksheets contain anything new or certainly anything revolutionary. Neither the single phases of managing a project nor the described working steps and methods are very special, and many people will surely have heard of them before. The new aspects of the Beccaria concept lie in the special design of the working materials, which meet the special needs of local crime prevention initiatives. The working materials provide local initiatives with everything they need in order to undertake a crime prevention project from the very beginning until the end. The working materials manage to do this in a manner that appeals to any target group. The contents are reduced to the most important and most central aspects of successful project management. Everyone will find the time to read them and everyone will be able to understand them quickly. Reading a leaflet while enjoying a cup of coffee takes less effort than poring over books trying to find appropriate target group definitions. The leaflet is deliberately designed in a very practice-oriented manner.

For example, the leaflet asks its readers questions in order to get them thinking instead of just giving »smart advice«. The content of the leaflets can be understood intuitively and has the function to creating interest in the issue of quality in crime prevention. To make the leaflet more of an eye-catcher than most info materials, it is the size of a mobile phone, in order to easily fit into any pocket or bag. The leaflet is designed to create interest especially among those who have little experience in carrying out a project and wish to get help from working materials and other forms of support. The leaflet also should raise interest among people who have only heard little about these issues yet. Good project management has already started when a person reads the leaflet and starts to wonder at step 1 »What is the exact problem?«. In local crime prevention, the objective of a project often remains unclear, making the implementation of the project rather difficult and its evaluation almost impossible. After all, a person who does not know where to go must not be surprised if he never gets anywhere. However, these problems are home-made. Luckily, no one has to get into complicated project management theories in order to conduct a successful crime prevention project. The compact 7-step leaflet aims to prove this. By supplying these working materials, the Lower Saxony Crime Prevention Council wants to achieve a consciousness for quality issues among players in the field of local crime prevention and to support them when it comes to actually achieving a certain quality standard. The central objective is to provide uncomplicated and practical help for the successful realisation of prevention projects and to respond to Dölling's[17] demand for an »evaluation for practitioners«. Erroneous prejudice among crime prevention practitioners has to be decreased and the development of a culture of evaluation has to be supported. The broad distribution of the materials should further the general acceptance of well-conducted project management and project revision.

The application of the 7-steps actually reflects the procedure of a real crime prevention project:

Step 1: Establishing and describing the topic
Step 2: Identifying the causes
Step 3: Specifying the goals
Step 4: Developing possible solutions
Step 5: Constructing and implementing the project plan
Step 6: Reviewing the impact
Step 7: Documentation and conclusions

For each of the 7-steps introduced in the leaflet, complementary worksheets are available as downloads on the Beccaria website. This is meant to improve the quality of project planning, implementing and evaluating a crime prevention project. Accordingly, the worksheets which com-

[17] Please see: Dölling, 2005, p. 22

plement the leaflet offer a relatively detailed and understandable but not complicated overview of the methods and techniques of successful project management. In order to make these worksheets as understandable as possible, no terms are used that are too complex or possibly have a negative connotation.

The special features of the worksheets are their comprehensibility and the easy way of accessing them. Free of charge and within seconds, one can download a questionnaire which relates to the individual project phase and is fast and easy to answer. This assures a basic evaluation of any crime prevention project and establishes the basis for a deeper evaluation of processes and effects. Since August 2005, already filled-in example sheets can also be found on the Beccaria website. The example sheets cover a local crime prevention project which aims to tackle bullying in local schools. The responsible project managers used the 7-step materials and have filled in the complementary worksheets.

These sheets can now be used as an example by others who wish to use the 7-step materials but still find the worksheets a little too abstract to fill them in right away. The Beccaria website therefore not only offers support for one's own project work but also offers a real-life example which shows that project management does not have to be complicated or very demanding by any means. The example sheets are currently only available in German. However, if the need for examples from other European countries or in English becomes apparent, the Beccaria team will surely provide them. Generally, any further developments and further steps undertaken by the Beccaria Project will be heavily determined by the users' feedback.

Future perspectives

The 7-step concept of the Beccaria Project only represents the beginning of a long way towards better quality in crime prevention. Certainly it only represents one of many possible ways of approaching the problem. The Beccaria Project can provide minimal standards for successful and effective crime prevention and make quality management an integral part of any crime prevention project. However, the provision of support in the form of working materials surely has to be complemented by further offers. Apart from providing possibilities to obtain help from professional evaluators and experts, it is also important to complement the 7-step concept with the provision of personal advice on the local level.

The need for face-to-face contact has also been mentioned by various crime prevention practitioners in the context of the Beccaria questionnaire carried out at the beginning of the project. Especially when using the 7-step concept for the first time, many individual questions come up and have to be answered. An appropriate personal and free service is necessary to show local crime prevention initiatives how to use the 7-steps. Such a consultant would provide support in finding individual, local solutions rather than dictate standardized formulas. The Lower Saxony Crime Prevention Council is keeping this aspect in mind when working on the further development of the 7-step concept. On a European and international level, it will have to be considered whether personal support could be provided via a telephone hotline. The perspective is to appropriately qualify all actors in the field of crime prevention and to develop appropriate European standards. In the long term, only comprehensive training in project management, theoretical and methodological basics as well as structural and juridical aspects based on European standards will be able to guarantee quality in crime prevention.

The Beccaria-Online-Evaluation-Agency: Getting Users and Providers together

Evaluation represents a rather delicate issue not only in crime prevention but in general as well. There is a common fear that evaluation may result in cuts in resources or even dismissals, which causes it to be broadly rejected. At the same time, the chances that can result from evaluation, such as an increase in project-work quality, are only considered to a small extent. Examples outside of Europe show that this need not be the case. The Australian Institute for Criminology, for example, offers special training courses («Training crime prevention specialists for the modern world«) for various target groups. Evaluation methods are taught in order to further the use of modern project-management strategies in crime prevention. In Canada, evaluation is a priority of the National Crime Prevention Strategy (NCPS). In Europe, it is probably the Home Office Crime Prevention Centre/UK which pays the most attention to the issue of evaluation in crime prevention. Generally, a lack of scientific methods in practical crime prevention can be noticed in many European countries, which becomes especially apparent when it comes to evaluation. An institution which supports the co-operation between scientists and practical crime prevention on a daily basis is needed. Scientists should become an integral part of practical crime prevention and should use the opportunity to test their methods in real crime prevention work. This is where the Beccaria Project comes in: from the very beginning it has been clear that the objective of the Beccaria Project to increase quality in crime prevention is not possible without an increase in co-operation between experts and crime prevention practitioners at the same time.

On the other hand and especially in terms of evaluation, it is important to transfer methodological competencies into practice through training. On the other hand, people who lack scientific knowledge should also approach experts about evaluation or methods in order to accompany and to support quality-increasing processes. Practical players in the field of crime prevention have a great interest in profiting from experts' scientific (but still practice-oriented) knowledge, especially when it comes to project quality and evaluation.

The need for a better co-operation with evaluation experts also becomes very noticeable when one looks at the analysis of the questionnaire that was submitted to crime prevention professionals at the beginning of the Beccaria Project. When asked what sort of general support was needed for crime prevention projects, the majority of participants mentioned a better support of their work by evaluation experts. Generally the participants expressed the need for more scientific support in practical crime prevention. The majority of participants favoured support in form of a »guide« which lists experts for project planning, implementation and evaluation. Therefore it had to be concluded that the development of some sort of evaluation »contact pool« would be useful in order to bring together those in need of support and those offering this support. Correspondingly, the Beccaria Project aims to develop a network for experts and prevention practitioners in order to achieve a lasting improvement in practical crime prevention work.

The Beccaria Online Evaluation Agency

Since July 2005, the Beccaria Online Evaluation Agency is being realised at www.beccaria.de. The aim of the Beccaria Online Evaluation Agency is to bring users and providers together. The original meaning of the term »agency« is to accelerate the progress of something. In the context of the evaluation agency, the aim is to accelerate the progress of evaluation within the field of crime prevention. Furthermore, the term »agency« stands for the imparting of knowledge. In a figurative sense, the evaluation agency imparts evaluation experts. The intention is to open new ways of research for scientists and to provide players in the field of practical crime prevention with the contact details of possible partners for co-operation and support, such as experts, research institutes and universities at the same time.

The agency is a support service offering an information system for evaluation on the Internet. It leads those seeking advice directly to someone able to provide competent support. According to their individual needs, the users of the agency receive an overview of professional evaluators and contact details of institutions which either perform external evaluations or offer support in planning, implementing and evaluating crime prevention projects. In the long term, the aim is to develop a network on the national and international level which brings together the providers and users of evaluation.

During the initial phase of the agency, the majority of registered providers will be German; however, further development on a European scale is already planned. One perspective could be to develop the agency along the line of a European »marketplace« for international expert knowledge on evaluation in crime prevention. The Beccaria Online Evaluation Agency offers support on issues such as:

- Where can I find help to check on the effect of crime prevention projects?
- Who is responsible and competent for helping me out with problems and for answering my questions?
- What sort of support is generally available?

The database of the Beccaria Online Evaluation agency is part of the Beccaria website www.beccaria.de. The possibility of permanently updating and developing the online database is one of the agency's crucial advantages. It is possible keep up to date with the latest developments among the registered providers at all times. Furthermore, the fast access for users, relatively low running costs and the almost limitless possibility to extend the agency are definite advantages of the Beccaria Online Evaluation Agency.

Using the Beccaria Online Evaluation Agency

Everyone in search of support for evaluation in crime prevention or related issues is a part of the Beccaria Online Evaluation Agency's target group, potential users of the database. On the other hand, the agency addresses qualified providers of corresponding services, who can leave their profile with the agency. The users will then be able to get in contact with providers with suitable profiles. Therefore, the providers, i.e. partners for evaluation, are key players in making the Beccaria Online Evaluation Agency work. Interested providers can easily join the agency by typing in their contact details and information about their services in the entry mask. The provided information will then be revised by the

Beccaria team and finally posted with the online agency. The providers will be given a password via e-mail that enables them to enter their account and update their information at all times. However, in order to assure the quality of the agency's services, the providers have to commit to upholding certain quality principles themselves.

If one user's search criteria match the profile of a certain provider or several providers, the corresponding data will directly show up on the Beccaria website. The user can then contact the provider directly. Users can organise their search according to the provided standard data such as city, region, country, certain services such as advice, evaluation, scientific support or by typing in any other keyword into the search bar. Joining the Beccaria Online Evaluation Agency as a provider or conducting a search is possible by entering the German or the English version of the Beccaria website www.beccaria.de. In order to get the agency's services running as soon as possible, the Beccaria team has contacted relevant institutions all over Germany and encouraged them to provide their services via the Beccaria Online Evaluation Agency. The aim of creating a balanced offer comprising various services was kept in mind when contacting these institutions. The agency is now able to offer different services for different needs. Apart from university faculties, public and private institutes as well as qualified freelancers have been contacted. The Online Agency can now satisfy different demands in terms of contents, geographical factors or different financial backgrounds.

In most cases, private institutions will have to work in a profit-oriented way. Universities on the other hand will often be able to combine a project evaluation with their own research. This will occasionally result in the opportunity to get quality support at a cheap rate.

The quality commitment of the Beccaria Online Evaluation Agency

The providers enter their data into the agency's database independently, and it is important to consider appropriate control mechanisms in order to ensure the quality of the service. After all, it is the users' perfect right to expect that recommended evaluators, experts and institutions commit to certain quality principles. Therefore, the Beccaria team has applied the following measures. The providers are required to supply comprehensive additional information about their services. This assures transparency for those seeking information. The quality of the providers can be checked, and it is clear who is behind what service and what qualifications can be offered. The users get the chance to draw a detailed picture of the services provided via the Online Agency. Furthermore, the providers commit themselves to upholding the following Beccaria principles, which assure that a certain quality is met by each provider who joins the agency.

Quality Control
The providers systematically check the effectiveness and efficiency of their own services on a regular basis.

Transparency
The providers are prepared to give additional information about themselves and their services on request. This will provide transparency to those seeking information and underline the quality of the information provided. Detailed information on the provider is essential for the users to judge whether the provider actually offers what they are seeking.
This encompasses transparency on:
- The provider, profile, legal form
- the organisation behind an online offer for evaluation, whether a research institute, university etc.
- the services provided
- support in planning, implementation and evaluation of crime prevention projects
- scientific support
- evaluation
- advice on evaluation
- purpose (specifications concerning purpose and objectives may also be required for legal aspects, such as liability)
- specific target groups

Usability
The provider's own website is user-friendly in terms of navigation and design. The website contains no barriers that prevent users from browsing the entire website. The provider's personnel can be contacted via mail, telephone, e-mail or personally and are prepared to answer questions.

Up-to-dateness of the supplied information
Services and information are regularly checked to make sure they are up to date at all times.

Reliability
All information provided on the Internet is factual, comprehensive and precise.

Comprehensibility
The information is provided in an appropriate fashion in order to reach the target group.

The application of these measures ensures a minimum quality for services of the Online Agency.

The further development of the Beccaria Online Evaluation Agency

The Beccaria Online Evaluation Agency is a so-called »learning project«. The described aim to develop a network among the providers and users of evaluation in crime prevention is only a first step. The users' feedback is of great importance to develop further services with the aim of supporting local crime prevention initiatives in order to conduct their own quality management. It is crucial to continually optimize the Online Agency's services. Therefore, the users are strongly encouraged to provide feedback when visiting the Beccaria Online Evaluation Agency at www.beccaria.de. Additionally, the Beccaria team will use the number of users as well as the inquiries made via the web-provider for internal evaluation.

Conclusion

The Beccaria Online Evaluation Agency is a further measure to complement the Beccaria Project's overall objective to achieve better quality in crime prevention. The Online Agency's central aim is to improve the practical work of local crime prevention initiatives as well as in crime prevention generally. Currently one often finds only insufficient methodological and conceptual knowledge on project planning and implementation among players in the field of crime prevention. This especially applies to evaluation. The Beccaria Online Evaluation Agency can help to find competent support which meets the individual demands of local crime prevention projects. The long-term objective is to develop the Beccaria Online Evaluation Agency into a European platform for expert knowledge and evaluation. Such a platform could bring together crime prevention initiatives seeking information and experts who provide this information on an international level.

The 7-step concept and the Beccaria Project's concept of further training needs in crime prevention are complemented by the Beccaria Online Evaluation Agency which helps to find professional support. The 7-steps are a supportive measure enabling players in crime prevention to help themselves. The measure with the most sustainable outcome, namely training, will enable all players in the field of crime prevention to carry out quality project management independently and to extend their competencies.

Literature:

Dölling, D.: Zur Qualität und Evaluation von Kriminalprävention. In: forum kriminalprävention. Zeitschrift der Stiftung Deutsches Forum für Kriminalprävention, 1/2005, S. 421–424

Landeshauptstadt Düsseldorf: Düsseldorfer Gutachten über empirisch gesicherte Erkenntnisse kriminalpräventiver Wirkungen, Düsseldorf, 2002

Landespräventionsrat Nordrhein-Westfalen (Hrsg.): Leitfaden kommunale Kriminalprävention. Ein Leitfaden zur Planung, Durchführung und Evaluation kriminalpräventiver Projekte. Erstellt von Dr. Jörg Hupfeld unter Mitwirkung von Dr. Rainer Strobl, arpos Institut e.V., Hannover in Verbindung mit der Arbeitsgruppe Evaluation des Landespräventionsrates Nordrhein-Westfalen unter der Leitung von Prof. Dr. Wolfgang Bilsky, Münster. 2004

Meyer, A., Marks, E.: (Mehr) Qualität in der Kriminalprävention, In: Die Kriminalprävention 11/2004, S.16–20

Meyer, A., Linssen, R., Marks, E.: Das Beccaria-Projekt: Visionen für eine bessere Qualität in der Kriminalprävention. In: forum kriminalprävention, Zeitschrift der Stiftung Deutsches Forum für Kriminalprävention, 31/2004, 31–34

Polizeiliche Kriminalprävention der Länder und des Bundes, ProPK (Hrsg.): Qualitätssicherung polizeilicher Präventionsprojekte. Eine Arbeitshilfe für die Evaluation. Stuttgart 2003

Perspective 2005–2007:
Beccaria-Center: Professional Training in Crime Prevention

The State Prevention Council of Lower Saxony/Lower Saxony Ministry of Justice plans to set up a European Beccaria Center, in order to advance the campaign for quality in crime prevention that was started in 2003. The Beccaria Center is a cooperative network with eight European partner organizations. The goal of the two-year project for the center is to enhance the professional skills of crime prevention workers by establishing a range of qualification offers for basic and further training.

The center is to help
a.) better meet the changing demand for specialists, directors and managers as well as
b.) increasingly standardize the training and education curricula for European crime prevention.

The central task of the Beccaria Center is to design a scientific, demand-oriented and professional range of qualification offers.

This comprises
1. the creation and establishment of a training program as well as
2. the development of an advanced Master's program (in-service).

The range of further training offers will be geared towards the transfer of knowledge and the improvement of professional practice. Both of these aims require the development of a modular, interdisciplinary curriculum with bilingual teaching contents that relate to the local region as well as to Europe. Transparency and international comparability are ensured by orienting the planned Master's program to a performance point system (ECTS). First of all, a demand analysis and a feasibility study will be carried out in the course of strategic planning. The observance of standards is ensured by checking and evaluating the quality of the course of study – also in the form of a subsequent, obligatory accreditation of the program and the system.

(Abstract of the Applicat Form Programme AGIS 2005)

Lawrence W. Sherman
University of Pennsylvania, USA

Enlightened Justice: Consequentialism and Empiricism from Beccaria to Braithwaite

German-speaking criminology has done more to keep the spirit of Beccaria alive than any other chapter of our science. Not only is the very practical and modern Hannover conference on crime prevention named in Beccaria's honor. The New German Society of Criminology has also, for years, honored the work of outstanding criminologists with the Beccaria medal. There are many German criminologists, such as Franz von Liszt, who could also merit a medal named in their memory. The choice of an Italian for the NKG medal therefore reflects a very great deal of respect for the unique role of Beccaria in the history of criminology.

We may therefore ask, in the spirit of the Enlightenment of which Beccaria was a part, just why is this so? Why should Beccaria deserve such respect in the 21st century? What did he do, for that matter, that would make him relevant to discussions of situational crime prevention and other technical matters? Alfred North Whitehead has counseled that »a science that hesitates to forget its founders is lost.« So why should we not just forget about Beccaria? He was, after all, not much of a reformer, refusing invitations from European monarchs to travel abroad as an advisor on redrafting of penal codes. He was hardly an empirical researcher, doing almost no field work for his 1764 treatise. As a causal theorist, he said little that was new, including the deterrence doctrine central to his work. As a jurisprude, his ideas of proportionality were first published by Montesquieu in 1748. His opposition to the death penalty had been long preceded by Quaker theology in England and America. Even the formulation of the greatest happiness for the greatest number, often attributed to him (Gay, 1969) was actually published in Edinburgh decades before 1764 by the philosopher Frances Hutcheson (Buchan, 2003).

Three reasons provide a robust response to such skepticism. First, Beccaria is a symbol of the Enlightenment. Second, he was the most influential leader of the cause of »consequentialism« in justice, arguing that the moral basis of punishment was not the past crime but the future crime *prevention*—thereby making him a very appropriate hero for any discussions of crime prevention. Third, he was the architect of the »science of justice,« a vision that the consequences of justice decisions could be discovered and catalogued with »geometric precision.«

These reasons are all the more appropriate in this new century, in which many commentators suggest that the Enlightenment is growing dark. From evolution (vs. creationism) to religious tolerance (vs. intolerance and theocracy), there is evidence that the Western world increasingly struggles with Enlightenment principles once thought to be settled. The increasing rates of imprisonment in the US, UK and elsewhere raise questions about whether retribution has banished the goal of prevention. The hostility to science and empirical evidence articulated by so many politicians and even university students suggests that Beccaria's science could become politically irrelevant.

A New Beccaria? To these emerging problems of the 21st century, we have a living criminologist who provides a renewal, indeed a bulwark, against attacks on the Enlightenment. The collected work of John Braithwaite provides an enlightened perspective on reason and emotion, on sense and sensibility, and moderated consequentialism without the inflexibility of pure utilitarianism. He is also, perhaps less usefully, a moderated empiricist, with somewhat higher tolerance for threats to internal validity in scientific inference about causation than may be wise for evidence-based consequentialism.

John Braithwaite is a criminologist at the Australian National University whose influence has spread well beyond the English language and all across the globe. His most famous book, the 1989 *Crime, Shame and Reintegration*, re-examined the role of shame in relation to moral judgment. His theory of reintegrative shaming essentially claims that social control works best when it condemns the sin but supports the sinner. When punishment is required, he suggests, so too is reintegration. His more recent book *Restorative Justice and Responsive Regulation* (Braithwaite 2002) is a very broad-ranging moral and empirical analysis of ways of creating

compliance with law – another way to say crime prevention. It applies to corporations, to environmental pollution, and a very broad range of behaviour. What he has said in these books and other writings, inter alia, is this:
1. justice should not expel citizens from society, physically or socially; it should not be in the business of creating outcasts who, 650,000 times a year in the United States, come back from prison to live in my neighbourhood, and neighbourhoods across America, and as Jeremy Travis has said, they all come back – even some who are set to be on death row, when we find out they were innocent.
2. Justice should reintegrate, because criminological theory and evidence predicts that reintegration will reduce or prevent crime better than expulsion.
3. In the process of dealing with individual offenders, justice should use progressively more severe sanctions, starting with processes of restoration, and then imposing more coercion and restraint if voluntary compliance fails. One model of restoration, which Braithwaite says should be the »default« or initial automatic response to rule-breaking, is one that I have been involved in testing for about ten years. In this model, victims, offenders, and their families sit in a circle for several hours and talk about the crime and the harm it caused, then agree upon how the offender could repair the harm.

These ideas matter, I think, not necessarily because they are all correct, but because the Enlightenment is under threat. They matter because the President of the United States has been abusing religion in order to deny facts, and inspiring Americans to decide they should *not* think for themselves – they should listen to their President. Braithwaite is a bulwark of enlightened justice against that view and in favour of letting people directly affected by a crime think for themselves in each case. Whether or not this approach will consistently produce the consequences he suggests they might, the »restorative values« he has articulated are directly premised on Enlightenment values. In that respect, Braithwaite helps to preserve what Beccaria helped to create in the first place: enlightened justice.

By integrating the work of Beccaria and Braithwaite, we can suggest a 21st-century definition of enlightened justice as
a. the administration of sanctions under criminal law, guided by invi-

olate principles of human rights (banning torture, the death penalty, and procedural unfairness to victims and defendants)
b. aimed at producing consequences that reduce human misery, guided by the best available
c. empirical evidence on justice choices that work best to reduce human misery

This definition of enlightened justice can be justified, as well as placed into context, by the remaining discussion of this paper. That discussion shows how, in parallel, both Beccaria and Braithwaite constitute symbols of the Enlightenment, leaders for consequentialism, and defenders of empiricism.

Symbols of the Enlightenment

> »[Beccaria] was deeply indebted to the Enlightenment;
> the Enlightenment came to be deeply indebted to him.«
> Gay (1969: 438)

What is Enlightenment? Historians today debate its meaning and definition, but at its height in the 18th century, Immanuel Kant summarised it as »daring to know,« or »having the courage to use your own understanding:«

> Was ist Aufklärung? Aufklärung ist der Ausgang des Menschen aus seiner selbstverschuldeten Unmündigkeit. Unmündigkeit ist das Unvermögen, sich seines Verstandes ohne Leitung eines anderen zu bedienen. Selbstverschuldet ist diese Unmündigkeit, wenn die Ursache derselben nicht am Mangel des Verstandes, sondern der Entschliessung und des Mutes liegt, sich seiner ohne Leitung eines anderen zu bedienen. *Sapere aude!* Habe Mut, dich deines eigenen Verstandes zu bedienen! ist also der Wahlspruch der Aufklärung.«
> Kant (1784)

Peter Gay has an even more aphoristic summary of the Enlightenment: »the recovery of nerve.« This phrase is drawn from Gilbert Murray's analysis of Europe from the late Roman Empire, in which the sapping of human vitality and rationality led to asceticism and mysticism, pessimism and loss of self-confidence, loss of hope, loss of faith in human effort, as well as despair over patient inquiry, leading to human yearning (as I see in America today) for infallible revelation – the truth of the word – and indifference to the welfare of the state. The 18th century was important, for the first time in almost 2000 years, for its advances in both reasoning and emotional sensitivity to the pain and suffering of others. As Gay says, it was a time when it finally became more fashionable to *help* victims than to *create* them. There was just beginning to be a rebellion against militarism, and the worship of the strong. It was a time of scientific advances in theory, medical advances in practice, inventions of machinery. All of this provided visible evidence that human effort matters. The egalitarian view that all individuals matter – that they can all be achievers, they can all be victims, fostered our capacity to be empathetic and aware of the suffering of others.

This brought Beccaria to the stage to reinvent justice around the rational management of emotions, not with blindness, but with ultimately statistics as a way of seeing what effects justice had on human misery (Sherman, 2003). His 1764 treatise was a tipping point that ultimately led to widespread abolition of capital punishment and torture and secret trials – had less effect on this idea against retribution and in favour of prevention. He reinvented justice with both a moral and empirical theory, and with some descriptive research and some innovations as a blue-print for going forward. But his curse was that he confused the moral and the empirical (despite David Hume's strong contemporary argument against such confusion). He engaged in no experimentation. He stated theories in a way which would be difficult to falsify. He set a template for the way in which politicians, law professors, and even some social scientists muddle together what they believe is right, and what they can document based on scientific evidence.

Henry Fielding: The Inventive Enlightener

Beccaria's ivory tower isolation from empirical evidence provides a sharp contrast to another criminologist, Beccaria's contemporary, who could be more properly viewed as the founder of criminology (Sherman, 2005). You may know him as the author of the novel »Tom Jones.« He was also the stipendiary Magistrate (judge) at Bow Street Court, where he met and punished hundreds of criminals. He also became the first criminologist to publish in English, with his influential treatise on the recent increase in robberies (Fielding, 1751). This treatise focused on such environmental theories as the availability of cheap gin, a high concentration of bars in a very small area, a big influx of the rural poor from the enclosures. It also led directly to Fielding's biggest experiment, funded by what is now called the Home Office, in the wake of a murder wave. When asked what could be done about it, he said he could create England's first professional police force. The idea of having *paid* people on patrol to go looking for criminals had to be kept a secret. The government of the day did not want to broadcast the fact that the English Government was »spying« on people with a Police patrol. But Fielding's police did arrest a gang that had committed the wave of murders, a success that was followed by many months in which London experienced no murders at all (Fielding, 1755).

Fielding was also an inventor who came up with crime reporting, crime analysis, and rapid response on horseback to crimes that had just occurred. He kept the Bow Street Runners (his Police force) going by what he called a no-cost extension in grant funds past his death when his brother John Fielding took over. His clear focus was on prevention of crime, not revenge. He was a very empathetic person who actually wrote about the state of poverty that many Londoners lived in. His general view was the medical attitude of the 18th century, which is »don't think – try.« That was the instruction to the inventor of smallpox vaccine, Edward Jenner, by his medical mentor, John Hunter (Barry, 2004), who invented organ transplants. Jenner, who discovered that milkmaids who had contracted cowpox never contracted smallpox, inoculated people with cowpox. By 1977 this method had led to the worldwide eradication of smallpox.

Jenner worked in the same era in which James Lind discovered that limes prevented scurvy. Lind discovered this by some thinking, but much more by trying. He was a ship's doctor in the US Navy who tried out five different diets to cure sailors suffering from scurvy. One of the diets included orange juice and lime juice. Even with a small sample size, the fruit juice diet prevented much better than the alternatives. He then presented the results to the officials of the British Navy, who said »thank you very much« and did nothing for forty-two years. When the officials finally handed out limes to British sailors, they became known world-wide as »limeys.« Yet the fate of evidence-based policy was hardly smooth. I think we agree that evidence does not lead to policy in an automatic sense, and that 42 years may in some circumstances be considered as fast as lightning.

So who had more effect? Was it Beccaria in his library (like Voltaire) or Henry Fielding in his court room and his secret police (like Jenner and Lind)? That may be the wrong question. Beccaria shows the power of theory; Fielding shows the power of experiment. Imagine combining the spirit of both these Enlighteners to create the modern conception of enlightened justice.

Both Beccaria and Fielding: Braithwaite. That is, in fact, what we find in the work of John Braithwaite. He has worked with equal diligence in reviewing research reports and in instigating experiments. He has observed justice in field settings from Afghanistan to Minnesota, while digesting theories and data from a wide range of scientific disciplines. He has made normative arguments to the Chief Justice of Australia, while giving practical advice to police sergeants on how to increase offender compliance with agreements. It is just this connection between theory and practice that is essential for the modern Enlightenment to work.

Making Consequences Matter

»To revenge crime is important, but to prevent it is more so.«
Conan Doyle (1927)

The second reason to celebrate Beccaria's contributions to the modern world is his lasting effect on consequentialism in penal principles. While Beccaria did not invent Utilitarianism, he remains important as the most effective advocate of making crime prevention consequences matter. To this day, his aphoristic treatise provides the most quotable, digestible, and emotionally persuasive case for making crime prevention the only goal of punishment. His condemnation of retribution as immoral has had less effect, with modern criminal codes designed on the premise that retribution and prevention are entirely compatible – espite substantial empirical evidence to the contrary (Sherman, 1993). Nonetheless, Beccaria helped to make the world safe for the long-term institutionalization of Fielding's inventions, especially the police (not firmly established in London until 1829). Beccaria's claim that it was better to prevent crimes than to punish them, echoed two centuries later in a Sherlock Holmes story by Arthur Conan Doyle (1929), allowed Patrick Colquhoun (1795) and then Sir Robert Peel and the founders of the Metropolitan Police in London to say that you do not prevent crime by hanging more and more people. The declining use of the death penalty, in fact, may have resulted more from the creation of preventive social control (like the police) than it did from the force of any moral arguments (Eisner, 2003).

The theory that Beccaria was building on came first from Montesquieu (1748), in the *Spirit of Laws,* in which he condemned the will to punish which we still see in many nations today. In both the United States, where I live, and the United Kingdom, where I often work, we see a zeal to punish. Montesquieu saw in that zeal a form of witchcraft, the idea that by punishing criminals we may »avenge the deity.« This idea, implicitly, still prevails today. Montesquieu's point was that if you want to honour the deity, do so, but try not to avenge the deity – the deity does not need it.

Beccaria's opposition to the idea of »just deserts« was consistent with his emphasis on prevention. He opposed any punishment exceeding that needed to deter. By extension, he implicitly recommended that the severity of the punishment should be made to fit the offender, not the offense. So that as the architect of the science of justice, he called for sentencing guidelines that were based on the post-sentence impact of punishments on crime: whether the sentence would help to prevent this offender and all potential offenders from committing this crime, or specific and general deterrence. No matter how surprising or counter-intuitive the evidence would be, he would say, »take that sentence which prevents the most crime, as long as the evidence is reliable«.

All of that assumes that consequentialism is reasonable. Braithwaite says it is reasonable both for agents of the state, as well as for offenders, victims and other citizens. If offenders can fully understand the consequences of crime for their victims, he suggests, they will have more empathy for the victim. If victims can gain understanding of why the offender came to be an offender, they may be able to integrate with each other to build a stronger community and perhaps prevent crime. All of this harkens back to the Scottish Enlightenment's views of empathy as a very powerful emotion, notably by David Hume and Adam Smith (see

Buchan, 2003: 136). Smith even hoped that empathy would be discovered as a kind of unifying force of the social universe, as gravity is in the physical. Braithwaite once viewed the emotions of shame in a similar way, but has also placed more emphasis in recent times on empathy. The fact that he has moved this way with the research is a further indication of an empirical stance that is not wedded to the theory's defense at any cost.

This philosophy makes the world safe for experiments in justice, of the kind that Fielding did, of the kind that von Liszt (1882) proposed, of the kind that Herbert Sturz undertook in the 1960s in New York, when he found that if you let people go before trial, if they had community ties (a place to live or a job) that they would come back to court to stand for trial – even if they had not posted money bail (Ares, Rankin and Sturz, 1963). This finding prevented millions of months of pre-trial imprisonment (in each case up to several months before trial), with the idea of »ROR« (release on recognizance) now spread across the world. It is not clear that such bold attempts to change longstanding practices would have ever been possible without the rhetorical force of Beccaria's writing.

Beccaria has also made the world safe for the ideas of John Braithwaite. The goal of crime prevention, seen more broadly as the reduction of human misery, is one that Braithwaite has been able to promote in such radical proposals as non-custodial sentences for sex offenders, or even homicides. The argument that such practices could actually save lives, or prevent rapes, has been made so strong by Beccaria that it is now hard to assail on purely philosophical (as distinct from empirical) grounds. It is a rare retributivist indeed who does not just *assume* that retribution deters and prevents crime, rather than arguing (against Beccaria) that consequences are morally irrelevant.

Retributivists have been able to take this stance partly, but not entirely, due to the small number of controlled experiments in justice policies. For even when research does find a failure of retribution to deter, there is a common tendency to rebut the research results on the grounds of poor methodology. In a recent public lecture at the University of Pennsylvania, for example, a prominent law professor simply asserted that there is no research on human beings that adequately measures the effects of criminal sanctions (Robinson, 2005), without even mentioning – let alone engaging – the many experiments that show criminal sanctions to increase crime rather than reducing it (Sherman, 1993). It is therefore essential that Enlightened Justice contain the third and modern element that Beccaria never imagined, but Braithwaite did from the very start.

Architects of the Science of Justice

> »Crime reduction should not simply be asserted by program advocates, but should be studied under rigorous conditions, with no guarantees in advance that positive results will be found.«
> Ruth and Reitz (2002).

In the history of science, much has been made of the need for independent testing and replication of theories. In the history of justice, little if anything has ever been said on the subject. If an enlightened approach based on consequences is to be guided by scientific evidence, then the transparency of science must be brought to bear on every recommended program of crime prevention. Field tests may be conducted by proponents of programs, just as Australian doctor Barry Marshall infected himself with ulcers and cured the ulcers with antibiotics (winning a shared 2005 Nobel Prize in Medicine). But it is only by adding the independent replications by others besides the author or inventor of a program that widespread confidence may be granted to the results. That was manifestly the case with Marshall's plan for gastric ulcers (Monomaney 1993). It is also manifestly the case for Marshall's fellow-countryman, John Braithwaite.

As Henry Ruth and Kevin Reitz (2002) discuss at length in *The Challenge of Crime*, Braithwaite is a moral entrepreneur who has the courage to place his program to independent empirical test. While they criticize Braithwaite's shifting terminology sometimes »mystifying,« they praise his clearly testable and falsifiable hypotheses. Most of all they praise his acceptance of the moral duty to experiment. As a key Watergate prosecutor who brought down Richard Nixon, Henry Ruth and his colleague mince no words. They say that the most remarkable thing about Braithwaite's program is its linkage to a long-term program of empirical testing. Since they wrote, the program has expanded even more, into the courts and prisons of England, as well as other settings. Building on Braithwaite's success in funding the RISE (Re-Integrative Shaming Experiments) in Canberra, the Jerry Lee Program of Randomized Controlled Trials in Restorative Justice now has 12 completed field tests of Braithwaite's approach to restorative justice for different kinds of crimes, criminals, victims, and stages of the criminal justice process http://www.sas.upenn.edu/jerrylee/research/rj_jlc_rct.pdf.

The most important thing about these results is that they are highly mixed. Some findings support the predictions of Braithwaite's theories; other findings falsify the theories. The fact that Aboriginal youth become much *more* likely to be arrested after restorative justice than after conventional justice is perhaps the greatest disappointment in the entire body of research (Sherman, et al, 2004). At the same time, it may offer the greatest theoretical opportunity to discover why »RJ« works for some people and not for others. More specifically, it may unravel the complex connections between legitimacy of law, legitimacy of sanctioning agents, and compliance with or defiance of the state's requirements not to commit crimes against fellow-citizens.

Braithwaite's response to all this has been as open-minded as scientific values require. While the program (which I co-direct with Braithwaite's ANU colleague Heather Strang) has been slow to get the results into peer-reviewed journals, there has been much discussion of it in government circles. In none of these settings has Braithwaite ever sought to attack the findings, or to defend the theory from empirical falsifications. In his own work, he has done just the opposite: revising the theory in light of new empirical evidence from the independent research program (Braithwaite and Braithwaite, 2001). This is truly an enlightened response in world beset by an adversarial approach to both justice and science, one in which even an »open-society« advocate like Karl Popper could not stand anyone criticizing his work.

Two years ago I was invited to a German state, where the Minister of the Interior called all the Police Presidents into the room and he announced to them that »starting today, we will evaluate all crime prevention. Do not just believe crime prevention, prove crime prevention works through evaluation.« It is striking that even in the 21st century, a Minister of the Interior has also accepted the moral duty to test the effects of crime response programs. He thereby says, in effect, that Beccaria was right, and that in the modern context whenever large human consequences are an issue in crime response programming, methodologically sound research should be undertaken – unless a good reason can be cited to explain its absence. Then he echoes Braithwaite's approach to the balance of reason and emotion, not because of its logical analysis, but because of the emphasis on the testing that would be done.

Thus the modern Enlightened Justice represented in John Braithwaite has both sense and sensibility. It offers *sense* in the reason to face facts and consider alternatives to current justice practices. It offers *sensibility* to, and empathy for, the pain of others, and not just moral outrage at the rage to punish. It offers *balance* to keep the two separate, letting sensibility serve as the engine driving the effort to impose »common sense« on the reduction of harm.

Conclusion

As moral and empirical architects of the science of justice, Beccaria and Braithwaite both offer the emotional foundation for an immense superstructure. If »geometric precision« in an individualized response to each crime, let alone criminal, is ever to be constructed, it will require an immense superstructure of empirical facts. Only by adding the sum of these facts together in ways propagated by the Campbell Collaboration (see http://www.aic.gov.au/campbellcj/) can we hope to build an enlightened justice in the 21st century. Such efforts as have already been attempted (Sherman et al, 1997) will constitute a drop in the ocean of facts that must emerge to guide an enlightened justice. A huge pile of so many facts thus runs the danger of a Tower of Babel, crashing down around us because no one can understand all the facts, let alone languages, that have been placed on top of one another. What we will continue to need is a clear and emotionally satisfying vision of reducing human suffering, making the world a better place. That is what Beccaria has given us to this day. And for those who cannot or will not consider words written by dead white European males in white wigs, it is important to have a contemporary voice to describe that vision, using modern examples, modern policy debates, and modern research results.

Since Voltaire fueled Enlightenment empathy by telling stories about individuals, we have known that such anecdotes are a powerful way to spread an idea. Hagiography is not written for the subjects of the praise. It is written to inspire the acts of the readers who may emulate what they read about. The purpose of this essay is to do just that. The challenges of criminology require far more emotional support and inspiration than most secular criminologists would ever admit. In the ritual of recognizing the great good created by individual criminologists, we may all be inspired to continue against the constant challenges and obstacles to an enlightened justice. As Beckett reminds us,»To all mankind they were addressed, those cries for help still ringing in our ears,« from crime victims, from offenders in prison who are also victims of crime, and from their loved ones. Yet without criminology, all humankind together may neither hear nor answer those cries. Our job, as Beccaria and Braithwaite so powerfully remind us, is to provide the light to guide the way. For of all the things that may be said of what we do, perhaps the most valued would be this: »they were enlighteners.«

References

Ares, Rankin and Sturz (1963). »The Manhattan Bail Project: An interim report on the use of pre-trial parole.« New York University Law Review 67:38.
Barry, John (2004). The Great Influenza. N.Y.: Viking.
Beccaria, Cesare (1764) Of Crime and Punishment. Milan.
Braithwaite, John (1989). Crime, Shame and Reintegration. Cambridge: Cambridge University Press. (2002). Restorative Justice and Responsive Regulation. Oxford: Oxford University Press.
Braithwaite, John and Valerie Braithwaite. (2001). »Shame, Shame Management and Regulation.« pp. 3–68 in Eliza Ahmed, Nathan Harris, John Braithwaite and Valerie Braithwaite, Shame Management Through Reintegration. Cambridge: Cambridge University Press.
Braithwaite, John and Philip Petit (1990). Not Just Deserts. Oxford: Oxford University Press.
Buchan, James (2003). Crowded With Genius. The Scottish Enlightenment and Edinburgh's Moment of the Mind. N.Y.: HarperCollins.
Colquhoun, Patrick (1795). A Treatise on the Police of the Metropolis. London. Reprinted at Montclair, New Jersey: Patterson-Smith, 1969.
Conan Doyle, Arthur (1927). »The Adventure of the Illustrious Client,« in The Sherlock Holmes Case-Book. London: John Murray. Text on-line at http://www.bakerstreet221b.de/canon/illu.htm .
Eisner, Manuel. 2003. »Long-Term Historical Trends in Violent Crime« Crime and Justice; A Review of Research, Vol. 30, pp. 83-142 (U. of Chicago Press).
Fielding, Henry. 1751. An enquiry into the causes of the late increase of robbers, &c., with some proposals for remedying this growing evil. In which the present reigning vices are impartially exposed; and the laws that relate to the provision for the poor, and to the punishment of felons are largely and freely examined. London.

Gay, Peter (1969). The Enlightenment. Vol. 2: The Science of Feedom.N.Y.: Alfred A. Knopf.

Kant, Immanuel (1784). Quotation reproduced as an epigraph in Gay (1969) at forepage.

Liszt, Franz von (1882). The Marburg Program. Marburg: Phillips University of Marburg.

Montesquieu, Baron de (Charles de Secondat). (1748, trans. 1752). De L'Esprit des Lois. http://socserv2.socsci.mcmaster.ca/~econ/ugcm/3ll3/montesquieu/spiritoflaws.pdf

Monmaney, Terence. 1993. »Annals of Medicine: Marshall's Hunch.« The New Yorker. Reprinted on-line, Oct. 7, 2005.

Robinson, Paul (2005). »Does Giving People the Punishment They Deserve Help Reduce Crime?« The 2004–2005 Albert M. Greenfield Memorial Lecture on Human Relations, University of Pennsylvania (see http://www.sas.upenn.edu/jerrylee/programs/greenfield_lecture.htm)

Ruth, Henry S. and Kevin Reitz (2003). The Challenge of Crime. Cambridge, Mass.: Harvard University Press.

Sherman, Lawrence (1993). »Defiance, Deterrence and Irrelevance: A Theory of the Criminal Sanction.« Journal of Research in Crime and Delinquency 30:445–473.

Sherman, Lawrence (2003). Reason for Emotion: Reinventing Justice With Theories, Innovations and Experiments: The 2002 American Society of Criminology Presidential Address. Criminology 41: 1–38.

Sherman, Lawrence (2005) »The Use and Usefulness of Criminology, 1751–2005: Enlightened Justice and Its Failures« Annals of the American Academy of Political and Social Science 600: 115–135.

Sherman, Lawrence, Denise Gottfredson, Doris MacKenzie, John Eck, Peter Reuter and Shawn D. Bushway (1997). Preventing Crime: What Works? What Doesn't? What's Promising? Washington, D.C.: Office of Justice Programs, U.S. Department of Justice (see http://www.ncjrs.org/works/).

Paul Ekblom,
Central St. Martin's College of Art and Design, University of the Arts, London[18]
The 5Is Framework:
Sharing Good Practice in Crime Prevention

Introduction

Evaluation is a demanding task. It takes expertise, time, money and commitment to give results which are reliable enough for policymakers and practitioners to use with confidence. Therefore, our supply of good evaluations is so far pretty limited. However, we are now seeing a steady growth in the evidence base that evaluation aims to build. Thanks to people like Larry Sherman and his colleagues,[19] we now have good evidence in principle that diverse kinds of crime prevention can successfully, and even cost-effectively, reduce crime. And these methods have the potential to make a significant difference to people's quality of life – if the approaches are based on reliable evidence, and if they are implemented well.

The Beccaria Project rightly focuses on the intimate relationship between evaluation and quality of crime prevention. A key link in this relationship is knowledge and how we handle it.

Defining, capturing, storing, retrieving and transferring knowledge of good practice is a difficult process. Even medicine finds it a challenge to become a fully evidence-based discipline. But for the softer, social science approaches central to crime prevention, it is even harder

---

[18] Examples of CSM's work on Design Against Crime are at www.arts.ac.uk/research/dac
[19] Sherman, L., Gottfredson, D., MacKenzie, D., Eck, J., Reuter, P. and Bushway, S. (1997). *Preventing Crime: What Works, What Doesn't, What's Promising* A Report to the United States Congress. Available at www.cjcentral.com/sherman/sherman.htm . Goldblatt, P and Lewis, C (eds.) (1998). Reducing Offending: An Assessment of Research Evidence on Ways of Dealing with Offending Behaviour. Home Office Research Study No. 187. London: Home Office. www.homeoffice.gov.uk/rds/pdfs/hors187.pdf.

to achieve. How do we take rigorous knowledge of what works in crime prevention, capture what has been implemented, make good practice available to practitioners and policymakers, and ensure it is used, both in individual projects and large-scale programmes?

An evidence-based approach

There is growing awareness that knowledge does not flow like water naturally from source to mainstream, but has to be actively moved uphill. Passive dissemination is not enough to ensure that practitioners adopt an evidence-based, problem-oriented approach. We already see great efforts to *generate* knowledge through research, development and evaluation; and to *integrate* this knowledge through high-quality *systematic reviews* of evidence of effectiveness, such as through the Sherman Report and the Campbell Collaboration[20]. Now, we are also seeing explicit efforts to *transfer and apply* that knowledge. Now, there is increasing activity involving education and training, practitioner networks, toolkits and the establishment of knowledge bases. *Beccaria* is a very welcome part of this tendency.

This trend towards actively organising the transfer of knowledge is accelerating. This is especially because we are now more conscious that social and technological change, and adaptive, innovative criminals can make what *currently* works in preventing crime, irrelevant or obsolete in the future. What used to work is no good. We have to *catch up*, and then *innovate* faster than the criminals can.

But we should not accelerate *blindly*, but first pause to think. When *designing* any knowledge base or setting out any training curriculum, we must be very clear *why* we are doing it, and exactly *what* we are hoping to transfer. To rush into construction is to risk wasted expense and effort on the part of the designers and builders, and confusion, and lost opportunity, for practitioners. Past attempts at knowledge bases have not always succeeded.

Help is, though, available from one particular direction. ›*Knowledge management*‹ appears to have emerged as a discipline almost overnight, to cater generically for an increasingly knowledge-driven society. In principle this approach is vital. But is it enough? I would argue strongly

---

[20] www.campbellcollaboration.org

that it is not sufficient, because it is *content-free*. We need to put some of that content back, and that's what I'm going to talk about now.

So here are the key questions I am going to pose.
What is the knowledge for?
What types of knowledge fulfill that purpose?
What form/s should the knowledge take to be fit for purpose in a practical context and to reflect the real nature of crime prevention activity?

The purpose of crime prevention knowledge

So we begin with the fundamental question, what is the purpose of knowledge? In the present practical context, I take the purpose to be *improving, extending and sustaining performance in crime prevention.*

A huge variety of people and institutions, private, public and commercial, act as purposeful crime preventers who carry out tasks which deliver crime prevention interventions, or support them. These tasks can range from formal and professional policing, probation and the punishment and rehabilitation of offenders, to dedicated private security services, to the design of products and environments against crime, to surveillance and site management by employees (such as railway station staff), to the self-protection and informal social control that ordinary citizens do every day.

Improvements in the performance of these individuals and institutions in their crime prevention roles involve making better judgements, decisions and actions. We can look closer at the concept of performance itself.

Cost-effectiveness is at the heart of the ›what works‹ mission, but there is much more to performance than this. There are also:

Better responsiveness to individual crime problems and to the problems of an area as a whole. Responsiveness in turn covers several things:

Prioritisation of prevention in relation to the consequences of different crimes, and people's needs for protection

Accurate targeting on needs of victim and wider society, and on causes of crime;

More complete coverage on the ground – can practitioners cost-effectively tackle all burglaries, say, or only those in the worst-hit areas or certain types of burglary? and wider scope, in terms of the range of different crime problems preventers can tackle – highly specific or broad-spectrum? Timeliness – of implementation, impact greater sustainability – how long the implementation of the crime prevention activity can be maintained, or how long the crime prevention effect itself lasts. Perhaps a new neighbourhood Watch group gives up after a few months. Maybe a CCTV camera only deters criminals for a few weeks until they get used to it.

Avoidance of significant undesirable side-effects of action – such as stigmatisation of areas or people, interference with other values and policy areas such as privacy, or environmental pollution, or even displacement of crime onto more vulnerable victims.

Greater legitimacy or acceptability of crime prevention actions, within the wider population, within minority subgroups, or even among offenders themselves. It is pretty obvious how closely this analysis of performance relates to the Beccaria Project's concept of quality.

Money, staff, legitimacy and motivation are all needed to achieve good performance, combined with the right occupational culture, organisational procedures, structures and management frameworks. But none of these are much use, without reliable knowledge. Knowledge is not merely an extra component, of course, but something which provides the core substance and connects the whole show together.

The content of crime prevention knowledge

What, then, can we know about crime and its prevention, so we can improve our performance? We can actually identify seven distinct types of knowledge:

Know about crime problems, and their costs and wider consequences for victims and society; ... offenders' modus operandi, legal definitions of offences, patterns and trends in criminality, risk and protective factors,... and theories of causation.

Know what works – what crime prevention methods work, against what crime problem, in what context, with what side-effects and what cost-effectiveness.

Know how to put into practice – knowledge and skills of implementation and other practical processes, and methodologies for research and analysis.

Know who to involve – contacts for advice, potential partners and collaborators who can be mobilised as formal or informal preventers; service providers, suppliers of funds and equipment and other specific resources; and sources of wider support.

Know when to act – there's always a right time to make particular moves – the climate has to be right, other initiatives need to be coordinated with etc.

Know where to target and distribute resources – this is obvious.

Know why – this sounds a bit existential – but it's really about the symbolic, emotional, ethical, cultural and value-laden meanings of crime and preventive action, including fairness and justice. Failure to address these issues can cause even the most rational and evidence-based actions to be rejected. The classic example is the public outrage sometimes caused by expensive sporting activities for young offenders.

Implementation failure

Now for some bad news from the battlefront. Many crime prevention projects, it must be said, have a number of quite significant limitations – this is the world of implementation failure. Single demonstration projects, often designed and implemented by top academics and practitioners, usually work well – but when such success stories are replicated or rolled out in the mainstream of a programme, they frequently fail to meet expectations. This is serious!

Medical science gives some useful terminology here, referring to the difference between *efficacy* – the results in principle, from a laboratory trial – and *effectiveness* in practice, as constrained for example by patients' unwillingness to take their medicine as instructed.

Routine replication/mainstreaming of ›success stories‹ is difficult

Long and depressing experience shows some typical limitations of ›mainstream‹ projects. Many of these stem from poor management, but I will focus on those associated with poor knowledge and a weak conceptual framework:

First, we find superficial interventions with no clear understanding of the causes of the crime problem, and a lack of focus on either the fundamental principles of crime prevention or the detailed causal mechanisms by which the methods are meant to work. An example we often see is

›this project is about working with young people‹. Now, this could equally be a good intervention or a poor one; it is certainly a poor description. What *exactly* is the project trying to do – and how *exactly* does it work? Both questions need an answer before you can reliably replicate.

Sadly, therefore, we find many cookbook replications – which do not copy these fundamental principles of an intervention, or the intelligent process of going from analysis to intervention to implementation. Instead, they only copy its external form. They also fail to recognise that a method may work well in one social context, but not in others. Crime prevention methods are not like pesticide which can be sprayed uniformly over all the fields and have the same effect.

We also find limited innovation. Creativity, too, comes from a head full of organised principles and ability to mix them together to suit specific cases, rather than from a random idea generator or a fixed repertoire.

Similarly, we often find weak impact evaluations from which no reliable knowledge is accumulated – this is sometimes due to poor methodology, but often through insufficient focus on causal mechanisms.

Looking at the body of evaluated knowledge as a whole, there is also a lack of synthesis of the results – knowledge should be a properly constructed building rather than a disconnected pile of bricks.

Under all these circumstances, we would do better to arm our practitioners with a set of *generic principles* of prevention and knowledge of the *process* rather than supply them merely with large numbers of fixed solutions. This is because fixed solutions may not always fit, and worse, they become obsolete as said earlier. More broadly put, we have to help practitioners to think less like *technicians* selecting a simple prepackaged remedy from a limited menu, like a service engineer with a broken washing machine; and more like *expert consultants*, using these principles to customize to context, to innovate and reconfigure their diagnoses and solutions as they go. Again, I think this is consistent with the Beccaria project's vision.

A knowledge base that is fit for purpose

So what are the features of knowledge that we have to capture if our knowledge base is to be fit for purpose? Perhaps my most important message is this. What-works knowledge is essential, of course, but for successfully sharing and replicating good practice lessons we need that knowledge in a lot of detail – and we need a great deal more than What-works too. Our knowledge base must attempt to describe process in a way that promotes the *intelligent reconstruction* of crime prevention actions by describing every stage of developing and delivering them. Given the importance of process, we should be able to retrieve *good practice elements of action* derived from each stage of a project. For example, if a burglary scheme has a rather unimaginative intervention, it may still have an extremely useful and novel method of mobilising the local community – this is an element of good practice which could be used in a range of other circumstances – such as in tackling car crime.

The knowledge base must extract information on the original *context* of the project, and how that context was thought to contribute to successful analysis, intervention, implementation and impact. One important factor to capture in adapting to different contexts is what I call *Troublesome Tradeoffs*. By these, I mean the tricky balances that must be creatively resolved in designing any crime prevention activity. How do we maximise security for reasonable cost, whilst also respecting convenience, privacy, aesthetics, environmental issues, social exclusion and sales figures? The general principles behind a new replication may be similar to the original project that is being copied. But the pressures, constraints and possibilities for realisation may be very different in new contexts, leading to rather different solutions in practice.

The knowledge base needs a certain kind of *structure*, too. It must help practitioners to flip between thinking at several levels. From an immediate, implementation perspective, we have to help practitioners think, and share information about practical, tangible *methods* – like running particular activities in youth clubs, or fixing gates on the alleyways behind houses. From an analytic perspective we have to try to extract information on higher-level *principles* such as surveillance and even on *theories* like social learning theory (theories are the ultimate in compressed knowledge), and on very specific *causal mechanisms* – how principles actually combine and play out in detailed configurations in the particular context.

The lack of consistent terminology limits what can be described and retrieved in a knowledge base. This is especially a problem with *international* knowledge bases, like the one that is now emerging through the EUCPN, or indeed through Beccaria. And underneath clear terminology, there has to be a clear *conceptual framework,* to support the capture, storage, retrieval, transfer and application of knowledge. This is far more important than just gathering isolated facts. It is about supplying people with *tools for thought.* The lack of a conceptual framework has several other serious consequences for the performance of crime prevention:

It inhibits communication and collaboration between diverse partners: the police may use one term, local government officers a different one.

It affects clarity of planning preventive action, and quality assurance of implementation.

It prevents integrated, strategic thinking about causes and solutions – some people speak only a judicial and law enforcement language, others the language of civil prevention. And some people focus exclusively on situations, others just on offenders.

It weakens education and training – learning works best when practitioners have a complete mental schema with which they can organise their knowledge, and assimilate new facts. In this respect we need to strive to build a schema that is collective and cumulative, rather than reinventing our terminology with every publication. Ron Clarke's attempt to do this with the techniques of Situational Crime Prevention has been heroic – now they are 25.[21]

Campbell (systematic) Reviews – necessary, but not sufficient?

At this point we should make a brief diversion into Campbell country. The Campbell approach, as mentioned above, involves conducting systematic reviews of all available evidence on effectiveness and cost-effectiveness, for a range of social interventions, including crime prevention. The academic standard of evidence is rightly high – it is intended to guide national or international policy and public expenditure. The Campbell approach is, therefore, pitched at a level of generality that makes it very suitable to inform such policy – for example, that ›street lighting can be a cost-effective crime prevention strategy‹. But this generality makes it insufficient for supporting practical replication. How do practitioners put together a working lighting scheme that is fit for context and purpose? Knowledge of what works is currently collected

---

[21] See R.V. Clarke and J. Eck (2003) *Become a Problem-Solving Crime Analyst (in 55 small steps)* www.jdi.ucl.ac.uk/publications/manual/crime_manual_content.php

in insufficient detail, with insufficient synthesis of theory and mechanism, and insufficient sensitivity to context. And what works knowledge is insufficiently balanced by attention to the other dimensions of knowledge that I described earlier. These limitations also feed back up from the practical level to constrain strategic delivery. This is because governments need to know more than comparative cost-effectiveness – they also need to know about implementability of preventive methods – what are the constraints and risks in getting from policy to practice? What is needed to establish the supporting infrastructure in training, information, guidance and organisational development to make mainstream programmes succeed?

But I should restate here that Campbell-type approaches are completely necessary – they just need development and extension to support implementation through replication and innovation.

Happily, some of the approaches to systematic review have begun to develop in these directions. For example, one study in medicine[22] systematically reviews the evidence on the effectiveness of the processes of transferring knowledge to practitioners. (Here, the outcome measures of the evaluations reviewed are not reduced illness, but improved performance of medics ... which hopefully *does* lead to reduced illness if the impact evidence base is also sound).

What users of knowledge bases need

That's the philosophy, but the immediate purpose of knowledge bases, of course, is operational. Most of what I have to say applies to crime prevention practice out there in the field, but we can identify equivalent messages for the kind of knowledge that *policymakers* need when they are undertaking their own practice.

When ground-level practitioners log into a knowledge base, they will have some clear needs and expectations. After *defining their problem* they want to *select* preventive methods, which are both evidence-based and suitable to tackle their own crime problems in their own regional and local context. After selection, they hopefully move on to intelligent *replication*. Where no direct good practice example fits, or can be adapted – which may happen often – a good knowledge base should not leave

[22] www.epoc.uottawa.ca/scope.htm

practitioners in the dark, but should still help them to bridge the gap by *innovation*. (Innovation in turn has to draw on high-level principles which are evidence-based or could be.) Interestingly, given the context-dependency of crime prevention activity, even the most mundane replication is far more like innovation than we may comfortably think.

Well, these are demanding specifications for a framework. The framework most people have been using in the English-speaking world over the last 15 years is SARA – Scanning, Analysis, Response and Assessment.[23] This originated in the world of problem-oriented policing and gave practitioners an easy-to-use starting platform. But is SARA up to it? I have to say, that I think SARA gave practitioners an excellent start, but it has insufficient depth of detail, and pays insufficient attention to the issue of the structure of action. As such, I think it now constrains practice as much as facilitating it – but that is a matter for debate.

The five Is: The steps of the preventive process

So far, I have discussed the nature and purpose of crime prevention knowledge, identified some pervasive problems with performance of crime prevention and the replication of good practice, and set out a design specification for a framework for knowledge. This also serves to specify a methodology for doing crime prevention in a quality-sensitive way. Now, though, it is time to present the framework which I have begun to develop, which aims to satisfy that specification.

The 5Is framework for crime prevention comprises a series of steps:

Intelligence is about gathering and analysing information on crime problems and their causes and consequences.

Intervention is about action to block, disrupt or weaken those causes and risk factors, in ways which wherever possible are evidence-based and appropriate to the crime problem and the context.

Implementation involves making the practical methods happen – putting them into action on the ground.

Involvement covers mobilising other agencies, companies and individuals in the community to play their part in implementing the intervention, and it also covers the more symmetrical partnership.

Impact and cost-effectiveness evaluation.

---

[23] See www.popcenter.org

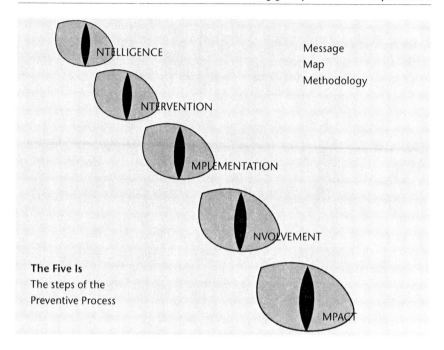

The Five Is
The steps of the
Preventive Process

To help communicate the framework, 5Is has three levels of understanding. The 5 Is themselves are the Message. This is an easily-remembered slogan which communicates the basic concept in everyday language to a wide range of users. The next level of detail is the Map – a detailed list of headings under each of the 5 Is. This is suitable for managers and supervisors to be familiar with. The final level is the Methodology. This is the detailed guidance and knowledge that appears, or will appear, under each of the headings of the Map. It's for the professional practitioners. I haven't the time to go through the whole Map, and certainly not the Methodology. Besides, it is still under development. But I can illustrate it with some examples. You can find example descriptions of projects using 5Is on the EUCPN website, and more guidance material on the UK Crime Reduction website.[24]

As you can see, 5Is completely maps onto the SARA process, although

---

[24] www.crimereduction.gov.uk/learningzone/5isintro.htm

it greatly expands SARA's ›Response‹ stage into 3 separate activities. 5Is is also pretty close to the 7 Steps of the Beccaria Project. Dropping down to the map and the methodology levels reveals that these similarities are even closer, although Beccaria's final step on *documentation* is a useful extra.

Example of zooming in: Intelligence

Here is one example of zooming in.
Message: Intelligence
Map: Causes, risk factors
Methodology: This can include the *Problem Analysis Triangle,*[25] which again is excellent for beginners but quickly becomes constraining or the *Conjunction of Criminal Opportunity*

Describing causes of crime
The Conjunction of Criminal Opportunity (CCO), my preferred framework, sets out 11, generic, immediate causes of the crime problem being tackled. These range from the *offender* side – such as their personality and their immediate motivation, which is influenced in turn by their current life circumstances such as drug addiction or poverty – to the *situational* side – what aspects of the environment and the people in it make crime more risky, less rewarding and more effort to commit. CCO also involves two other sets of roles than the offender – *preventers*, who make crime harder, and *promoters*, who make it easier. Preventers and promoters can be public, commercial or police, prison, probation or drug treatment officers. The benefit of this framework is that it gets practitioners to think across two major professional cultural divides – between *situational and offender-oriented prevention*, and across *justice and civil prevention*. We will revisit these causes, in the case study.

Describing crime prevention interventions

We can also describe Interventions using the CCO framework. Take the example crime problem of robbery in a car park.
   This shows how a crime prevention intervention (trimming bushes in the wider environment) has blocked one of the causes (environmental

[25] www.popcenter.org

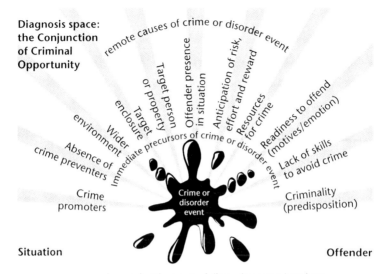

www.crimereduction.gov.uk/learningzone/cco.htm

concealment), leading to a disruption of the Conjunction of Criminal Opportunity, to decreased risk of the criminal event happening (ie prevention), and in this case to successful reduction in crime, and to wider benefits such as increased perception of safety, and social and economic regeneration.

We can extend this diagram to systematically map the entire range of generic families of intervention principles onto the generic causes of crime that they aim to block. CCO aims to cover both civil and enforcement-based interventions, and both situational and offender-oriented ones, so it truly attempts to integrate the field. The intervention ›families‹ are listed on the UK Crime Reduction Website.[26]

That was the complete map of ›intervention space‹.[27] Now for the issue of multiple levels.

[26] www.crimereduction.gov.uk/learningzone/cco.htm
[27] There are extensions which cater for interventions in higher-order markets, networks etc – see Ekblom, P (2003) ›Organised Crime and the Conjunction of Criminal Opportunity Framework‹, in A. Edwards and P. Gill (eds.) *Transnational Organised Crime: Perspectives on global security*. London: Routledge, pp. 241–263; and Roach, J, Ekblom, P and Flynn, R (2005) ›The Conjunction of Terrorist Opportunity‹ (accepted for *Security Journal*).

Any practical crime prevention method is likely to act through several of these immediate intervention principles. For example, hardening a target enclosure by building a high wall may physically block theft, deter the offender from selecting that enclosure, and help preventers do their work of surveillance. In some cases, the interventions will be quite remote, and involve a whole chain of cause and effect before the immediate precursors to criminal events are changed.

In the real world, a crime prevention scheme or operation may combine several methods in a *package* to tackle multiple causes of a crime problem, or to block offenders' obvious displacement routes. It may tackle multiple scenes in a complex organised crime, or simultaneously disrupt several aspects of a market for stolen goods. It may address multiple crime problems if, say, they involve the use of a common resource such as forged passports, or a criminal network.

Example of zooming in: Involvement

Under the heading of *Involvement*, the subhead of *Mobilisation* involves several linked activities:

Clarify the crime prevention tasks that need to be achieved (intervention, specific facilitation of interventions by others or more general climate-setting), or roles and responsibilities that need to be taken on.

Locate the preventive agents – identify institutions and individuals with the appropriate qualities to carry out the crime prevention tasks, because of their assets (competences; wider resources including staff; significant positions of influence), their acceptability for the role and their interests. Once located, secure their cooperation and enhance their performance in pursuit of the designated goals by:

Alerting them about the crime problem, that they or others might be affected by it, that they might be contributing to its cause and/or might be capable of contributing to its cure.

Motivating them to take on the crime prevention task – through inherent acceptance of its worth, exercise of responsibilities and duties, self-interest in its achievement or compliance with external incentives and sanctions linked to regulations and standards.

Empowering them – building capacity and alleviating constraints by supplying operational resources such as funds, staff and information; appropriate legal powers; competence; and technical aids. (Of course, empowerment should have a second edge – checking that powers granted are not exceeded through over-zealous actions such as vigilantism.)

Directing them (where appropriate) through objectives and standards, including quality standards.

Given the way society works, we are unlikely to succeed by atomistic approaches that rely on influencing individual agencies in isolation. This CLAMED approach has to bring together a range of agencies in an integrated system of influence and support. And there is a need, also, to establish a receptive *climate*.

Case Study: Operation Moonshine

So now for an example of a 5Is project description.[28] We collected this information in a 3-hour semi-structured interview with the practitioners using 5Is as the schedule. At the end of the session they were astonished at how much they had achieved during the project, because they had never articulated it before.

The project was about anti-social behaviour and consumption of alcohol by under-age drinkers in a small housing estate in the South of England.

Intelligence

THE GENERAL CONTEXT OF THE PROBLEM

The Borough of Test Valley, Hampshire is primarily rural. Valley Park, the project area, has around 7.5k residents. It is quite well-off – little unemployment. One per cent of the working age population were unemployed. Nationally, Valley Park is among the 5% of least deprived neighbourhoods.

EVIDENCE OF THE CRIME PROBLEM –
SOURCES OF INFORMATION AND ANALYSIS

Crime data in this study involved recorded crime (mainly criminal damage, shoplifting, commercial burglary) and what the force termed ›Crime and Disorder Act nuisance incidents‹ (mainly juvenile nuisance,

---

[28] The complete 5Is project description is available on www.beccaria.de

minor public disorder and noise nuisance). The data was collected in a computerised crime reporting system and put on a map. People were reluctant to report this kind of crime, partly because they felt that the police were not doing anything to tackle the disorder issues; so the crimes recorded only represented a fraction of the picture.

The local youth club was used to hold a focus group to identify their needs. And the team defined acts of disorder as ›anything that you can think of that would impact on your quality of life without being a criminal offence‹.

THE CRIME PROBLEM THAT THE PROJECT AIMED TO TACKLE

At the time the baseline data was collected in early 2002, during each month there were around 70 antisocial incidents and crimes.

The *offenders* were male and female, aged between about 12 and 18. The local ones were from relatively rich families in the London commuter belt. There was also a less wealthy set of migrant offenders who came from further afield including Southampton.

In terms of *Modus Operandi*, groups of youths up to 50 strong would congregate around the shopping centre, drinking alcohol which made them progressively noisy and disorderly, eventually leading in some cases to violence (particularly where local groups of youths interacted with others from outside the area). Criminal damage was perpetrated on any street items that got in their way. Youths targeted one specific shop, as it had a broken door, which was repeatedly kicked in so they could steal alcohol and food. There was evidence of significant use of recreational drugs by a few youths.

SIGNIFICANT CONSEQUENCES OF THE CRIME PROBLEM

All these events had a negative impact on the community's *quality of life*. The problem was not so much that particular people were being victimised, more that the young people were persistently acting in a disorderly way for the entire weekend.

The public's *perception of safety* was severely diminished and they felt intimidated. Customers were deterred from visiting the shops, as they saw the large numbers of intoxicated and loud youths gathering on the flowerbed as a threat.

The misbehaviour also took a lot of *police time* for dispersing youths and dealing with incidents.

SIGNIFICANT CONSEQUENCES FOR FURTHER OFFENDING
There was no evidence so far that the antisocial behaviour specifically led individuals to a criminal career, or to the development of a criminal subculture. But the presence of youths themselves in large numbers did attract the attention of drug dealers.

Now we move onto *causes* and use the headings of CCO.

WIDER ENVIRONMENT
The raised flowerbed attracted youths to assemble on the flattened earth to drink their alcohol. The rough state also encouraged littering.

A shop close by provided light, and shelter from a canopy.

Migrant offenders were attracted to the area because of the presence of the wealthier local youths, who had money for alcohol.

OFFENDERS' PRESENCE IN CRIME SITUATION
Some of the youths involved in the trouble in Valley Park lived nearby. The influx of youths from the surrounding areas led to conflicts with the local male youths over the local females.

TARGET ENCLOSURE (BUILDINGS, COMPOUNDS ETC)
Already mentioned is the shop with poor external security measures.

RESOURCES FOR COMMITTING CRIME (TOOLS, WEAPONS, KNOW-HOW)
Loose bricks within the flowerbed were used in vandalism.

Some of the migrant offenders turned up with golf clubs and other weapons.

Mobile phones were sometimes used to draw gang members together and coordinate escape from the police.

READINESS TO OFFEND (immediate motivational and emotional factors)
One obvious motivating factor was boredom through *inadequacy of local leisure* facilities. The absence of legitimate entertainment on which to spend their sizeable disposable incomes may have led them to spend it on alcohol.

The youths also had difficulty getting *access to leisure facilities* further away. The nearby towns did offer some entertainment for this age group, but travel involved money and time; also the transport system was not good.

Underage consumption of *alcohol* acted in the all-too familiar way, to increase the readiness of the youths to misbehave. It also seemed to play a symbolic role, for expressing their independence.

How did they get hold of the booze? Some stole it from the ›soft target‹ shop, but others got it indirectly through the inaction or action of various crime preventers and promoters.

CRIME PREVENTERS – PEOPLE WHO MAKE CRIME LESS LIKELY TO HAPPEN
Numbers of staff in some of the local shops were insufficient to control theft.

CRIME PROMOTERS – PEOPLE WHO MAKE CRIME MORE LIKELY TO HAPPEN
Some local retailers illegally *sold alcohol* to under-18s. They also saved money by employing younger, lower-wage workers, and paid *inadequate attention to security*.

Young people placed orders for drinks with a 17 year old youth from outside the local area, and the drinks were distributed from the back of a car. His age meant he couldn't be arrested. The police were just waiting for his 18th birthday!

Older youths had purchased the alcohol legally and supplied it to their younger peers/siblings.

The offending youths harassed the general public to purchase alcohol on their behalf.

Parents acted as negligent promoters. Often both parents worked and commuted long hours, and required a break on returning home. The parents therefore did not wish to experience teenage angst, so sent their children out giving them (often plenty of) money to amuse themselves.

Peer pressure also served to encourage those who would not normally engage in antisocial activities, to join in.

Higher-level cause – drug market
An influx of drug dealers from outside the area resulted from the increase in numbers of accessible wealthy youths.

Intervention

So we move on to *Interventions*. Interventions are how the action *works* in terms of cause and effect.

Interventions can be described on both *practical* and *analytical* levels – respectively methods, and principles – both kinds of information are necessary for intelligent replication of good practice, and 5Is tries to reflect this.

Here are the interventions we extracted from the practitioners.

1. Modification of carrier bags
2. Targeted high visibility police patrols
3. *Acceptable Behaviour Contracts*[29] for persistent offenders
4. Target hardening of retail store to prevent alcohol theft
5. Removing flowerbed from the front of row of shops
6. Community clean up
7. Youth shelter
8. Mobile recreation unit
9. Arresting/Cautioning of Anti Social Behaviour offenders
10. Drop in centre for youths
11. A healthy living centre for youths
12. A forest location as alternative place for youths to gather
13. Disrupting a possible drugs market targeting youths

I will just describe some of these to show the kind of information we captured.

INTERVENTION 1: MODIFICATION OF CARRIER BAGS

Method: Modification of plain carrier bags to branded bags
Principles: Reducing readiness to offend (removing supply of alcohol); Deterring and incapacitating crime promoters (shopkeepers) and converting them to preventers; Mobilising preventers (parents); Empowering preventers (police).

Retailers who were selling alcohol to underage youths, were identified through the plastic bags that they gave to customers for their shopping. Police officers then went to the relevant stores and seized CCTV footage

---

[29] Acceptable Behaviour Contracts (ABCs) are written agreements between a young person, the local housing office or Registered Social Landlord (RSL) and the local police in which the person agrees not to carry out a series of identifiable behaviours which have been defined as antisocial. The contracts are primarily aimed at young people aged between 10 and 18.

of the sale. This footage was then used both to remind the retailers of the liquor licensing legislation and to mobilise them as preventers. CCTV footage (where of good enough quality) was also used to inform the parents of the offender(s) who often did not believe their dear child was buying alcohol. The carrier bags of certain retailers were also modified from plain white to ›branded‹ bags.

Risk to method 1: countermove by offenders

Following these modifications to carrier bags, youths subsequently used their own bags brought from the big supermarket chain Tesco's. The police, when confiscating these bags, checked at the local Tesco store for CCTV footage and confirmed that this was *not* where the alcohol had been bought. The police then re-established with the offender the true location of the alcohol purchase, and visited the shops.

INTERVENTION 5:
REMOVING A FLOWERBED FROM THE FRONT OF ROW OF SHOPS

Method: Removing the flowerbed from the row of shops
Principles: Environmental design; Restricting resources for crime; Deflecting offenders from a crime situation; Reassurance

They removed the flowerbed, which was actually spoiling the image of the area, not improving it. This prevented the youths from misusing the loose bricks. The area no longer attracted gatherings of youths as there was now nowhere to sit. The action also meant that shoppers no longer had to squeeze past the crowd of youths to reach the shops.

Risks of method 5:

Local retailers were concerned that removal of the flowerbed would take away the protection from ram-raiders. So bollards were placed at frequent intervals on the paved area to prevent ram-raiders targeting the shops. But these bollards could be misused as seats, so they were given pointed heads.

INTERVENTION 6: COMMUNITY CLEAN-UP

Method: Community clean up of Valley Park
Principles: Reassurance; Deterrence; Motivating preventers

Community wardens and some members of the public cleared up litter and generally tidied up the area by Valley Park shops. This apparently boosted reassurance (although it is difficult to measure direct impact), through the visible presence of community wardens and an apparently cleaner and safer place. It may also have engendered feelings of ownership and augmented ›social capital and collective efficacy‹. Removing the ›signs of crime‹ and establishing standards, may also be seen as applying ›Broken windows‹ principles to reduce misbehaviour and set rules. The clean-up also served the ›involvement function‹ of mobilising/engaging residents.

INTERVENTION 7: YOUTH SHELTER

Method: *Youth shelter for local juveniles*
Principles: *Diverting offenders from the crime situation and from alcohol; Reducing readiness to offend by meeting needs legitimately*

The project team installed a youth shelter that provided a personal space for young people to gather in and socialise without being a nuisance to others. This was intended to divert youths from hanging around the shops and also to keep them away from sources of alcohol. The shelter was installed as a result of consultation with youths carried out by the social services.

Risks

When the youth shelter was set up the police told the youths that it was their property so they had to take responsibility for it. If the shelter was destroyed, the police would remove it. The shelter did get graffiti from the youths, but the police considered this to be acceptable in principle, unless the message was obscene or racist. Then, the local bobby sprayed it out with a can which he carried in his bicycle saddlebag .

INTERVENTION 9: ARRESTING/CAUTIONING OF ASB OFFENDERS

Method: *Arresting/cautioning of ASB offenders*
Principles: *Removing offenders from the crime situation; Giving offenders resources to avoid offending (education); Deterrence and discouragement; Mobilising preventers (parents); acting as a gateway to CJS; and to youth services*

The police used cautions for the first and second time ASB offenders, which involved threatening the offender with arrest if they continued to commit offences. For more persistent offenders the police arrested them and sent them to the youth courts. In either case the police would recommend the youth in question to seek youth services – which offered advice on citizenship, drugs and alcohol, etc. This process was boosted by the police approaching the offenders' parents and showing them video footage to confirm their child's involvement in ASB. This helped engage this group to tackle their children's offending.

Risks of method 9: Attempting to arrest offenders – countermoves by offenders

Youths often resisted arrest – using mobile phones to warn of impending approach, and ›starbursting‹, running in every different direction. They hid in bushes. They also used hedges to conceal their alcohol, so that if caught they no longer had it in their hands. The council dealt with this by lowering the height of hedges and bushes and clearing rubbish.

INTERVENTION 12: A FOREST LOCATION AS ALTERNATIVE PLACE FOR YOUTHS TO GATHER

Method: A part of the local forest was given over for use by the local youths
Principles: Removing offenders from the crime situation; Rule setting; Reducing readiness to offend by meeting offenders' needs

The Tree Conservation Volunteers Group together with the police made available a portion of a local wood to use as a gathering place, particularly in the summer holidays. Ground rules were established about acceptable behaviour (e.g. about littering).

Risk to method 12: offenders ignore rules

Some youths, of course, ignored the rules. Then, encampments that had been built were taken down and the area left as it was originally. After this had happened several times, the youths accepted that they needed to comply to retain the encampments.

Implementation

Implementation involves converting the in-principle interventions into practical methods, and putting them into effect in ways which are appropriate for the local context. There is only space to give a couple of examples. Headings include:

Converting the method into action on the ground – management, planning and supervision

Targeting of the action on the crime problem, offender, place and victim

Inputs of £, human resources, capacity-building
Monitoring, quality-assuring and adjusting the action in the light of feedback
Outputs achieved – for each method
Risks/blockages in implementation
Exit strategy/expansion

Lessons learnt from the implementation process included:

The need for Adaptability. There was a degree of learning from what didn't work, so that the eventual project was a result of having tried out different options.

The practitioner team judged on past experience that the interventions would only be effective for 3–5 years, because of changing fashions in antisocial behaviour – so to sustain the project, they had to *continually re-assess alternatives*.

Involvement

Involvement is about partnership, mobilisation and climate setting.
There were lots of partners, as you can see.

Partners
Hampshire Police Force
Test Valley/Eastleigh Borough Councils
Neighbourhood Wardens
Representative from a local shop
Residents Association
Youth Service
Local Landowners – of the parade of shops
Parish Council

CLIMATE-SETTING

Climate setting involved some tricky work managing the public's expectations about the police response to antisocial behaviour and there was mobilisation of parents, other residents, shopkeepers and others. I have a framework for this, too, but I don't want to strain your patience!

Risks and blockages included the conflict between the young and old –

and the project team arranged some successful mediation – including inviting the elderly residents to the opening of the youth shelter.

Who did what
Here are some of the many crime prevention tasks carried out or led by the police.

Hampshire Police Force
Crime reduction officer and police beat constable formed the core project co-ordinating team
Monitored changes in ASB offences and CADA incidents
Offered advice on prevention to the other key partners
Chaired the steering group/committee meetings
Located sources of funding for the project
Local basic command unit – carried out targeted police patrols involving a mixture of covert and overt observations of the crime/ASB problem.

And this is what the local councils did.

Local Councils
Test Valley/Eastleigh Borough Councils
Community safety officer and relevant services attended committee meetings
Funded alterations to the local community centre
Supported additional services for youths at leisure centre
Provided the supporting use of neighbourhood wardens
Involved in representing the local council's views at the committee meetings
Consulted on developing council owned land
Willing to support ABC contracts and ASBO
ASBO officers showed videos of offending to parents

Impact
Here are the main headings for Impact.
  Intermediate outcomes
  Ultimate outcomes

Sustainability of implementation
Sustainability of impact
Replicability

Replicability is particularly important. The aim is to try to identify any special contextual conditions at each stage of the project, from Intelligence through to Involvement, which were vital to make the project work, but which may be hard to establish in other places.

RESULTS

And here are some impact results of the ongoing interventions. We estimated the reduction in antisocial behaviour incidents in the immediate project area to be about 75% fewer than expected on the basis of background trends. More details follow below.

This is a fairly ›soft‹ evaluation that we did retrospectively. But that does raise a serious issue, namely that trying to obtain examples of good practice that have been evaluated to even the lowest standard, is extremely difficult. It's a big challenge for a knowledge base.

DETAILED RESULTS

Recorded crime fell from 74 offences (covering mainly criminal damage, shoplifting, burglary from a shop), in January–December 2002 to 53 offences in the same period in 2003, equating to just under a 30% decrease in these offences not considering background effects. Incidents (mainly youths gathering in intimidating numbers, noise disorder, minor public disorder) showed a substantial reduction of around 79%, falling from 68 incidents in Jan-December 2002 to 14 in the same period for 2003, not taking background changes into consideration. Following the interventions in The Close there were 75% fewer ASB incidents there (51 fewer cases in 15 months) than expected on the basis of past levels and background trends. Overall falls in Valley Park as a whole may partly be attributable to the spillover of the effects of action within The Close – a case of diffusion of benefit. Taking displacement/diffusion of benefit into account, *net* reductions in ASB incidents in the whole of Valley Park attributable to the project action were estimated at 44% (106 cases in 15 months).

Burglary and shoplifting were included in the analysis of ASB in this study, as these related to the acquisition of alcohol, which as described above was an important contributory factor to ASB in the area. There is anecdotal evidence that police patrol time and overtime was reduced as a result of the project; it was noted that an expected migration of the residents away from the area as a result of increasing ASB had not occurred as a probable outcome from the interventions.

The rest of Valley Park (the buffer zone) appears to follow the trend in the background comparison area – there is no overt evidence of displacement from the target area. Rather, the steeper fall in the buffer zone relative to the background comparison area (44% versus 20% from Phase 0 to Phase 1) suggests either a local background trend in the whole of Eastleigh that was coincidental to the intervention; or diffusion of benefit, where the action in the target area was having a wider than intended effect. If the former, this would imply the net impact of the intervention was less than the *gross* 75%/51 incidents figure above. If the latter, it would be more. The latter seems more plausible in this case.

WIDER USES FOR 5IS PROJECT INFORMATION

When we collect information on individual projects, there are many wider uses for it if the quality is good enough.

We can undertake synthesis and testing of principles and theories, and convey this information through toolkits and training. Extracting and synthesising knowledge from many projects is important and probably a more efficient way of organising knowledge to guide practitioners than a purely case-study approach, though electronic versions mean that we can flip from one to the other quite readily.

Police and others are notorious for not learning from their mistakes. They talk about ›reinventing the wheel‹, but they continually reinvent the flat tyre. You can do failure-mode analysis at each ›I‹ and each subhead – what went wrong, what can be learned? In this respect 5Is offers far more detailed analysis than the familiar ›theory failure, implementation failure, measurement failure‹.

You can use this information to support gap analyses for research, and strategic overviews for creating policies and designing their effective delivery through mainstream programmes. The recent Home Office Burglary Reduction Initiative[31] certainly revealed enormous gaps in the process information collected by the evaluators – if only they had had something like 5Is to guide them at the time of data collection, not to mention in writing up the site reports – the information was all over the place and virtually had to be beaten out of the documents sometimes.

Most of these uses of 5Is are retrospective – after the projects have been implemented and evaluated. But the same framework *could* be used prospectively as a tool for business-planning and option appraisal, for project development and for implementation. This is very close to the quality-assurance interest of the Beccaria Project. To add to the previous if-onlys – if only some of the Burglary Reduction Initiative practitioners had had this kind of guidance, their projects would have been easier to evaluate and perhaps more worthwhile doing so!

The Question of Simplicity

A knowledge management framework has to be communicable, understandable and memorable in itself. Considered alone, this argues for simplicity. But more fundamentally, as we all know, crime prevention itself is complex. Just ask the practitioners! And simple frameworks do not so far appear to have succeeded in penetrating below the level of *slogans*, to communicate seriously detailed knowledge which can be acted upon to deliver reliable results.

The philosophy behind 5Is is that a high level of *investment* in concepts, knowledge, training, guidance and other infrastructure is necessary for a high *yield* in terms of successful *performance* in crime prevention. *There is no point in dumbing-down the language to describe and guide good practice so that more people can understand it, if what they understand cannot then deliver useful crime prevention.* So we must make the language that we use, fit for purpose.

5Is of course is not simple. However, its complexity is *not* like that of quantum mechanics. It is more like that of a tree – with simple branches that each split into further simple branches. 5Is has been designed to cope with the tradeoff between simplicity and complexity by ›zooming‹ in and out with message, map and methodology. It's probably the case that 5Is will work best if practitioners are trained in it quite intensively, as part of their ›foundation training‹ – once they have the schema in their heads, it should simply become their *way of looking at the crime prevention world*.

Finally, there's one more practical problem – *retrieval*. Detail is necessary, as said. But practitioners don't want to have to go through 12 or 14 pages just to find one element of good practice. Having a well-designed structure facilitates retrieval.

Conclusion

I hope that this presentation has made clear the conceptual and practical connections between knowledge, evaluation and quality, as illustrated by the 5Is framework.

I welcome the Beccaria programme and will continue to watch its progress, and support it where I can. The important objectives of developing professional quality, establishing common frameworks and terminologies and advancing the practice of evaluation are all vital if crime prevention is to make a serious and lasting contribution to quality of life in Europe and beyond. To this end, I think we all need to work towards developing one, collective framework rather than having several alternatives. I think we can all agree on many of the details, even if we have not yet decided on the main headings – 5Is, SARA, 7 Steps or whatever. Let's get to work!

5Is documentation and examples

March 2005
- Overview of 5Is, at www.crimereduction.gov.uk/learningzone/5isintro.htm
- Definitive and detailed set of headings for 5Is _ EU guidance note. Available from paul.ekblom@homeoffice.gsi.gov.uk Needs update.
- Detailed background paper Towards a European Knowledge Base including worked example of a 5Is project description, available from Paul Ekblom
- Background paper presented at EU Beccaria conference, Hanover 2005, with Eastleigh Drink and Disorder case study www.beccaria.de/downloads/pres_ek.ppt
- Examples of original EU 5Is project descriptions at http://europa.eu.int/comm/justice_home/eucpn/practices.html
- BURGLARY http://europa.eu.int/comm/justice_home/eucpn/docs/aalborguk2.pdf
- MOBILE PHONE national initiatives http://europa.eu.int/comm/justice_home/eucpn/docs/aalborguk1.pdf

- YOUTH INCLUSION PROJECT http://www.adobe.com/products/acrobat/readstep.html
- links to further UK *burglary* examples at www.crimereduction.gov.uk/burglary60.htm and
Reducing Burglary Initiative Project Summary Bacup
Reducing Burglary Initiative Project Summary Ladybarn
Reducing Burglary Initiative Project Summary Rusholme
Reducing Burglary Initiative Project Summary Stockport
Reducing Burglary Initiative Project Summary Stockton
Reducing Burglary Initiative Project Summary Stoneferry, Hull
- Case studies on CCTV from evaluation of Home Office CCTV Initiative at
http://uk.sitestat.com/homeoffice/homeoffice/s?rds.rdsolr1305pdf&ns_type=pdf&ns_url=%5Bhttp://www.homeoffice.gov.uk/rds/pdfs05/rdsolr1305.pdf%5D
http://uk.sitestat.com/homeoffice/homeoffice/s?rds.rdsolr1205pdf&ns_type=pdf&ns_url=%5Bhttp://www.homeoffice.gov.uk/rds/pdfs05/rdsolr1205.pdf%5D
http://uk.sitestat.com/homeoffice/homeoffice/s?rds.rdsolr1105pdf&ns_type=pdf&ns_url=%5Bhttp://www.homeoffice.gov.uk/rds/pdfs05/rdsolr1105.pdf%5D
- other 5Is case studies
- Gateshead Metro Centre *car crime* www.crimereduction.gov.uk/iex/htmlfiles/ideas/201.shtml
- Luton *car crime* www.crimereduction.gov.uk/iex/htmlfiles/ideas/202.shtml
- Leicester *mentoring* www.crimereduction.gov.uk/iex/htmlfiles/ideas/203.shtml
  - Slough Trading Estate *CCTV* available from paul.ekblom@homeoffice.gsi.gov.uk
  - Other CCTV case studies available late Feb 05
  - Eastleigh *Antisocial behaviour/drinking* at www.crimereduction.gov.uk/gpps05.htm (scroll to bottom for full document and powerpoint presentation)
- 5Is top-level headings used on ›Together‹ – UK website for good practice on Anti-Social Behaviour. See eg www.together.gov.uk click on ›case studies‹, and format at www.together.gov.uk/addcasestudy.asp

- Reference at Youth Justice Board
  http://www.youth-justice-board.gov.uk/YouthJusticeBoard/Research

Ekblom, P. (2004) ›Le Cadre des 5 I‹ dans Bruston, P. et Haroune, A. (éds.) *Réseau européen de prévention de la criminalité: (REPC) Description et échange de bonnes pratiques*. Paris: Délégation Interministérielle à la Ville. [English & français].

Original ›think piece‹ on knowledge and replication issues in crime prevention:

Ekblom, P. (2002). ›From the Source to the Mainstream is Uphill: The Challenge of Transferring Knowledge of Crime Prevention through Replication, Innovation and Anticipation.‹ In: N. Tilley (ed.) Analysis for Crime Prevention, Crime Prevention Studies 13: 131–203. Monsey, N.Y.: Criminal Justice Press/Devon, UK: Willan Publishing.

Ronald V. Clarke
Rutgers State University of New Jersey, USA

Seven Principles of Quality Crime Prevention

On arriving in Hanover, I was a bit alarmed to find that the Beccaria-Project had its own »7 Steps to a Successful Crime Prevention Project«. What if these were exactly the same as my »seven principles«? Might it not look as though I had copied the Beccaria-Project? Or that I had nothing to add to the discussion – that my participation in the conference was fraud? Worse, perhaps, my seven principles might be completely different from the Beccaria-Project's seven steps! This would be embarrassing for both me and the staff of the Beccaria-Project, suggesting that we had learned different things from the literature and our own experiences.

Fortunately, neither of my concerns was warranted. There is considerable overlap between the 7-steps and the 7 principles (see Table 1). Both focus on *project* management, not the development of a program of crime prevention or a crime prevention capacity, and both follow a similar progression of systematic stages. However, they differ in small ways, which may reflect my specialized background in situational crime prevention and problem-oriented policing. In what follows, I will expand on each of my principles in turn and will try to show why each is important.

Table 1: Comparison of the Seven Steps and the Seven Principles

	7 Steps to a successful Crime Prevention Project (Beccaria-Project)	7 Principles of quality Crime Prevention (Clarke)
1	Establishing and describing the project	Be clear about your objectives
2	Identifying the causes	Focus on very specific problems
3	Specifying the goals	Understand your problem
4	Developing possible solutions	Be skeptical about displacement
5	Devising and implementing the project plan	Consider a variety of solutions
6	Reviewing the impact	Anticipate implementation difficulties
7	Documentation and conclusions	Evaluate your results

1. Have Clear Objectives

Preventing crime is very difficult and your project will only succeed if crime reduction is the principal goal. Too often, crime prevention projects try to meet other goals at the same time. These might include improving social conditions, reducing fear, showing official concern about crime and building partnerships with community »stakeholders«. These are legitimate goals in their own right and they might sometimes be a desirable by-product of a crime prevention project. But do not expect to serve all these goals *and* reduce crime in the same project. This is because choices of what to do must always be made in undertaking a crime prevention project. Unless you are firmly focused on crime reduction, you might make a choice that will ultimately not serve this goal.

A related danger is of »goal drift,« substituting some other objective when it becomes apparent that the original crime reduction goals of the project will not be met. Rather than yield to this temptation, it is better to abandon the project, learn from the failure, and conserve your energy for some new attempt to reduce crime.

In order to keep on track, and resist goal proliferation and goal drift, it is important to specify a realistic target for crime reduction. Do not be overly ambitious or you might be forced to admit failure, even when you had in fact achieved some modest but worthwhile reductions in crime. To specify a target reduction, you must of course have some reliable measure of crime and an evaluation plan (see 7 below).

2. Focus on Very Specific Problems

Your crime prevention project is most likely to succeed when it is focused on a specific category of crime, such as juvenile joyriding, rather than some broader category of crime such as »juvenile delinquency« or »car thefts.« This is because each specific category of crime is often quite different from another one that seems superficially similar. It may be committed for different motives, by different offenders with quite different resources and skills. This would be true, for example, of different forms of car theft such as stealing a car for one's own temporary use and stealing a car for export to former Soviet-block country. In-built vehicle security might be needed to prevent both forms of theft, but preventing the export of stolen cars would require other measures in addition, including improved owner registration procedures and documents. This point holds even when the same group of offenders is involved in two quite different kinds of crime such as shoplifting and burglary; there may be some overlap in the preventive measures needed (those focused on the offenders), but other (situational) measures will need to be closely tailored to the nature of the problem.

These points can be illustrated by research on residential burglary undertaken by Poyner and Webb (1991) in one British city. They showed that burglaries committed in the suburbs were quite different from those committed in the city center. Burglaries in the city center were committed by offenders on foot who were looking for cash and jewelry. Because most of the housing was built in terraces they could only get in through the front door or a front window. The burglars operating in the suburbs, on the other hand, used cars and were targeting electronic goods such as videocassette players and TVs. They were as likely to enter through back or side windows as through the front. They needed cars to get to the suburbs and to transport the stolen goods. The cars had to be parked near to the house, but not so close as to attract attention. The layout of housing in the newer suburbs allowed these conditions to be met, and Poyner and Webb's preventive suggestions included ways to counter the lack of natural surveillance of parking places and roadways. Their suggestions to prevent inner city burglaries focused more on improving security and surveillance at the point of entry. As for disrupting the market for stolen goods, this approach had more relevance to the suburban burglaries that targeted electronic goods than to the inner city burglaries that targeted cash and jewelry.

3. Understand Your Problem

As I have already mentioned it is crucial to understand the nature of your problem before designing your intervention. A fatal mistake is to design a crime prevention project around an intervention (such as neighborhood watch or CCTV surveillance) rather than around a specific problem. It may turn out that the intervention is quite inappropriate for the local problems. Fortunately, many tools and concepts now exist to help analyze crime problems and I will discuss them under the following headings:
- Develop hypotheses
- Identify crime concentrations

- Use the crime triangle
- Adopt the offender's perspective

3.1. Develop Hypotheses about the Problem

Your analysis of the problem should be guided by hypotheses about its nature that you should continually test and refine with each new set of data you examine. Hypotheses help you to decide which additional data you need, and a well-founded hypothesis (or explanation) at the conclusion of your analysis helps you to think about possible solutions to the problem.

3.2. Identify Crime Concentrations

Crime is never uniformly distributed, but is always concentrated at particular times and places. Many studies have shown that it is also focused on particular targets or victims. This is popularly known as the 80/20 rule. Twenty percent of any group of people, targets or victims, experience eighty percent of the crime. Seldom is it exactly 20 percent and 80 percent, but crime is always concentrated in this kind of way.

This fact is of great importance for crime prevention because it means that crime prevention effort does not have to be spread evenly, but should be focused where it can achieve most benefits. The British call this »getting the grease to the squeak«, while the Americans call it »getting the biggest bang for the buck«. A second reason why the 80/20 rule is important is that comparison of the troublesome 20 percent with the remainder helps to identify reasons for the crime concentrations. An understanding of these reasons is crucial for designing interventions.

Useful crime concentration concepts include: repeat offenders; hot spots; repeat victims; hot products and risky facilities. The first three of these are well known and have been the focus of many targeted crime prevention efforts. For example, in the United States, Compstat tends to focus police attention on hot spots of crime, while in the U.K., many police forces offer a »graded« response to victims of burglary so that repeat victims get more crime prevention help than first time victims. The remaining two concepts, hot products and risky facilities, are newer and I will say a little about each of them.

HOT PRODUCTS
Hot products are those which are CRAVED by thieves because they tend to be concealable, removable, valuable, enjoyable and disposable

(Clarke, 1999). The hottest product of all is cash, which my Rutgers colleague, Marcus Felson, calls the »mother's milk« of crime. One important source of data about hot products is the British Crime Survey, which shows that, apart from cash, the items most often targeted in residential burglary are jewelry and various electronic sources of entertainment such as TVs and DVD players. Another useful source of information about hot products is the annual survey conducted in the United States of the most shoplifted items, which include tobacco, liquor, sneakers, brand name jeans, CD/cassettes and cosmetics. Finally, annual data are published in the U.S. (and now the U.K.) on the rates of theft of the various models of car on the road. These rates vary considerably, with some models being more than 30 times at greater risk of theft than other models. A Home Office study showed that there were similar variations in the risk of theft of lorries of different kinds (see Table 1).

Table 2: Lorries Stolen in the United Kingdom, 1994

	Number Stolen	Theft Rate per 1000
Livestock Carrier	156	56
Drop-side Lorry	582	27
Flat-bed Lorry	565	14
Garbage Truck	10	1

Source: Brown (1995)

The low theft rates of garbage trucks are not surprising since there would be little demand for these. The few that were stolen were probably stripped of their engines and other parts and then abandoned. The high rates of theft for livestock carriers may be partly explained by the fact that this category includes small horse boxes, for which there is a substantial second-hand market. A thriving second-hand market for a particular category of goods generally results in an increased risk of theft for those goods. Knowing which products are at risk of theft has several implications for prevention. In some cases, such as cars and mobile phones, pressure can be brought on the manufacturers to improve the security of these goods – which the government has done in the United Kingdom for both cars and mobile phones (Clarke and Newman, in Press). Owners of high-risk lorries can be warned to improve the security of vehicle storage yards or parking facilities. Police can advise shops at high risk of shoplifting because of the goods they carry to take additional security precautions, and if the shops are informed which of the items they carry are at greatest risk, then they can improve security for just these goods.

RISKY FACILITIES
Consistent with the 80/20 rule, it has been found that within any group of similar facilities – for example, convenience stores, banks or schools – a small proportion of the group (the »risky facilities«) account for most of the crime experienced by the whole group (Eck et al., in press). For example, in the United States, 6.5 percent of convenience stores experience 65 percent of all the robberies in convenience stores. In the United Kingdom, 4 percent of banks have robbery rates 4–6 times higher than other banks. Eight percent of Stockholm schools suffered 50 percent of the violent crimes reported in the 1993/4 school year. In Liverpool, 40 percent of vandal damage committed against bus shelters occurred in nine percent of the shelters.

Comparing the risky facilities with the other members of the group can be very helpful for crime prevention purposes since it can reveal layout and design deficiencies (for example, in parking lots or stores) or lax and ineffective place management (for example in pubs, apartment buildings or schools) that are promoting crime. Having identified the crime-promoting factors, pressure can be brought on the responsible authorities to change them, as in the following examples:

- In the United States, uncooperative landlords can be forced to improve rental apartment complexes by invoking code (maintenance) regulations.
- Police can bring indirect pressure to bear by publishing data on risks of theft in different car parks; or they might certify those that are »safer« (the British police operate a scheme like this).
- In Australia, »accords« have been reached between the managers of pubs and clubs in entertainment districts in Melbourne, Surfers Paradise, Geelong and elsewhere to reduce drink-related violence by cutting down on drinks promotions and through other codes of good practice.
- In Oakland, California, the police entered into an agreement with a motel chain that the chain would significantly reduce crime and disorder at one of its problem motels in the city. This agreement was

guaranteed by a »performance bond,« which required the chain to pay $250,000 to the city if the goal were not reached within two years. It was left to the motel chain to decide which security measures to introduce and it decided to upgrade lighting and fencing, replace the managers and security guards, conduct pre-employment background checks on all new employees, establish strict check-in procedures with a list of banned individuals, and prohibit room rentals for more than 30 days.

3.3 Use the Crime Triangle

The Crime Analysis Triangle

Source: Clarke and Eck (2003)

The latest version of the »crime triangle« (or problem analysis triangle) developed by John Eck is a valuable analytic tool that once again opens up possibilities for prevention (see Figure 1). Grafted onto the original triangle (consisting of offender, victim and place) is an external triangle of »controllers«:

- The »handler« is someone with a special relationship with the offender who might be able to exert some control (e.g. a teacher at school)
- The »guardian« affords protection to a particular place (e.g. your neighbor might help to protect your home from burglars)
- The »place manager« has some responsibility for the place where crime occurs (we have just seen how important these managers are in respect of risky facilities)

3.4. Adopt the Offender's Perspective

Consistent with the rational choice perspective, Paul Ekblom has argued that it is important to see the crime from the offender's perspective (a process which he calls »think thief«). This assists understanding of how and why offenders commit the crimes in question. You should try to imagine the steps that the offenders must take, but try also to interview a sample of them to clarify their modus operandi. The interviews should seek answers to questions such as: how are targets selected, victims subdued, police avoided and goods disposed of? Knowing the answers to these questions will assist you in devising preventive actions.

4. Be Skeptical about Displacement

Nothing saps preventive enthusiasm as much as the pessimism of the »displacement doomsayers«. Many criminologists fall into this group, but so also do the police who almost automatically respond to suggestions for reducing opportunities by arguing that the offenders will merely turn their attention to some other targets, will change their methods or will offend elsewhere. Underlying this pessimism is the view that offenders are driven inexorably to commit crime and will find their ways around any barriers. This ignores the considerable evidence that situational factors play an important part in causing crime (Felson and Clarke, 1998; Clarke, in press) and it also ignores common sense. For example, if casual shoplifters can no longer steal items from their local supermarket because of newly introduced security measures, it is most unlikely that they would begin to shop at some more distant and inconvenient store simply so that they could continue to shoplift. Even more unlikely is that they would begin to steal items from work to compensate for the ones they were no longer able to steal from the supermarket.

Nor is the supposed inevitability of displacement supported by the empirical research on the topic. The latest available meta-analysis of displacement studies (Hesseling, 1994) undertaken for the Dutch government reviewed 55 studies and found:
- No displacement in 22 studies
- Some displacement in 33 studies
- There was always more crime prevented than displaced

Many more studies have been published since Hesseling's review, and though I have not systematically reviewed these, I doubt very much that they would require any substantial modification of Hesseling's conclusions. Moreover, an increasing number of studies have found the opposite of displacement. They have found that, far from shifting crime elsewhere, targeted opportunity-reducing measures can result in crime falling beyond the direct reach of these measures – a phenomenon called »diffusion of benefits.« Here are some examples from well-designed studies (references can be found in Clarke, in Press):

1. Security added to houses that had been repeatedly burgled in Kirkholt, a council housing estate in the north of England, reduced burglaries for the whole of the estate, not just for those houses given additional protection.
2. When street lighting was improved in a large housing estate in Dudley, England, crime declined in both that estate and a nearby one where the lighting was not changed.
3. When »red light« cameras were installed at some traffic lights in Strathclyde, Scotland, not only did fewer people »run the lights« at these locations, but also at other traffic lights nearby. (In a smaller city, with more local traffic, this effect might be short-lived as people learned exactly which junctions had cameras).
4. CCTV cameras installed to monitor car parks at the University of Surrey reduced car crime as much in one not covered by the cameras as in the three that were covered.
5. As expected, electronic tagging of books in a University of Wisconsin library resulted in reduced book thefts. However, thefts also declined of videocassettes and other materials that had not been tagged.
6. When a New Jersey discount electronic retailer introduced a regime of daily counting of valuable merchandise in the warehouse, employee thefts of these items plummeted – but thefts also plummeted of items not repeatedly counted.
7. When vehicle tracking systems were sold in six large U.S. cities, rates of theft declined citywide, not just for car owners who purchased the tracking devices.
8. Widespread ownership of burglar alarms in an affluent community near Philadelphia resulted in reduced burglary rates for the community at large.

The most likely explanation of diffusion of benefits is that offenders learn that new preventive measures have been introduced, but are unsure of their extent and over-estimate their reach. If this proves to be a general phenomenon, as the above list suggests it might be, it would substantially enhance the value of focused crime prevention efforts.

5. Consider a Variety of Solutions

When it comes to finding solutions, experience suggests that it is usually better to introduce a package of measures, each of which is addressed to a different component of the problem, than to rely on a single measure. Furthermore, there is never just one way to reduce a crime or disorder problem. In order to broaden the choice of possible measures, I have worked over the years with various colleagues (including Derek Cornish, Mike Hough, Ross Homel, Pat Mayhew and Richard Wortley) to develop a classification of opportunity-reducing techniques. The latest version of the classification (see Table 3) consists of 25 techniques arranged under five main headings: increase the effort needed for crime, increase the risks, reduce the rewards, reduce provocations and remove excuses.

You should assess the possible solutions you identify in terms of their economic and their social costs, the latter to include inconvenience, intrusiveness, aesthetics and social exclusion. In making your choice of solutions, it is better to choose those that address what Paul Ekblom calls the »near« (usually situational) causes of the problem, rather than the more distant social and psychological »root« causes. This is because there is a more certain and immediate result of focusing on near causes (crime is reduced now, not in the distant future) and it is easier to demonstrate that your actions were effective.

6. Anticipate Implementation Difficulties

Do not underestimate the difficulties of implementing solutions. Most of the literature emphasizes the need for a project coordinator (preferably full time) and the need to form partnerships with community agencies to assist implementation. While I agree with the need for a project coordinator, be careful not to rush prematurely into forming a partnership. Ideally, you should delay your choice of partners until you are reasonably sure they will have a direct role in implementation. This means waiting until you have a clear idea of the problem and the best means of responding to it. Forming a partnership before you reach this point can waste time in unproductive meetings and can also lead to implementing measures that have no real prospect of success, simply to give partners some role in the project – a classic example of goal drift.

Even if you can avoid this danger, you can expect many other implementation difficulties. This is especially the case when a solution, (1) needs coordinated action among different agencies to be implemented, (2) takes a long time, (3) requires a series of steps, (4) is implemented by staff with little understanding of the problem or the solutions, (5) lacks a champion among the project team and (6) lacks the support of top administrators. Also expect difficulties when the solution is implemented by an agency that is in turmoil or is poorly resourced, that is outside the partnership and that gains little direct benefit from the work.

7. Evaluate Your Results

Do not be put off by the prescriptions for a »scientific« evaluation laid out by some criminologists, which can include the need for random allocation of treatment conditions. In fact, it is rarely possible to meet these prescriptions in a small crime prevention project, but it is still important to make the best evaluation that you can. This will enable you, your partners and your sponsors to learn from the project. If you publish your results, you will also play your part in assisting the development of crime prevention theory and practice.

You might be able to obtain advice in conducting the evaluation from a nearby university department and you should try to enlist their participation right from the beginning of your project. You should establish a quantifiable goal for the reduction of the problem and you should collect reliable data about the problem that will enable you to make a comparison before and after the implementation of solutions. Ideally, you should also be able to make quantifiable comparisons with a control group.

8. Conclusions

It is frequently said that crime prevention is »not rocket science«, but even so it is remarkably difficult to undertake a successful crime prevention project. While many successful projects have been reported in the literature, equally many or perhaps more projects have failed.

The Beccaria-Project's »7-steps to a successful crime prevention project« and my »7 principles of quality crime prevention« both attempt to distill practical advice for conducting successful crime prevention projects from the now quite voluminous literature. While differing in detail, the lists are in substantial agreement about the steps that should be taken in a successful project. Following them will not guarantee success, but it should make it more likely. If we document the results of our projects, and continue to learn from their successes and the failures, we will be able to refine the two lists of seven and, ultimately, work more successfully to reduce crime and disorder. Rocket science this may not be, but it is still a vitally important human endeavor.

9. References

Brown, R. (1995). The Nature and Extent of Heavy Goods Vehicle Theft. Crime Detection and Prevention Series, Paper 66. Police Research Group. London: Home Office.

Clarke, R.V. (1999). Hot Products: Understanding, Anticipating and Reducing the Demand for Stolen Goods. Police Research Series, Paper 98. London: Home Office.

Clarke, R. V. (In Press). ›Seven Misconceptions of Situational Crime Prevention.‹ In: Tilley, N. (ed.) Handbook of Crime Prevention and Community Safety. Cullompton, UK: Willan Publishing.

Clarke, R.V and J. Eck (2003) Become a Problem-Solving Crime Analyst – In 55 Steps. London: Jill Dando Institute of Crime Science, UCL.

Clarke, R.V. and G. Newman (in Press). Designing out Crime from Products and Systems. Crime Prevention Studies, Volume 18. Monsey, NY: Criminal Justice Press.

Cornish, D.B. and R. V. Clarke (2003) ›Opportunities, Precipitators and Criminal Decisions‹. Crime Prevention Studies, Vol 16. Monsey, NY: Criminal Justice Press.

Eck, J., R.V. Clarke and R. Guerette (in Press) ›Risky Facilities: Crime Concentrations in Homogeneous Sets of Establishments and Facilities.‹ Crime Prevention Studies, Monsey, NY: Criminal Justice Press.

Felson, M. and R.V. Clarke. (1998) Opportunity Makes the Thief: Practical Theory for Crime Prevention. Police Research Series, Paper 98. London: Home Office.

Hesseling, R. B. P. (1994) ›Displacement: A review of the empirical literature‹, Crime Prevention Studies, vol. 3. Monsey, NY: Criminal Justice Press.

Poyner, B. and B. Webb (1991). Crime Free Housing. Oxford UK: Butterworth Architect.

Table: Twenty Five Techniques Of Situational Prevention

Increase the Effort	Increase the Risks	Reduce the Rewards	Reduce Provocations	Remove Excuses
1. Target harden • Steering column locks and ignition immobilisers • Anti-robbery screens • Tamper-proof packaging	6. Extend guardianship • Go out in group at night • Leave signs of occupancy • Carry cell phone	11. Conceal targets • Off-street parking • Gender-neutral phone directories • Unmarked armored trucks	16. Reduce frustrations and stress • Efficient lines • Polite service • Expanded seating • Soothing music/muted lights	21. Set rules • Rental agreements • Harassment codes • Hotel registration
2. Control access to facilities • Entry phones • Electronic card access • Baggage screening	7. Assist natural surveillance • Improved street lighting • Defensible space design • Support whistle-blowers	12. Remove targets • Removable car radio • Women's shelters • Pre-paid cards for pay phones	17. Avoid disputes • Separate seating for rival soccer fans • Reduce crowding in bars • Fixed cab fares	22. Post instructions • »No Parking« • »Private Property« • »Extinguish camp fires«
3. Screen exits • Ticket needed for exit • Export documents • Electronic merchandise tags	8. Reduce anonymity • Taxi driver IDs • »How's my driving?« decals • School uniforms	13. Identify property • Property marking • Vehicle licensing and parts marking • Cattle branding	18. Reduce temptation and arousal • Controls on violent pornography • Enforce good behavior on soccer field • Prohibit racial slurs	23. Alert conscience • Roadside speed display boards • Signatures for customs declarations • »Shoplifting is stealing«
4. Deflect offenders • Street closures • Separate bathrooms for women • Disperse pubs	9. Use place managers • CCTV for double-deck buses • Two clerks for U.S. convenience stores • Reward vigilance	14. Disrupt markets • Monitor pawn shops • Controls on classified ads. • License street vendors	19. Neutralize peer pressure • »Idiots drink and drive« • »It's OK to say No« • Disperse trouble-makers at school	24. Assist compliance • Easy library checkout • Public lavatories • Litter receptacles
5. Control tools/weapons • »Smart« guns • Restrict spray paint sales to juveniles • Toughened beer glasses	10. Strengthen formal surveillance • Red light cameras • Burglar alarms • Security guards	15. Deny benefits • Ink merchandise tags • Graffiti cleaning • Disabling stolen cell phones	20. Discourage imitation • Rapid repair of vandalism • V-chips in TVs • Censor details of modus operandi	25. Control drugs and alcohol • Breathalyzers in bars • Server intervention programs • Alcohol-free events

Sources: Clarke and Eck (2003); Cornish and Clarke (2003)

Britta Bannenberg,
University of Bielefeld, Germany

Strategies for Effect-Oriented Crime Prevention[30] – The »Düsseldorfer Gutachten«

Empirical Effects Research

Practically no empirical research has yet been undertaken on crime prevention. No systematic evaluation of the crime prevention measures in place has been carried out to date.[31] Almost all we have are project reports and theoretical concepts without any reliable research into effects. There are many reasons for this situation, including a lack of research resources, little criminological engagement in this difficult field, and practitioners' reluctance to face up to the meagre results of their efforts. On the basis of the many studies into the causes of crime and theoretical concepts of primary, secondary, and tertiary crime prevention, many practical approaches were developed, initially in the United States, then in neighbouring European countries, and finally in Germany. Well-founded evaluation of prevention projects, without which the empirical effectiveness of crime reduction cannot be proved, has been neglected everywhere. Simply to rely on the well-meaning argument that prevention is better than repression is the wrong strategy, also in view of the possible waste of resources and effort or even the failure to recognise the role played by the consolidation of criminal structures – in peer groups, for example – in encouraging criminality. To take stock of crime prevention efforts and at least recommend guidelines for practitioners, reviewing the widespread but isolated empirical findings of effects research in Germany on the lines of the »Sherman Report«[32] in the United States is helpful.[33]

[30] Published in: Deutsche Zeitschrift für Kommunalwissenschaft, Vol. 142 (2003), No 1. http://www.difu.de/index.shtml?/publikationen/dfk/en/03_1/03_1_bannenberg.shtml
[31] BMI/BMJ 2001
[32] Sherman et al. 1997
[33] However, the same methodologically demanding criteria are not applied.

An attempt was made in this direction in 2001 for the Düsseldorf municipality.[34] The two-volume work, available to the general public[35], presents a broad secondary analysis of national and international effects research with the aim of pinpointing clearing recognisable effect factors in crime prevention for practical purposes. To analyse the current status of crime prevention and evaluate its success means tackling a difficult to manage, complex mass of material. Even if much detail needs to be filled in and precisely investigated, relatively clear structures and general lines in effective crime prevention can be identified. The report is based on a multi-level concept that aims to record congruent basic functions of effective crime prevention. The first part evaluates 61 studies on crime prevention distinguished by their interesting and up-to-date approaches, and especially by valid empirical back-up research. Local government policy can take such concrete and successful models as a guide, adjusting them to suit local conditions.[36] The second part contains excerpts from the Sherman Report, and part three provides specific findings of effects research on xenophobic and extreme right-wing violence.[37] Even if few evaluation studies are involved, certain recommendations can be made. Measures to reduce xenophobic attitudes, which can provide a breeding ground for concrete violence, should either make use of specific information on cultural differences and their causes or rely on contacts under favourable conditions. The school is a place where both attitude modification can be tackled and aggression and violence prevention programmes carried out.[38] Finally, part four investigates what policy conclusions for German cities are to be drawn from the largely American debate on »broken windows« and »zero toler-

[34] Rössner/Bannenberg 2002
[35] www.duesseldorf.de/download/dg.pdf for the over 400-page report and http://www.duesseldorf.de/download/dgll.pdf for the guidelines. Adobe 5.0. is recommended for downloading. Where this article refers to »studies 1-61« reference is to the report, Rössner/Bannenberg 2002. For details see there.
[36] It should be pointed out that, strictly speaking, the only projects that could be recommended for emulation are those that have proved lastingly effective in experimental tests in various places. On methodological prerequisites see Schumann 2001: 435 ff. However, there are no such projects in Germany, so that all that can be recommended is to try out the successful projects and later subject them to scientific assessment.
[37] Wagner/van Dick/Christ 2002: 265 ff.; Wagner/van Dick/Endrikat 2002: 96 ff.; Wagner/Christ/Kühnel 2002: 110 ff.
[38] Wagner/van Dick/Christ 2002: 324

ance«.[39] American conditions under which the establishment of formal order constitutes the basis for social control and a peaceable community cannot be compared with German conditions, so that »broken window« theories must be considered inappropriate crime prevention concepts for Germany. Fundamental structures of realistic crime prevention derived from the findings of these four parts are to be outlined below.[40]

The Possibilities and Limits of Effects Research in Crime Prevention

An examination of effects research reveals a distinction, which, while attracting hardly any attention, is crucial in evaluating crime prevention. Are measures intended more generally and unspecifically to establish beneficial conditions for socialisation, the basis for acquiring behavioural and value orientations as well as knowledge about and a feeling for social situations and for conformity behaviour, or are they planned and targeted, specific courses of action to reduce crime, i.e. specific crime prevention? Primary socialisation and education as well as secondary socialisation in kindergartens and schools naturally have a considerable influence on children and adolescents, i.e. on their development and resistance to criminality. But such general foundations for successful integration into the community are almost impossible to measure or determine. Societal change, manifest in the loosening or dissolution of family structures and cohesion in the immediate social milieu, and the loss of ties with societal institutions, e.g. local authorities, churches, clubs, cannot be influenced by isolated, specific crime prevention measures. Specific crime prevention can be concerned only with positive change in particular conditions that manifestly deviate from »average« socialisation in a given society. It should be remembered that intensive and hardened criminality is a relatively stable »5-per-cent problem« under a wide range of societal conditions. Neither »all« children and adolescents nor members of any other age group are habitually criminal; a minority of intensive offenders (some 5 per cent in male groups, far fewer among girls and women) display a syndrome of social deficiencies that apparently influence their behaviour. The main elements of this syndrome are a dysfunctional family; lack of control and of care and attention in the family; changing or violence-ori-

---

[39] Laue 2002: 333 ff., 424 ff.
[40] For details see Rössner/Bannenberg 2002

ented educational behaviour by parents; substantially deviant behaviours like truancy and aggression at school; no school-leaving qualifications or vocational training; no supportive human relationships; incapacity for emotional communication.[41]

Overall, it appears that unspecific crime prevention measures cannot be isolated from complex socialisation processes and are therefore scarcely accessible to targeted effects research. This is not to say that by ameliorating societal conditions and remedying shortcomings in basic socialisation »unspecific« prevention has no impact. On the contrary. But these underlying conditions are not amenable to specific effects research. One example is provided by the recent ban on corporal punishment for children. It is considered certain that the physical maltreatment of children or adolescents correlates with later aggressiveness[42] but the general consequences of this amendment to legislation are practically impossible to investigate empirically.

These considerations have been empirically confirmed: the negative findings of the most important prevention study yet undertaken, the Cambridge Somerville Youth Study[43], show that even where a range of social help is available, specific crime reduction effects are not necessarily demonstrable in the dominating overall process of socialisation. The ineffectiveness of measures designed to change public attitudes and behaviour demonstrates the failure to influence overall societal processes. All the studies looked at in this area, some involving elaborate and costly media campaigns, come to similar conclusions. Information disseminated through the mass media cannot prevent crime, although it might have other positive effects. But it has no specific preventative impact, which must be taken into consideration when appropriating resources for costly poster, film, or exhibition campaigns. Effects research shows that open thematization, strict application of rules, concentrated counteraction, support for victims, and the surveillance of dangerous areas have a marked impact in preventing crime, especially violent crime.

---

[41] Göppinger 1997: 252 ff.; Kaiser 1996: 523 ff.; Marneros/Ullrich/Rössner 2000: 5 ff.
[42] Pfeiffer/Delzer/Enzmann/Wetzels 1998
[43] Powers/Witmer 1951

Guidelines for Applied Crime Prevention

Specific crime prevention addresses children and adolescents at risk in the family, at nursery school, kindergarten, and in the community. Crime prevention measures designed to prevent recidivism address delinquents who have already been convicted and thus require resocialization. Effective crime prevention is characteristically intervention that focuses directly on the punishable behaviour, that either takes early, intensive, and comprehensive effect in multi-problem cases, or tackles specific deviant behaviours (intervention programmes). Such intervention takes norm clarification as the basis for all social control.[44] Social integration is to be achieved through broad, multi-level concepts ensuring targeted, supportive socialisation at the macro-social level, through family and school influences, and at the level of the individual personality.

Development-related criminality must be treated differently from predictably consistent development towards criminality in the context of a given lifestyle. Any development towards habitual crime involving the above risk factors needs urgent intervention in socialisation at an early stage, for example in the family or at school. Media campaigns, like appeals against violence, do not influence serious delinquent developments.[45]

Intervention Programmes Directly Addressing Delinquent Behaviour

Informal social control in as orderly an environment as possible has a specific effect at all levels and in all societal institutions.

In the family, all effective multi-systematic treatment also relies on strictly non-violent but more intensive control over the child or adolescent. Parents should be neither aggressive nor inconsistent in educating their offspring, nor should they be too lax. Limits must be set and desirable behaviour encouraged. Parental supervision of the child is thus a vital preventive factor.[46] Clear standards and limits in orderly structures are also important factors in early substitute upbringing in homes.[47] And even more clearly, the control of deviant and endangered adolescents in foster families, who, together with a permanent child welfare

---

[44] Hassemer 1999: 23 ff.
[45] For details see the studies in the report Rössner/Bannenberg 2002.
[46] Fend 2000: 451
[47] Lösel/Bliesener 1994: 753 ff.

careperson, ensure that rules are obeyed strictly and meticulously for six to nine months, constitutes the core element of a successful and currently much lauded programme in the United States.[48] Once again, rule learning proves to be highly effective in almost all social relations.[49]

Apart from the family, prevention is most important at school, and crime prevention programmes are accordingly most advanced in this field. [50]

Particularly successful multi-level concepts like the Olweus programme use the school as the level of intervention where social norms and basic rules are learned (e.g. not to attack anyone, to help victims of attack, not to exclude anyone). For children and adolescents this first level is decisive for the experience of encountering the same rules everywhere and, where they are strictly applied, of learning to rely on them. This very first element of the multi-level concept develops crucial preventive force in the field of informal sanctions – with »offender-related« acute norm intervention and long-term educational measures, as well as »victim-related« acute protection reactions and long-term reinforcement relating to school, the school class, and the individual. An ideal combination combines offender and victim-related measures in offender-victim mediation or conflict resolution programmes. Offender-victim mediation offers a non-violent model for conflict resolution and for strengthening empathy as a protective factor against crime.[51] The biggest problem in practical implementation is apparently to persuade the people and institutions responsible (school directors, teachers, parents, youth welfare office, youth welfare services, the police, etc.) to acknowledge the problem and to ensure their cooperation. Crime prevention councils could assume an enormously important mediating role in this regard. The people involved are often surprised that a problem like violence at school, which takes the form of blackmail, threats, and bodily harm, and where victims are usually younger and weaker students, is also a matter of concern in other institutions, and only the interlinking and coordination of countermeasures offers any real prospect of success in containing this deleterious behaviour.

[48] Schumann 2001: 435 ff.
[49] On the criminological explanation of social norm learning, which confirms the positive evaluations of both intervention and integration programmes, see Rössner/Bannenberg Leitlinien 2002: 13-21.
[50] Olweus 1978; 1995; Noltin: 249 ff.; Nolting 2001; Schubarth/Ackermann 2000. See also the findings of the 13 studies in the report, Rössner/Bannenberg 2002; Knopf 1998.
[51] Simsa 2001

Sport offers similar possibilities with the necessary and inevitable linkage between physical exertion and obedience to rules. Sport provides a relatively comprehensible and simple illustration of a system for regulating violence. It includes the experience of physical stress situations and a knowledge of the resulting emotions and their physical processing. The limited preventive effect of sport programmes shown by effectiveness studies, e.g. midnight basketball, or a one-off event like a football tournament, is, in contrast to school programmes, due mostly to the lack of a multi-level concept and too low a level of intensity. If it is to contribute to preventing crime, sport must be used to develop lasting, stable ties with endangered juveniles.

In the neighbourhood, orderly conditions and constructive, informal control are fully effective factors in regional crime prevention, as an overview of individual studies[52] and the comparable analysis contained in the Sherman Report show. The civic and community commitment of the following programmes is particularly worth noting.

In publicly assisted housing estates, control by so-called »social caretakers« in cooperation with residents can prevent some offences in housing complexes.

In the broader neighbourhood, projects to reduce opportunities for crime in high-rise housing estates are advisable; combinations of police foot patrols and activation of the public to reduce opportunities for various types of criminal offence; neighbourhood-watch programmes, improvement of social ties, cooperation with the police, especially to improve burglary prevention. It should be noted that, depending on how these measures are implemented, they can produce a negative side-effect in the form of a rise in the fear of crime.[53]

In the community as a whole, prevention efforts need to be supplemented and interlinked. Here, too, success has been achieved, for example with safer cities programmes[54] against various types of crime like burglary, family violence, assault and battery, car theft, shoplifting; with coordinated campaigns to reduce crime opportunities; and with offender-related measures.

---

[52] Rössner/Bannenberg 2002 Gutachten Studie 5, 11, 21, 25, 29, 30–34, 40, 41, 47, 49, 50, 52, 53, 55, 56, 58, 59, 61.
[53] Kohl 2000: 752 ff.
[54] Rössner/Bannenberg 2002 Gutachten Studie 61.

Particular forms of criminality demand special forms of intervention that have a promising effect in a certain field of delinquency. Studies on such special situations show this quite clearly. They include drug crimes (combined control strategies of the police and trained teams from municipal institutions to stop drug trafficking); xenophobic, racist violence (permanent combined measures like improving offence reporting behaviour, security plans involving the police, victims, landlords, psychological advisory services, offender-related measures and police specialisation); domestic violence (intervention programmes)[55]; vandalism (technical prevention to reduce offence opportunities and offender-oriented measures). It is apparent everywhere that well-structured programmes that take a differentiated approach to a particular crime problem produce better results than less structured approaches.[56]

However, in all these social fields, courageous people are needed who are willing to face up to the problems and who are not prepared to accept social and individual harm. A culture of looking the other way[57] stops the discussion of crime prevention, which has a fatal effect in relatively closed social spaces. The messenger, i.e. the person who reports an offence, must not be condemned for disturbing the community: the message and how it relates to reality are what is important. Anyone in a system under the rule of law who for moral reasons publicises a criminal offence – for example at school or in the home – is not an informer but a responsible citizen concerned to protect the victims.[58]

Reinforced informal and constructive social control in various spheres of life apparently performs an essential role in crime prevention. As empirical studies on the effectiveness of criminal law show, it seems to be far more important than formal control – especially that exercised by criminal justice[59] The preventive force of criminal law lies in more intensive prosecution and in the risk of discovery and not, for example, in the extent or severity of punishment. This is where promising community policing approaches fit in.[60] Criminal law is an important ele-

---

[55] Bannenberg/Weitekamp/Rössner/Kerner 1999; Schweikert 2000
[56] Lösel 1996: 57 ff.
[57] Schwind et al. 1998
[58] For a detailed treatment of the problem of whistle blowing in the case of corruption, cf. Bannenberg, 2002: 375 ff. The principles can be transferred to other social areas.
[59] Rössner 2001: 978 ff.
[60] Kube 1999: 71 ff. See also the compilation of worldwide projects by the United

ment of the state's monopoly of force with the task of isolating breaches of the norm to nip spiralling crime in the bud and to afford justice and protection to the victim.[61]

The preventive necessity of criminal law intervention and constructive conflict resolution offering opportunities for social learning is best illustrated by the institution of offender-victim mediation (also conflict regulation, reconciliation). Offender-victim mediation is better suited than any other reactive measure to make the offender aware that he has breached elementary rules of behaviour and has to take responsibility for the consequences. This assumption of responsibility also satisfies the norm clarification function of criminal law relating to young offenders without having a de-socialising and disintegrative impact. Offender-victim mediation is the classical case of an integrative sanction.[62] It can be particularly useful in furthering the following preventive functions: limit-setting (norm clarification) through confrontation with adverse consequences; the model function for the pro-social assumption of responsibility; social learning; and reinforcing acceptance of non-violent solutions and integration. Offender-victim mediation is thus the only (criminal law) reaction that can introduce important countervailing aspects, because the offender takes cognisance of the victim and, if the process is successful, acknowledges him as a person, for he has to concern himself intensively with the suffering of the victim, his guilt and responsibility. There is now evidence for the positive impact of this approach in crime prevention. According to international research[63] and comparable studies on the use of »mild means« in the context of diversion[64] it can be assumed that OVM is at least equally as effective and that the constructive elements have a positive impact. At any rate, first studies on recidivism show a positive trend.[65]

In problem-oriented crime prevention, CCTV surveillance for high-risk public spaces, particularly favoured in the United Kingdom, has

Nationals Interregional Crime and Justice Research Institute (UNICRI), Preventing Crime: Citizens Experience across the world, 1997
[61] Schöch 1990: 95 ff.
[62] Rössner 1992; 1998; 1999
[63] Weitekamp 1990
[64] Heinz/Hügel 1987
[65] Schütz 1999; Busse 2001

proved extremely successful (critical comment[66]). As a purely technical control tool, its effectiveness is only limited in comparison with stronger informal controls, but there is empirical evidence that legally unobjectionable video surveillance by the police does reduce crime in clearly definable, high-risk spaces in the community. Image transmission to a manned monitor plus recording puts the offender doubly at risk of discovery, which clearly influences his decision on whether to act because he is more likely to be punished: he must reckon with immediate arrest and with easier identification through the recording. Possible displacement effects (which have to be considered in the case of other measures to reduce opportunities for crime, as well) still have to be investigated. However, there are indications that even where displacement does take place, the reduction effect is greater.

Social Integration Programmes

Leaving aside these programmes, which tend to be oriented on (constructive) intervention, intensive social integration programmes can be expected to have a positive preventive effect in relation to individuals at multiple and high risk of delinquent development if they begin either at a very early stage in childhood or address very specific deviant behaviours.

Successful family programmes designed to promote the well-being of the child are available for the first alternative, providing intensive supervision and guidance in child-rearing, educational support in problematic cases[67], especially where there is a tendency towards violence against children[68] or – substantiated by a major longitudinal study[69] – by encouraging social responsibility and learning motivation in deprived kindergarten children through play pedagogy. Such concepts are favoured in all major studies in the field of intensive crime prevention. Often several approaches are combined, like parent and child training with the involvement of the school.[70] However, programmes should not, as in the not very successful Cambridge Somerville Study, be applied indis-

---

[66] Gras 2001: 12-15; Reuband 2001: 5 ff.
[67] Study 46; Butler 1994
[68] Study 45
[69] Study 42; Schweinhart/Barnes/Weikart 1993
[70] Lösel 2000; McCord/Tremblay 1992; Schneider 1999

criminately: they must be targeted and intensive. Isolated interventions have hardly any lasting effect. In practical implementation, attempts have been made, for instance in Denmark, to bundle efforts in so-called SSP programmes (social services, school, and police) and, in particular, to incorporate targeted programmes. Legislation has even required the actors involved to cooperate.[71] The problem of interlinkage has not been solved elsewhere, either.

The elaborate but exemplary American project to support young offenders in the community through specially trained foster families[72] shows that, in the secure atmosphere of suitable foster families, basic catch-up socialisation is possible in general personality development and social skill acquisition even in adolescence (15 to 19), bringing a marked reduction in delinquency.

Otherwise – if individual problems are not deeply grounded in failed basic socialization – programmes address delinquency-related problems as specifically as possible. Although much research still needs to be done in this area, the effects of such measures can no longer be ignored. Our analysis shows positive effects of specific drug therapy – possibly because the focus has so far been on problem-oriented programmes.[73]

The greatest success has been achieved by multi-level, longer-term intervention specifically addressing the criminally inclined juvenile and a supportive community with supervision by mentors[74], or the particular problem of domestic violence. Stand-alone social training courses that are limited and not very integrative have less chance of succeeding.[75]

In the case of severely delinquent children and adolescents, especially if they have no more links at all with a structured life, constructive residential care can succeed in the last resort and be a first step towards integration. For young offenders between the ages of 14 and 18 sentenced by a juvenile court this can offer a useful alternative to penal detention, which is dominated by young adults.[76] With a great deal of pedagogical

[71] Ive 1999: 267 ff.
[72] Study: 47
[73] Studies 1-7, 9, 11, 12
[74] Study 44
[75] Studies 18, 60
[76] Rössner 1991. The Baden-Württemberg Ministry of Justice is currently implementing a »Project Opportunity« model as an alternative to penal detention for young prisoners.

input, difficult children and adolescents can be stabilised in such small institutions. In a country under the rule of law that is concerned for the welfare of its citizens, it is no alternative to simply stand by and watch the complete social disintegration of young people by the age of 14 and their consequent incarceration.

Good residential care can now be a viable alternative even for severely delinquent juveniles because of the protection it can offer: a permanent significant person as educator, social support from non-dissocial persons, clear norms and structures in the institution as well as the development of cognitive and social skills plus the experience of self-efficacy, coherence, and structure in life.[77] Despite the high cost of such institutions, the necessary crime-prevention resources should be provided for the few people involved in dealing with most difficult cases in the community.

Finally, major countereffects of prevention through social integration must be pointed out: criminal attitudes and behaviours among young people are determined relatively strongly not only by family and school but also by equally close peer groups.[78] They provide models and reinforce a deviant lifestyle. This means that in crime-prevention programmes that work not with the individual but with (deviant) groups, peer-group effects may obstruct positive aspects of integration or even be negatively superimposed on them. This danger is particularly acute for less deviant persons if they are brought together with severely deviant cases.[79]

---

[77] Lösel/Pomplun 1998
[78] Hawkins/Herrenkohl/Farrington 1998: 106 ff.
[79] Schumann 2001: 442

Bibliography

Bannenberg, Britta (2002), Korruption in Deutschland und ihre strafrechtliche Kontrolle, Neuwied und Kriftel (BKA Band 18, Reihe Polizei und Forschung).

Bannenberg, Britta/Weitekamp, Elmar/Rössner, Dieter/Kerner, Hans-Jürgen (1999), Mediation bei Gewaltstraftaten in Paarbeziehungen, Baden-Baden.

Bundesministerium des Inneren (BMI)/Bundesministerium der Justiz (BMJ) (ed.) (2001), Erster Periodischer Sicherheitsbericht, Kurzfassung, Berlin, www.bmj.bund.de or www.bmi.bund.de.

Busse, Jochen (2001), Rückfalluntersuchung zum Täter-Opfer-Ausgleich: eine statistische Untersuchung im Amtsgerichtsbezirk Lüneburg, Marburg.

Butler, S. (1994), Radford Share Care Project, University of Nottingham.

Fend, Helmut (2000), Entwicklungspsychologie des Jugendlichen, Opladen

Göppinger, Hans (1997), Kriminologie, 5. Aufl., München.

Gras, Marianne (2001), Videoüberwachung in Großbritannien, in: Neue Kriminalpolitik, Heft 4, 12–15.

Hassemer, Winfried (1999), Neue Ansätze der Kriminalpolitik, in: Rössner, Dieter/Jehle, Jörg-Martin (eds.), Kriminalität, Prävention, Kontrolle, Heidelberg, 3–24.

Hawkins, NN./Herrenkohl, NN./Farrington, David P., et al. (1998), A review of predictors of youth violence, in: Loeber, NN./Farrington, David P. (eds.), Serious and violent juvenile offenders, 104–146.

Heinz, Wolfgang/Hügel, Christine (1987), Erzieherische Maßnahmen im Deutschen Jugendstrafrecht, informelle und formelle Erledigungsmöglichkeiten aus empirischer Sicht, Bonn.

Ive, NN. (1999), Public/Private Partnerships in Crime Prevention. The SSP-Co-operation in Denmark, in: Joutsen, Marc (ed.), Five Issues in European Criminal Justice, 207–146.

Kaiser, Günther (1996), Kriminologie, Ein Lehrbuch, 3. Aufl., Heidelberg.

Kohl, NN. (2000), Veilig Wonen – erfolgreiche Einbruchsprävention in den Niederlanden, in: Kriminalistik, 752–756.

Kube, Edwin (1999), Kriminalprävention – konkrete Ansätze für die Praxis, in: Rössner, Dieter/Jehle, Jörg-Martin (eds.), Kriminalität, Prävention und Kontrolle, Heidelberg, 71–88.

Laue, Christian (2002), Broken windows und das New Yorker Modell – Vorbilder für die Kriminalprävention in deutschen Großstädten?, in: Rössner, Dieter/Bannenberg, Britta/Landeshauptstadt Düsseldorf (eds.), Düsseldorfer Gutachten: Empirisch gesicherte Erkenntnisse über kriminalpräventive Wirkungen, Düsseldorf, Teil IV, 333–438.

Lösel, Friedrich (2000), Risikodiagnose und Risikomanagement in der inneren Sicherheit, in: Neuhaus, Helmut (ed.), Sicherheit in der Gesellschaft heute, Erlangen, 43–90.

Lösel, Friedrich (1996), Working with young offenders: The impact of meta analysis, in: Hollin, Clive Ronald/Howells, Kevin (eds.), Clinical approaches to working with young offenders, Chichester, New York, 43–90.

Lösel, Friedrich/Pomplun, Oliver (1998), Jugendhilfe statt Untersuchungshaft. Eine Evaluationsstudie zur Heimunterbringung, Pfaffenweiler.

Lösel, Friedrich/Bliesener, Thomas (1994), Some high-risk-adolescents do not develop conduct problems, in: International Journal of Behavioral Development, 753-777.

Marneros, Andreas/Ullrich, Simone/Rössner, Dieter (2000), Das Hallenser Angeklagtenprojekt, in: Marneros, Andreas/Rössner, Dieter/Haring, Annette/Brieger, Peter (eds.), Psychiatrie und Justiz, München und andere, 2-12.

McCord, Joan/Tremblay, Richard Earnest (eds.) (1992), Preventing antisocial behavior, New York et al.

Nolting, Hans-Peter (2001), Lernfall Aggression. Wie sie entsteht – wie sie zu vermindern ist, Hamburg (1. Aufl. 1997).

Nolting, Hans-Peter/Knopf, Hartmut (1998), Gewaltverminderung in der Schule: Viele Vorschläge – wenige Studien, in: Psychologie in Erziehung und Unterricht, 45. Jg., 249-260.

Olweus, Dan (1995), Gewalt in der Schule. Was Eltern und Lehrer wissen sollten – und tun können, Bern.

Olweus, Dan (1978), Aggression in the schools: Bullies and whipping boys, Washington.

Pfeiffer, Christian/Delzer, Ingo/Enzmann, Dirk/Wetzels, Peter (1998), Ausgrenzung, Gewalt und Kriminalität im Leben junger Menschen, Baden-Baden.

Powers, Edwin/Witmer, Helen Leland (1951), An experiment in the prevention of delinquency: the Cambridge Somerville Youth Study, New York.

Reuband, Karl-Heinz (2001), Was die Bürger von der Überwachung halten, in: Neue Kriminalpolitik, Heft 2, 12-15.

Rössner, Dieter (2002), Reform des Jugendstrafvollzugs, Plädoyer für Modellversuche, in: DVJJ-Journal.

Rössner, Dieter (2001), Die besonderen Aufgaben des Strafrechts im System rechtsstaatlicher Verhaltenskontrolle, in: Schünemann, Bernd, et al. (eds.), Festschrift für Claus Roxin zum 70. Geburtstag, Berlin/New York, 977-987.

Rössner, Dieter (1998a), Rechtsgrundlagen und Rechtspraxis, in: Dölling, Dieter (ed.), Täter-Opfer-Ausgleich in Deutschland, 49-119 (Schriftenreihe des BMJ).

Rössner, Dieter (1998b), Die Universalität des Wiedergutmachungsgedankens im Strafrecht, in: Schwind, Hans-Dieter/Kube, Edwin/Kühne, Hans-Heiner (eds.), Festschrift für Hans Joachim Schneider zum 70. Geburtstag, Berlin/New York, 877-895.

Rössner, Dieter (1992a), Mediation und Strafrecht, in: Strempel, Dieter (ed.), Mediation für die Praxis, Ort, 42-54.

Rössner, Dieter (1992b), Strafrechtsfolgen ohne Übelzufügung, in: Neue Zeitschrift für Strafrecht (NStZ), 409-415.

Rössner, Dieter (1991), Reform des Jugendstrafvollzugs, Plädoyer für Moedellversuche, in: DVJJ-Journal, 219-221.

Rössner, Dieter/Bannenberg, Britta/Landeshauptstadt Düsseldorf (eds.), Düsseldorfer Gutachten: Empirisch gesicherte Erkenntnisse über kriminalpräventive Wirkungen, Düsseldorf 2002 (free of charge from www.duesseldorf.de/download/dg.pdf or Landeshauptstadt Düsseldorf, Arbeitskreis Vorbeugung und Sicherheit, Zollstraße 4, 40200 Düsseldorf).

Rössner, Dieter/Bannenberg, Britta/Landeshauptstadt Düsseldorf (eds.) (2002), Düsseldorfer Gutachten: Leitlinien wirkungsorientierter Kriminalprävention, Düsseldorf (free of charge from www.duesseldorf.de/download/dgll.pdf or Landeshauptstadt Düsseldorf, Arbeitskreis Vorbeugung und Sicherheit, Zollstraße 4, 40200 Düsseldorf).

Rössner, Dieter/Bannenberg, Britta (2002), Empirisch gesicherte Leitlinien der Kriminalprävention, in: Kühne, Hans-Heiner/Jung, Heike/Kreuzer, Arthur/Wolter, Jürgen (eds.), Festschrift für Klaus Rolinski, Baden-Baden, 459–469.

Schneider, Hans Joachim (1999), Neue Wege der Kriminalitätskontrolle, in: Universitas, 819–835.

Schöch, Heinz (1990), Zur Wirksamkeit der Generalprävention, in: Frank, Christel/Harrer, Gerhart (eds.), Der Sachverständige im Strafrecht. Kriminalitätsverhütung, Berlin et al., 95–109.

Schubarth, Wilfried/Ackermann, Christoph (2000), Forschungsgruppe Schulevaluation, Aggression und Gewalt, 45 Fragen und Projekte zur Gewaltprävention, Sächsische Landeszentrale für politische Bildung, Dresden (1. Aufl. 1998).

Schütz, NN. (1999), Die Rückfallhäufigkeit nach einem Außergerichtlichen Tatausgleich bei Erwachsenen, in: Österreichische Richterzeitung, 161ff.

Schumann, Karl F. (2001), Experimente mit Kriminalprävention, in: Albrecht, Günter/Backes, Otto/Kühnel, Wolfgang (eds.), Gewaltkriminalität zwischen Mythos und Realität, Frankfurt/Main, 435–457.

Schweikert, Birgit (2000), Gewalt ist kein Schicksal, Baden-Baden.

Schweinhart, Lawrence J./Barnes, Helen V./Weikart, David P. (1993), Significant benefits: the high-scope Perry Preschool study through age 27, Michigan.

Schwind, Hans-Dieter, und andere (1998), Alle gaffen... keiner hilft: unterlassene Hilfeleistung bei Unfällen und Straftaten, Heidelberg.

Sielert, Uwe (1999), Evaluation des Projekts »Sport gegen Gewalt, Intoleranz und Fremdenfeindlichkeit«, Projektbericht der Christian-Albrechts-Universität Kiel, Institut für Pädagogik.

Simsa, Christiane (2001), Mediation in der Schule, Neuwied.

Wagner, Ulrich/van Dick, Rolf/Christ, Oliver (2002), Möglichkeiten der präventiven Einwirkung auf Fremdenfeindlichkeit/Antisemitismus und fremdenfeindliche/antisemitische Gewalt, in: Rössner, Dieter/Bannenberg, Britta/Landeshauptstadt Düsseldorf (eds.), Düsseldorfer Gutachten: Empirisch gesicherte Erkenntnisse über kriminalpräventive Wirkungen, Düsseldorf 2002, Teil III, 265–332.

Wagner, Ulrich/van Dick, Rolf/Endrikat, Kirsten (2002), Interkulturelle Kontakte. Die Ergebnisse lassen hoffen, in: Heitmeyer, Wilhelm (ed.), Deutsche Zustände, Folge 1, Frankfurt/Main, 96–109.

Wagner, Ulrich/Christ, Oliver/Kühnel, Steffen M. (2002), Diskriminierendes Verhalten. Es beginnt mit den Abwertungen, in: Heitmeyer, Wilhelm (ed.), Deutsche Zustände, Folge 1, Frankfurt/Main, 110–122.

Weitekamp, Elmar (1990), Restitutionsprogramme für Erwachsene in den USA und Kanada, unpublished report for the Max-Planck-Institut für ausländisches und internationales Strafrecht, Freiburg im Breisgau.

Willemse, NN. (1994), Developments in Dutch crime prevention, in: Crime Prevention Studies, 33–47.

Lars Rand Jensen

Chairman of the National SSP Committee under the Danish Crime Prevention Council and Chief Constable of Odense, Denmark

Perspectives on Crime Prevention and Quality Management

Introduction

Establishing standards for developing the quality of crime prevention in Europe requires an examination of both the concept of crime prevention, itself, and of the basis for the further development of crime prevention initiatives as well as the ordinary constituent elements of prevention activities.

Perspectives on Crime Prevention

Prevention of crime forms an integral part of a variety of initiatives taken by all sectors of modern society. Consequently, crime prevention is related to all activities which aim at preventing, controlling, reducing and countering the incidence of crime. Primarily, this means that crime prevention is fundamentally related to *policing, crime control* and *social order*.

Crime prevention aspects are related as well to policing measures on crime control (or policy on crime), consisting of *preventive, proactive* and *reactive* elements as to the entire social order in society, especially within the areas of *care* and *order* as the fundamental conditions for a good social life.

At present these concepts are referred to, e.g. in the EUCPN Draft Work Programme, as *freedom, security* and *justice*. They are also, however, related to education, housing and ways of life etc. Crime prevention should be viewed in this broad context, and this is the context in which methods should be progressed in order to promote further development of quality in individual crime prevention projects.

This presents difficulties because we lack actual comparative methods of determining factors that are to be compared in individual countries, in projects, among countries and as a background for a common European quality development.

Some steps have been taken, however, towards improved comparability through common project descriptions, common evaluation standards, development through quality awards, as well as through a great number of attempts on benchmarking and the like.

Much has still to be done, however, for instance making a distinction between prevention and proactive initiatives. This also applies to descriptions of networks and setting out standards for evaluating networks, clarification of whether networks include public agencies alone or whether they include community involvement. There is, further, a tendency towards benchmarking *effectiveness* and not *effect*. Within the EU the Council of Ministers as well as the Commission, the EUCPN and working groups have launched activities directed towards formulating the basis for improved comparative statistics, developing standards of *crime proofing*, i.e. making legislation better equipped to prevent crime from being committed by way of evasion, distortion of competition etc., as well as towards securing consumer goods and tools so as to impede criminal acts. Both elements aim at reducing the steady increase in *crime potential*. Systematic work is also in progress on *monitoring* crime prevention elements in Member States' policies on crime.

In short, endeavours are directed towards developing comparability of countries' individual projects and initiatives in order to measure an activity that reduces criminogenic effects and ensures the effect of individual crime prevention measures.

In many countries, including the EU, work is being carried out within the fields of educational and social policies. In these policy areas there is a tendency to apply prevention concepts from the worlds of medicine, social policy and education and to rashly transfer prevention methods to the field of crime prevention.

It is highly uncertain whether prevention concepts can be transferred from the medical, social and educational sciences to crime prevention. As stated above, crime prevention finds itself in a different context. Crime prevention, for instance, sees a much greater connection to the control systems of society (police and the criminal justice system) and a connection to people's immediate desire for situational gratification of their needs, irrespective of whether the means are legal or not, or simply an expression of unacceptable behaviour. It is, for instance, a question whether there is a need to counter alcohol and drug abuse or a need for health promoting interventions to regulate the legal substance use in daily life and in larger segments of the society. It is urgently required to arrive at a more precise formulation of the concept of crime prevention as well as to establish the effects of individual prevention hypotheses.

The Role of the Police

The functions of the police and their potential for preventing and reducing crime are natural components of the concept of crime prevention. This applies to the delivery of core policing functions as well as to providing support to and cooperating with other agencies and with the population in the widest sense, including those groups that are not organised and are characterised by a certain degree of criminal activity, abuse and unacceptable behaviour. Such groups may also comprise subcultures and groups which are socially innovative.

The role of the police might be summarised in the following description of the problems and opportunities facing the police within the area of crime prevention:

The *growth* of crime and disorder in continental Europe, UK and other Western industrial societies is *not inevitable*. There is no doubt that these topics are breeding at present: growing public debate and divisions both as to their causes and as to the ways to *counter* and *prevent* them in the fields of crime control, order and care in society by support from the police.

Potential for crime and disorder comes from many quarters: from mass unemployment to mass consumer values; from family breakdown to drug abuse; from homelessness to failures in urban planning and housing policy. And this potential seems strongest where these and other associated factors meet and compound each other in environments of multiple disadvantage and added to it, in many countries and in various ways, the different kinds of multiethnic problems.

As potential for crime and disorder turns often into harsh fact (such as riots of diverse causes in many large cities) there is growing recognition that much current policing policy and practice is inadequate to check these rising threats to peace and order. The police themselves come under mounting pressure to rethink and remodel their strategies, priorities, organisational structures and use of resources. And as the limitations of their professional resources become increasingly apparent, they increasingly perceive needs to develop – in Sir Kenneth Newman's words (former Commissioner of the Metropolitan Police in England) »a co-ordinated strategy« against crime contributed to by government, police, social agencies and communities. And to this might be added: based on knowledge and research, and again comparative research.

Policy and *practice* along similar lines are now developing for almost identical reasons in *all* Western societies. These range from the work of the national Crime Prevention Councils in the Nordic countries and other co-ordinating structures elsewhere to the very comprehensive recommendations for social/economic/legal policies against delinquency recommended by the »Commission des Maires« to the Prime Minister of France followed all ready by the Decree of 1983 and before that the recommendation of the Peyrefitte Committee followed by the Decree of 28 February 1978. So there is a long story behind this thinking.

These views have most recently been laid down in the strategy plan (»Crime Prevention – Policing 2002–2005«) of the National Police Directorate of Norway.

Visions or strategy plans such as these are based more or less explicitly upon a description of three policing models set out in 1982 by the above Sir Kenneth Newman:
   the »crime control model« versus the »due process model«
   the »legalistic model« versus the »service model«
   the »reactive model« versus the »proactive model«
The three models are based upon a wide variety of Anglo-Saxon research from the 1960s and 1970s. They are also the basis for the formulation of the role of the police at local level which we have sought to apply in Denmark in recent years.

Community and/or Neighbourhood Policing

In Denmark we have stated our community policing strategy on the basis of the following assumptions regarding the elements comprised by the concepts:

- Area-based policing,
- Multi-agency partnership,
- Community-based crime prevention,
- Police-public contact strategies,
- Area-based foot patrols,
- Community involvement and consultation.

These are the six community policing models which have been described by, *inter alia*, Trevor Bennet in 1994. To these I wish to add some specific working methods, which are, at any rate, important for consideration in the Nordic countries:

- Problem-oriented policing
- Cross-sectoral and interdisciplinary preventive work and inter-agency cooperation
- Community involvement.

The Nordic Crime Prevention Model

Since 1971 all the Nordic countries have established national Crime Prevention Councils, most recently in Finland with the creation of the Crime Prevention Delegation, and with the establishment of an agency in Iceland under the Ministry of Justice and Ecclesiastical Affairs.

A common denominator for the national Crime Prevention Councils is an overall effort to develop and promote all types of crime prevention activity based on solid research with special attention directed towards local initiatives. The objective is to establish interagency and cross-disciplinary initiatives with the police service as an important and also equal partner in cooperation. Special efforts have been directed towards involving individual members of the public, for instance parents, in the activities.

A number of constant components are common to the Nordic views on crime prevention:

There exists a perception that the criminal justice system exerts only a restricted influence on the crime rate. Therefore, equal importance is attached to delinquency prevention and crime prevention. The incorporation of elements of social policy, not least targeted at reducing marginalisation and social isolation, receives high priority. Elements of social as well as cultural policies are incorporated especially to establish networks, so that all children and young persons may lead as good an everyday life as possible. »A good life« is a concept which is key to all the Nordic countries, especially in relation to children and young persons.

Throughout basic general education deliberate efforts are directed towards identifying methods that may contribute towards the shaping of norms and social skills which are also presumed to have a lasting crime prevention impact.

The great number of situational initiatives attempt to deliberately involve the general public and all types of organisation and group both regarding an improved quality of everyday life of children, young persons, and the elderly and regarding various forms of technical safeguarding, neighbourhood watch, and Operation Marking schemes. It is a distinctive feature that in the Nordic countries the police will be involved in initiatives within all the areas referred to. This is a result of a systematic endeavour to involve the police as an equal partner in those areas.

Special importance is attached to the involvement of the local community, its professionals and its residents in co-ordinated cooperation both as far as social and cultural policies and as far as situationally determined activities are concerned. Cross-sectoral and interdisciplinary working methods receive high priority, and at local level it is endeavoured to establish decentralised types of organisation which can promote these endeavours. Every attempt is made to coordinate public-sector and private initiatives.

Inherent in the shaping of crime preventive strategies in all the countries is the fact that it should be based on scientific research – both in the search for causes and patterns as well as in the assessment of the efficiency and effect of crime prevention initiatives. The crime prevention policies defined by central government, which are predominantly reactive, are deliberately complemented by a government-supported general crime prevention doctrine, defined by the respective national Crime Prevention Councils and their initiatives and guidelines. As the framework of this presentation does not allow going into further detail on this issue, I have, as an illustration, distributed a handout which describes these factors by way of examples from Denmark.

Crime Prevention in Denmark

Along the lines set out above we have in Denmark supplemented the reactive delinquency prevention policies, i.e. threat of punishment, defined by central government with a general crime prevention doctrine defined by the Danish Crime Prevention Council, established in 1971. It follows from this that there is a close connection between crime prevention activities of the Danish Crime Prevention Council, the Danish police districts, the local authorities and the various private organisations. The connection may initially be described as a fairly close and uniform network structure. The structure has been developed over a period of 30 years and is characterised by the fundamental values of cooperation, cross-sectoral and interdisciplinary co-ordination, mutual understanding, a tolerant understanding of people and training of professionals at all levels. The network is, moreover, based on a careful balance between demands for co-ordination and demands for autonomy. The network was introduced by the national level (top-bottom) but operates bottom-up in the daily work, i.e. with the national authorities and the Danish Crime Prevention Council as fora for compiling the experience gained at local level. The network model has been developed with full respect for all official and professional competencies; it rests on negotiated agreements and it is based locally on the so-called SSP network.

The Crime Prevention Council and the SSP Network in Denmark

»SSP« stands for a form of interdisciplinary and cross-sectoral cooperation involving schools and after-school programmes (S), the social services and health care services (S) and the police (P). The National SSP Committee under the Danish Crime Prevention Council was set up in 1975. The objective of the SSP committee is to guide and assist local authorities in establishing SSP cooperation in the communities. In 1996 the Committee expressed the declaration of intent for SSP cooperation in the following way: The central aim of SSP cooperation is to build up local networks that have a crime prevention effect on the daily lives of children and young people.

The National SSP Committee works primarily with planning initiatives that may reinforce interdisciplinary and cross-sectoral co-operation locally. The Committee encourages all municipalities to establish formalised SSP cooperation and offers advice and guidance to local authorities and the police on how the work may be planned and on which initiatives should be taken. More than 95% of the Danish municipalities have now established SSP committees in accordance with the guidelines laid down by the Crime Prevention Council.

The term »formal cooperation« is not legally binding. SSP cooperation will be based on municipalities' decisions to implement interdisciplinary and cross-sectoral activities.

Denmark's local government system precludes central demand that municipalities shall establish interdisciplinary and cross-sectoral cooperation. This would only be possible if the Danish Parliament (*the Folketing*) should pass legislation to that effect.

Legislation Governing SSP Cooperation

Danish legislation obliges the basic educational system, the social services and the police to carry out crime prevention work in its broadest sense.

This obligation is not expressly stated in the Primary Education Act. However, the objectives in the Act state that the individual pupil should acquire all-round personal development. This aim is very difficult to achieve if the young person is involved in alcohol and drug abuse or crime. Legislation on the social services obliges staff to supervise the conditions under which children and young people live. This includes the possibility of supporting them in creating the best possible conditions for growing up. Legislation covering the social services, health care and education ensures that the population can maintain a certain standard of living and receive free treatment under the National Health Service and free education in Danish primary schools. Legislation concerning housing regulations, including planning and urban redevelopment programmes, ensures healthy housing standards. All these factors form a long-term part of the endeavour towards reducing crime. The duties of the police are laid down in sections 1 to 3 of the Danish Police Act of 1 July 2004, under which the police must do whatever is necessary to prevent crime. It should be added that provisions in section 115b of the Danish Administration of Justice Act enable the laws concerning professional confidentiality to be derogated from to a limited extent in connection with SSP work.

SSP cooperation shall build up, use and maintain local networks that have a crime preventive influence on the daily lives of children and young people. The networks are also to be used to detect, at an early stage, danger signals and new tendencies in the development of crime. Moreover, they are able to monitor the development in the conditions of life for children and young people.

Another aim is to identify local prevention options on an interdisciplinary and cross-sectoral basis as well as at professional level in specific fields such as schools, social services, police, institutions, housing and recreational and cultural areas. Projects and specific efforts are directed towards attempting to prevent young people and groups of young people from engaging in inappropriate social behaviour, including criminal behaviour. And to prevent this type of behaviour from spreading.

Quality Development of SSP Cooperation

The Crime Prevention Council is working on a project in which the country's municipalities will be offered the assistance of consultants to develop plans of action for SSP cooperation. Eleven ad-hoc consultants have been trained, and they will support municipalities in the process of finalising their plans of action. Agreements have been made with 23 municipalities, large as well as small, across the country.

A member of staff from the Council will establish contacts with new local authorities and manage the corps of ad-hoc consultants.

As support to the ad-hoc consultants, »model plans of action« will be worked out for small, medium-sized and large municipalities.

Activities Relating to Young Persons over 18 (»SSP +«)

Another focus area of the Crime Prevention Council is work with the over-18 age group. It has been necessary to involve new partners in the cooperation scheme so that, in particular, young people with social problems may be given improved prospects for the future. For many years the Council has recommended – and contributed towards – organising crime prevention initiatives for both pre-school and post-school age groups, so the idea of working with a target group of over 18-year-olds was not a new one. It is, however, essential to discuss how traditional SSP cooperation can be developed to include other educational institutions than primary schools. The background for this is the circumstance that many state and county institutions (business schools, upper secondary schools, vocational colleges, production schools and others) have come forward with specific problems and have wished to be included in the existing SSP cooperation in their neighbourhoods.

Many local authorities have followed the Council's recommendations on involving new partners in the cooperation scheme. The results show that groups are chiefly set up with representatives from public services, educational institutions etc., all of which have in common the fact that they usually work with individual cases, counselling or education.

A typical group can comprise representatives from:

- Social Services
- Child and Youth Welfare Service
- Cultural Affairs Service
- Prison and Probation Service
- Police
- Integration Groups
- Outreach Youth Education Programmes
- Youth Schools
- Youth Guidance Service
- Production Schools
- SSP co-ordinators
- Consultants working with drug abuse
- Psychological advisors

not necessarily all of them, but put together on ad-hoc demands.

The SSP+ work can be characterised by the term »prevention of recidivism«, as many of the target groups or individuals have, in one way or another, been involved in criminal activities.

In short, in Denmark this currently means:

- Action against marginalisation and social isolation of children and young persons not comprehended by ordinary prevention activities.
- Handling socially unstable children and young persons who at an

early age fall outside the ordinary offers of help provided under special systems.
- Development of working methods and organisation of the work with young persons who socially are severely unstable and marginalised in relation to social initiatives in the broadest sense and who are in a situation where they are not within reach of even sophisticated prevention programmes of a socio-educational nature but rather need real treatment.
- Concretisation of cooperation relationships to be developed in regard to socially unstable young persons of 18 to 24 years of age.

The Concept of »Network« in Crime Prevention

As stated above, the concept of crime prevention should generally be viewed in a wider context. In Denmark, it is often characterised by cross-sectoral and interdisciplinary views and practices; it is marked by rather floating forms of cooperation involving a large number of interests and interested parties and we have, consequently, developed a working method along the following guidelines. If we were to form a general view of »a turbulent surrounding world« or »a complex and rapidly changing situation« against the background of such vague concepts as values, attitudes, view of human nature whilst at the same time taking decisions on institutions, communities of interest, »actors« and legal principles, it might be helpful to consider the totality as a network or a networking organisation. Such a consideration would mean that a problem might be formulated as a »network-reminder« as follows:

- Which degree of *co-ordination* is desirable and achievable?
- Which degree of *freedom/autonomy* is desirable and achievable?
- Which common interests and *principles* form the basis of the network?
- Which *competencies* and *legal principles* regulate the interaction between the separate constituent parts of the network?
- Which *fora/organisation* will co-ordinate the network and will ensure the appropriate autonomy for the separate constituents of the network?
- Which *communities of interests* can be identified?
- How are *common interests* and *principles* to be defined?

- *Who* is/are to define common interests and principles?
- How will common interests and principles be *safeguarded*?

Such, or similar, considerations will provide other approaches to a fundamental debate on cooperation. Hence, the following concrete questions may be posed as a basis for debate:

- What *basic values* are involved (e.g. democracy, human rights, market economy, social dimension, equality, environmental awareness, professional attitudes)?
- Which *actors* exist in the field of cooperation?
- Which degree of *co-ordination* is desirable?
- Which degree *of autonomy* is desirable?
- Which are the common *interests*?
- Which *competencies* and *legal principles*?
- Which *institutions, agencies, businesses*, spheres of authority?
- Which *communities of interests* (professional, cultural, religious, financial)?
- How, and by whom, are the various values, actors, interests and communities of interest to be *defined*?
- How will the various defined values, interests and communities of interests be *upheld and safeguarded*?
- How will the *balance be struck* between the numerous various interests and what *strategies* should be promoted?

Problem-Oriented Prioritisation

As crime prevention is so multi-faceted, an option might be to divide prevention initiatives into areas, for instance according to types of crime such as violence, acquisitive offences, economic crime, cross-border crime, organised crime etc. and then list potential prevention activities within the concept of *crime control*. Alternatively, distinctions might be made according to types of victim: young persons, the elderly, women, minorities, events etc. A second alternative might be to list the types of offender either to be induced to refrain from their actions or to be prevented from committing crimes.

In addition, priorities might be established for both types of victim and offender under the concept of *social order* or *security in society*, or a further step could be taken so as to focus on institutions, housing areas, businesses or the like.

Mention may be made of an example from Denmark, where we have attempted to prioritise »safer cities«. Under an umbrella-project we have implemented 12 well-documented projects during the years 2000 to 2004, following which we have attempted to extract the sustainable and transferable crime prevention *effects*. Ms Merete Watt Boolsen, sociologist and associate professor at the University of Copenhagen, Denmark, Department of Political Science, has been responsible for the work and the evaluation of the umbrella project.

This is the first time in Denmark that so many projects have been reviewed concurrently, systematically and with the application of sociological and crime prevention methodologies.

The objectives of the umbrella project are/were to »*implement, follow up and evaluate the subsidised projects with a view to identifying those crime prevention elements which are applicable to other projects/other areas*«.

It must be said forthwith: 12 projects constitute, of course, a flimsy basis for firm evaluations and conclusions. There is no reason to say otherwise! However, when the findings are considered in their entirety and when it appears that circumstances, conditions etc. repeat themselves in very diverse sub-projects under very diverse conditions (and are, moreover, supported by findings in other countries), then there are grounds for setting down perspectives which can be translated into concrete recommendations and guidelines.

Anyone who wishes to know the contents of the projects, their results and the crime prevention evaluation would be referred to the first part of the report on the umbrella project, which describes the approach towards »*implementing, following up and evaluating the subsidised projects...*«. The report describes the general approach and sets out the processes, experience and crime prevention evaluations of the individual sub-projects.

Anyone who is interested in the latter part of the objective of the umbrella project, i.e. »*identifying those crime prevention elements which are applicable to other projects/other areas*« would be referred to the report on *Crime prevention geometry: how to raise wolves, look after ducks and fit up caverns*. This report sets out a crime prevention philosophy which concludes in a number of practical and concrete guidelines on:

- how to work with crime prevention projects;
- how to prioritise interventions;
- how to implement good practice;
- how to proceed, practically and concretely.

The conclusions were the following:
The crime prevention evaluation of the »Safer Cities« projects indicates that the projects that have a comparatively larger positive effect (compared to other projects)

- are sub-projects of composite projects, i.e. in being well-integrated into a larger system where there already exists a »project framework« or a »project philosophy« which can be developed;
- are anchored in different networks (governmental as well as non-governmental) which are of relevance and importance to the projects and on the basis of which they can actively progress. The SSP cooperation scheme is singled out as an important network;
- involve more than one practitioner having the same role in the projects, i.e. there are »colleagues«;
- have developed short chains of command within the system (i.e. responsibility and competence are closely connected);
- operate in a preventive and inter-disciplinary way at a professional level;
- are methodologically grounded in a professional project culture.

The first four points concern, in the widest sense, various aspects of the *organisational structures* of the crime prevention projects and the two last ones deal with *practitioner competence*. The findings of the above mentioned umbrella project correspond with experience gained in various fields of evaluated projects over thirty years of crime prevention in Denmark under the crime council. Rather than benchmarking, these views represent an attempt at prioritising a defined, complex area and extrapolating the crime prevention effects. Or, as suggested by the EU-CPN within this field:

»There is currently *little methodological consistency* in the collation of good practice in crime prevention within the EUCPN.

The EUCPN is of the opinion that the Commission's proposal to have one EU-wide standard methodology is very ambitious. In the past the

EUCPN has tended to concentrate on small-scale projects. In future there should be a much broader scope that includes, among others, good practice in national *crime prevention strategies, policy-making, organisational structures, crime resistant product design* and development and *national crime proofing of legislation,* as well as *individual projects.*

This diversity of good practice suggests that one EU wide methodology would be unattainable. The aim of the EUCPN should be a diversity of methodologies, held together by common structural principles. These would range from rigorous academic descriptions and evaluations to peer evaluations and formats for narrative reports. Each of these and others can describe good practice and each is appropriate to the different forms it can take.«

Development of the Concept of Quality Management

The reflections above attempt to set out some approaches to the concepts which should form the basis of the way in which in Europe we develop the quality in crime prevention activities which are often in request and are considered necessary by many. Otherwise the term crime prevention would become a broad and quite undefined catchword.

How, then, do we develop a comprehensive professional approach which can be evaluated as to its effect and can form a comprehensive basis for further development of quality?

The answer would, to me, contain two basic requirements: One is to define ways in which we jointly arrive at some generally accepted *comparative methods* as a basis for common European evaluation standards. The other is to define ways in which to ensure the existence of an institutional framework for taking on this work and in relation to this, it should be determined where these efforts will be conjoined.

This and other conferences prove that tremendous and profound effort is being made in order to take forward the development of quality management as well at national as at European and international levels. Thus, for instance, as will appear from Recommendation 1531 (2001) of the Parliamentary Assembly of the Council of Europe, the Council has considered the establishment of a »European observatory«.

In my opinion such work should be based in a »unit« at an esteemed European university. Work on this topic was actually carried out from the

1970s into the 1990s by a fairly informal international interest group, which had accidentally chosen the name of Cranfield Conferences.

With much support from Cambridge University this informal interest group, consisting of a wide range of international partners, took steps towards realising an institutional framework for a unit at the Institute of Criminology at Cambridge University. I had the pleasure then of being the author of setting out the views of the group in concrete form as a proposal, the main elements of which were established at the Institute of Criminology, Cambridge, and funded by international trust. I would like to take this opportunity to reintroduce the proposal, which received a certain acclaim at the time but afterwards waned for a while:

Proposal

»Proposal: As new professional and inter-disciplinary and cross-sectoral approaches to crime control and prevention emerge in Western societies, so the need for an international structure with a comparative aspect to act as a common resource (base) for them becomes ever more plain. This need has been clearly identified by policy makers, practitioners and analysts from governmental, legal, police, social agency, community and academic backgrounds who have come together to discuss crime problems of common concern, and to analyse working models of policy and practice of common interest, in the series of Cranfield Conferences on European Strategies against crime.

These conferences have acted as springboards for fresh policy initiatives, new practical projects and original evaluative studies. They have been usefully complemented and reinforced by other »Cranfield« activities ranging from a postgraduate »problem-centred« research programme developed in partnership between academics and public service professionals, to seminars, workshops and publications on professional and inter-agency strategies for care and order in society.

A pattern of inter-dependent activities on similar lines recommends itself for an international structure for advanced police and crime preventive thinking and studies in social policies related to the above mentioned fields of interest. The purpose of this structure would be:

- *to create* a forum for inter-disciplinary/cross-sectoral and transnational thinking and action in this sphere through a programme

which links conferences, seminars and workshops developed in association with governmental, professional and academic institutions in Western societies;
- *to develop* research programmes in which academics and professionals from relevant disciplines can work in partnership to analyse crime and public order problems in key environments and to assess professional and inter-disciplinary strategies to counter or contain them. This research would aim to develop local, national and international perspectives and would be undertaken by »some kind« of permanent staff, by professional researchers on a contract basis, and by professionals from the public services within postgraduate research programmes;
- *to act* as an information and advice service for new preventive strategies; to provide consultancy services; to develop a series of publications from national and cross-national research and evaluation studies;
- *to liaise* with other institutions – governmental, professional, academic and research – in this sphere to create springboards for fresh practical initiatives and research studies. (Given the personal links and »network« already established with relevant institutions and professionals in Europe, as well as with European organizations, liaison of this kind could be e.g. the Council of Europe, the EUCPN, the Standing Conference of Local and Regional Authorities of Europe and other institutions within the framework of the European Community and the different programmes, e.g. the Beccaria programme.)
- *by the formation of a »Unit«*. The »Unit« e.g. research fellows and assistants, would be financed by funds or programmes and sponsored by the above-mentioned institutions and should be located at and work from an independent, major broadly recognised European university«.

I shall add today to *promote* solid comparative research to secure the development of *quality management in crime prevention*.

Ideas equivalent to these have been expressed by Dr. Joachim Jäger, Polizeiführungsakademie, Münster-Hiltrup, in a recent book *Effizienz von Kriminalprävention – Erfahrungen im Ostseeraum* (Schmidt-Römhild, Lübeck 2004) and presented at a conference under the umbrella topic of professionalization of practitioners in crime prevention.

Michel Marcus
European Forum for Urban Safety (EFUS), France

Evaluation: For what Purpose?

Evaluation is a political and technical process. This might seem obvious since it can be applied to many concepts used in science and technology. However, regarding the question of criminality and security, this has unexpected implications. It compels those who talk about evaluation to take into account its political aspect. Not to do so is to restrict the definition of evaluation to a mere technique of management, arbitrarily defined according to the interests of the security market, and to open the way to demagogy in political debates.

The political debate on crime largely heavily weighs on evaluation. Some think that it weighs so heavily that it leaves very little freedom to technicians and researchers. When Tony Blair's last election campaign laid insecurity as the priority theme, particularly that of anti-social behaviour, scientists' work will have trouble to be taken into account, even in a small portion, when determining priorities for national English policies. One can suppose that the political decision of Blair came about in part by studies highlighting the phenomenon. But it was basically nourished by the fundamental, completely subjective, observations of the English members of Parliament in their districts. The weight of such politics exists throughout Europe. If one can be pleased with the predominance of politics over the administrative and technical aspects, one should not forget that, in the field of security, demagogy and populism can easily grow to overcome all reason. For four years, France was afraid of its young people who were becoming particularly violent. Laws were implemented, plans elaborated, and a lot of money was spent. Four years later, new statistics showed that youth delinquency had not changed. No evaluation had been used to draft efficient measures, and there was no measure of the quality/cost ratio. Today the pressure has fallen.

Thus, doing an evaluation is far from being neutral. The process requires an agreement on the premises and on what one wants to demonstrate.

Furthermore, the priority given to evaluation differs according to the nature of the measures taken to ensure a safety policy. These measures concern the field of prevention as well as that of repression. The need for evaluation is not the same.

Prevention must prove that it has results, while repression seldom has to. Rarely will one evaluate the performance of the judiciary and police processes compared to their impacts on recurrence or on the satisfaction of the victims. Seldom will one perform an evaluation of the use of electronic processes for documenting people. It would technically be possible, as it is for prevention. It is rather the political intention that is missing. It is repression policies that benefit from the largest financial investments, without any comparison with policies of prevention. The European Parliaments do not feel they have a role to play in this type of control. This absence of curiosity may be due to the foundation upon which the system of repression rests, namely the ineluctability of prison. Prison has a history and therefore a beginning but it does not seem to have an end in our vision or scenarios for the future. The role of prison is never disputed, nor is its effectiveness especially with regard to second offense. Consequently, arresting people is the only objective of the system of repression.

In spite of its lack of means, prevention lives permanently with the requirement of proving its usefulness. This requirement operates as a permanent pressure on the actors of prevention. It is all the more unfair that the delivery delays of prevention actions are greater than those of repression and its success will depend on a great number of factors. In this regard, the evaluation of the impact of modifying the schedules of the police patrol for example, can be measured in the short term, while the evaluation of preventative actions is necessarily in the long term. This extension of analysis duration is inevitably fatal for the importance of the evaluation of prevention.

How can we achieve the objective of evaluating security if we only evaluate one of its pillars?

Another major obstacle to evaluating prevention is the complexity of the causes of criminality, and the multiplicity of actions coexisting in the same territory, at the same time, and often on the same person. How do we isolate the impact of one single action among multiple actions depending on different policies, such as cultural, educational, social and health policies? No local policy in the world can be reduced to only one type of action. Consequently, isolating one action through the evaluative process will lead to failure because of the need to introduce into the conclusive phase a variety of results coming from other actions.

Another difficulty of evaluating these types of measures is the lack of consideration for the changes induced in an institution by innovative measures. To introduce, in a general action against bullying at school, a partnership-based working method, involving parents in the life of the school, is almost as important as the methods of the action itself and is as important as its success. Alternative methods of working together may be the key to the success of other actions in the future. The quality of the institutional environment of an action is certainly the most ignored aspect of the evaluation process. It is certainly this aspect that explains the failure of systematized transfers. To take an action that has succeeded in a particular environment and decide to establish it in another city without worrying about the qualities of the partnership and administrative environment will undoubtedly lead to failure.

Safety and evaluation do not work well together. Politicians are not totally responsible for this; scientific methods of evaluation still need to become more precise and homogeneous.

Is it really necessary to evaluate safety policies? Do we not confuse the need for coherent tools for financial and administrative management of safety policies with an objective judgement on the efficiency of actions? Do we not confuse a management process with a tool for enabling citizens to control public policy and public spending?

Evaluating is an action aimed at having a greater knowledge of objectives, of expected results and of means of action. Such transparency facilitates political and democratic control. To accept the terms of the debate regarding democratic control implies finding new instruments of evaluation other than those scientific methods currently available. Organizing public debates with prepared citizens and supported by specialists is the way to follow. This would have the huge advantage of not leaving the question of safety in the hands of sometimes demagogic politicians and would give prevention the legitimacy it deserves.

Gorazd Meško[80], Mahesh Nalla[81] and Andrej Sotlar[82]
Slovenia/USA

Cooperation of Police and Private Security Officers in Crime Prevention in Slovenia

1 Introduction

Commonly referred to as »transitional economies,« numerous countries in Eastern Europe have made significant economic strides to become key players in global trade. Rapid economic development has been accompanied by changes in property relations and the identification of safety and protection as a commodity (Shearing and Stenning, 1983; Shearing, 1992). An offshoot of this development is the growth in the employment of private security personnel (Shearing and Stenning, 1983). Slovenia is merely one example. This country has also experienced significant growth in the number of agencies that provide security services as well as in the number of personnel employed in these industries (Nalla, Meško and Sotlar, 2004).

Interestingly, earlier work on police and security relationships centred on western capitalist societies where policing is generally acknowledged to serve the function of deviance control and order maintenance, and to provide a sense of security and safety to citizens. That is, citizens in western countries primarily view their law enforcement agencies as organizations that address community needs. The history, culture, and social context of police organizations in the United States, the United Kingdom, and Australia are similar in many ways. Distinct historical,

---

[80] Gorazd Meško, PhD, Associate Professor of Criminology, Faculty of Criminal Justice and Security, University of Maribor, Slovenia.
[81] Mahesh Nalla, Professor of Criminal Justice, School of Criminal Justice, Michigan State University, East Lansing, Michigan, USA.
[82] Andrej Sotlar, MA, Senior Lecturer in Security Systems, Faculty of Criminal Justice and Security, University of Maribor, Slovenia.

political, and cultural traditions unlike those of the U.S. or other developed capitalist societies have shaped the nature of policing in Slovenia (Pagon, 1996; Meško, Dobovšek, Pagon, 2004).

The present study explores the relationship between public law enforcement officers and private security personnel (security officers) in Slovenia. The specific aim of this study is to understand how police officers and security personnel perceive the working relationships between the two organizations, their attitudes to the professionalism of security personnel, their views on ways to improve the working relationship, and their perceptions of the future of public and private police relationships. The findings have implications for Slovenian society, given the rapid expansion of the private security industry in terms of both the number of vendors of security as well as personnel employed in this sector. Second, in general, many functions performed by the two organizations are more similar than different (Nalla and Newman, 1990). Third, law enforcement agencies are increasingly building partnerships with citizen constituents in developed and developing economies to harness social capital to deal with social problems (Nalla and Hummer, 1999a). This study will afford us the opportunity to examine the status of police/private security relationships and to determine to what extent the two organizations are ready to build bridges to achieve the common goal of public safety and order maintenance in Slovenia.

2 Prior Research on Police – Private Security Relations

The emergence of private security as a significant player in the regulation of social behaviour has led to inquiry into the nature of relationships between private security and policing. The first category of research focused on the conceptual framework for understanding partnership building between public and private sectors. More specifically, the research question related to the types of collaborative efforts between the government and private sectors (Bardach 1998, Teisman and Klijn 2002). The position adopted by these researchers is that public and private partnerships result in more efficient service to the clients or citizens and that these relationships are legitimate as well as effective. Sarre and Prenzler (2000) outlined various types of relationships in their work, which was more specific to relationships between law enforcement and private security. These include those relationships based on property, the division of labour and competitive forces on the one hand and relationships based on coordinated and combined partnerships on the other hand.

The second set of research is focused specifically on working relationships between law enforcement agencies and private security organizations. Examples of these studies include those that examined the distribution of police power to private security due to constrained police budgets (Stewart 1985, Walsh and Donavan 1989) and as an extension of state control through non-state agencies (Henry 1985). Others focused on case studies of police/security cooperative efforts in specific cities (Bocklet 1990, Cunningham et al. 1990).

Among the various studies that focused on police/security relations, very few examined police vis-à-vis security relationships. Of the various studies that examined police/security relationships in the U.S., most focused on topics peripheral to the issue of police and security officers' attitudes towards each other. One of the earliest studies by the *National Advisory Committee on Criminal Justice Standards and Goals* (1976) suggested that security professionals believe that police do not respect private security, law enforcement officers are less concerned with crime prevention and more focused on arrests, and that police officers seek information from private security but do not share information. In a national survey of police chiefs and security managers, Cunningham and Taylor (1985) also revealed similar findings. In a more recent study, Morley and Fong (1995) examined police/security relationships in California and found that security professionals were more optimistic concerning their relationship with police compared to police perceptions of security. In a more comprehensive examination of this issue, Nalla and Hummer (1999a) studied police/security relations in Michigan and found that overall, security professionals' perceptions of their relationship with police officers is positive. Interestingly, however, security officers believe that police officers do not view working with security professionals positively. Further, the findings from this study also suggest that police officers have a neutral view of security professionals while security professionals hold police in high regard. On the issue of working relationships, while police felt that the relationships were good, security professionals felt they were poor (Nalla and Hummer 1999a). Clearly, there were misperceptions from the point of view of security officers that may interfere with better relationships. In terms of strategies for improving relations, security personnel were more supportive of improvement initiatives than police officers (Nalla and Hummer 1999b). These trends suggest that there has been a gradual improvement in the police and security relationship over the last three decades.

Though much of this research is based on public/private partnerships in the U.S.A, research on private security as well as on law enforcement and private security relationships in some emerging markets have appeared in social science research in recent years. These countries include India (Nalla 1998), Singapore (Nalla and Christian 1996), and South Korea (Nalla and Hwang 2002). Findings suggest that with increases in the employment of private security forces in these countries, law enforcement agencies have begun to recognize the contributions of the private sector in their role as agents of social control.

These findings may be unique to the U.S., given its specific political, social, and cultural context. However, as a highly ranked transitional economy, Slovenia is rapidly making major political, social, and cultural transitions. The large numbers of security personnel increase the likelihood of personnel from both organizations coming in contact with each other. Thus, in this study we examine the nature of working relationships between private security personnel and police officers in post-independent Slovenia.

Studies on the role of private security agencies and policing in Slovenian society have been a matter of scientific interest at the Faculty of Criminal Justice and Security, which has organized several national conferences on private security (Anžič, 1997; 1998; 1999) and international conferences on policing (Pagon, 1996; 1998; 2000; 2002; Meško, Pagon, Dobovšek, 2004).

3 Community Policing and Cooperation of Police Officers with Private Security Officers

The democratization of Slovene society and the reformation of local self-government in the 1990s brought about changes in police organization. The new role accorded to the police was essentially different from that which the police performed before the change in the political system and before Slovenia gained independence in 1991. The approaches favouring new policing methods, such as community policing and problem-oriented policing, have gained wider publicity during the last decade. Among the many definitions of community policing, we find the most concise one to be that which was proposed by Trojanowicz and Bucqueroux (1994), stating that community policing is a philosophy and organizational strategy in which the emphasis is on cooperation between the citizens and the police. Within such a definition, the police and the community work in unison to identify problems, set priorities and find solutions to problems such as crime, drug abuse, fear of crime, social issues, ecological problems and other types of anti-social behaviour and nuisance in one's living and working environment. Community policing is characterized by a decentralized organization whereby police officers obtain legitimacy for their work from the community they serve in addition to the traditional sources of legitimization (e.g. laws, the ruling power and other political structures; Hahn, 1998). Under the community policing system, police officers are appraised and rewarded for their communication skills (sensitivity to cultural diversity, solutions to problems, mediation in conflicts etc.) and many other kinds of knowledge and skills otherwise excluded from the appraisal models used in traditional, paramilitaristic organizational systems (Pagon, 1998).

One of the »consequences« of the Police Act in the field of community policing is also the establishment of various counselling bodies in local communities in Slovenia. In the last five years, around one hundred and ten security/safety councils have been established in municipalities. The mayors are the founders in most cases, but there are a variety of different state and non-state bodies that also participate in these bodies. Along with the mayor and the representatives of the local police, there are furthermore representatives of schools, social services, companies, *private security agencies*, associations, NGOs, influential individuals etc. They all share the common idea of creating a safe local environment for the benefit of all residents in their local community. These bodies are, on the one hand, places in which participants can express some criticism of the police work, while on the other hand the police keep their autonomy because their work is based on legally defined competencies, which prevents them from succumbing to any pressure by individuals or institutions. The main tasks of the consultative bodies therefore are to discuss and to analyse the safety situation within the local community; to shape the strategy for suppressing the causes of criminal offences, to implement projects, to acquire the financial means and expert collaborators for the execution of projects, to establish work groups on the level of neighbourhoods, town precincts and local communities, to publish preventive materials (brochures, posters, videotapes), to organise panels, public discussions and to inform the public about the work of consultative bodies (The Slovene Police, 2003; Meško, 2004).

The nature of private security in terms of functions, services, and goals is fairly similar to that found in other European states, as well as American states. Meško (1997) identifies three categories of security services in Slovenia. The first category includes security companies that sell and provide a supply of physical and mechanical equipment for business premises and citizens' apartments. The second category includes services, such as alarms and related services. The third category involves the human element, which includes services supplied by security officers such as patrol and guard services. According to Meško, the underlying framework for security services in Slovenia is to provide security and protection, safeguard proprietary information and conduct surveillance, as well as to carry out prevention activities, which include investigation and detection.

The only empirical study on police and private security officers in Slovenia to date was conducted by Meško (1999), researching partnership and competitiveness between the police and private security officers. A questionnaire was used to collect information from police officers about their attitudes towards security officers, from security officers about their attitudes towards police officers, and information about the awareness of security, as well as possibilities for common endeavours to control crime and other problems in the security field. It has been found that we cannot speak about co-operation in Slovenia since the results show large obstacles in comprehending some of the basic characteristics of one or the other professional group. This also points to the conflict of understanding between the two profession groups. The obstacles are greater among the police, since they have a lower opinion of security officers than security officers do of them. In spite of the fact that ensuring security demands greater co-operation, results have shown that common endeavours for better security are still far off. The large number of security personnel increases the likelihood of personnel from both organizations coming in contact with each other. Thus, in this study we examine the nature of working relationships between private security personnel and police officers in post-independent Slovenia.

4 Preliminary Results of the Study on Police and Private Security Officers in Slovenia

Due to the presence of a large number of private and public order maintenance personnel, there are many opportunities for both formal and informal interactions. These include police as first responders to calls from security officers or interactions where the demarcation between private and public space is less distinct. For example, given that private security plays a visible and significant role in high rises with large numbers of housing units, they are often the first responders to crime scenes or may alert the police to disturbances.

We constructed a questionnaire based on a study conducted by Nalla and Hummer (1999a, 1999b) in the U.S.A. Respondents were asked to rank their opinions on Likert-type scales from 1 (strongly agree) to 4 (strongly disagree) on four specific areas. The first two areas relate to the nature of existing relationships between the personnel of both organizations and strategies for improving existing relationships. Correspondingly, we incorporated seven items on police/security relationships and nine items on strategies for improving police/security relationships from Nalla and Hummer's work (1999a,b). The third area relates to strategies for improving the professional image of security officers. Three items were included in this section.

The final substantive area was on the future of policing. Questions for this section were drawn from the theoretical contributions of Marx (1987) and Shearing (1992) and later expanded and tested by Nalla and Heraux (2003). The underlying conceptual premise is that the nature of the police and security relationships can be seen as *state-centred*, which suggests that law enforcement is the main framework for regulating society; it could be *laissez-faire*, which proposes private security is a commodity and police/security relations are that of senior/junior partners respectively; it could be pluralistic, which suggests that social regulation is managed by both public and private sectors with no central source of command; and, finally, it can be understood through the cryptic model, which suggests that the boundaries are blurred and the delineation between police and security will disappear. Based on this premise, we have adopted five items developed by Nalla and Hearux (2003) that tap into variations of this concept.

We constructed questions that were modified to suit the Slovenian context. The survey was translated into Slovene and then translated back into English to check for validity. The samples for security officers were drawn from 300 persons, and the police officers were drawn from 300 persons. Out of three hundred submitted questionnaires, two hundred seventy security officers replied (90.0%). The police officers were also given 300 questionnaires. We received two hundred fifty-one completed questionnaires (83.6%).

The results of this study show the importance of working relations, the improvement of relations between the police and private security officers, the futures of public and private policing and career satisfaction. In regard to the »*working relationship*«, private security officers have a better opinion about the police than vice versa; police officers believe that private security officers cannot be equal partners in crime prevention with the police; both groups expect more information about each other's powers; private security officers believe that the police should try to establish good/fair contacts with them; police officers do not believe that private security officers could take over some of the police control functions in public space. »*Relationship improvement*« is challenged by the following findings: Police officers disagree about the establishment of a common information database as well as about exchanging personnel for basic and advanced training in police and private security powers. Both groups agree that interagency communication should be improved but facilitated and approved by top management. »*Future of public and private policing*« is illustrated by the belief that police and private security will have to work closely in crime; policing will remain mainly the function of the state while private security will protect private premises and customers of all kinds of businesses; private security/policing will be understood as complementary policing to the public/state policing; and the delineation between public policing and private security will not vanish soon. »*Career satisfaction*« shows that more police officers identify with their organisation, like their work more than private security officers and are happier with their career than private security officers. The results also imply that the police career is more prestigious than the private security one.

5 Challenges for the Future

Private security is the fastest growing social control industry in Slovenia at the present time (Meško, Nalla and Sotlar, 2004). The paradox of underestimating the role of private security lies in the attitude towards such agencies. For example, students of criminal justice and other university students also believe that the public police deserve much more respect than private security officers and that private security officers are not trained properly in communication with people and show a lack of kindness in shopping centres and other facilities. On the other hand private security officers have to meet the requirements of new legislation on private security which is much stricter than in the past (ibid). Roughly the same negative attitude towards private security officers is found in the police professional culture as well as a mistrust of private security officers, who are considered more guardians of private interests than the common good. Following the idea of community policing in the Slovene police force, police have to seek partners in crime prevention. Since the police have started performing community policing, their perception of possible partners is about the same as the perception of private security officers. It is often related to high expectations and hasty actions in convincing possible partners for co-operation with them. On the one hand, the police sometimes meet people of good will who want to help them and support their control activities (i.e. responsible citizens). On the other hand, quite a huge number of citizens can be characterised as moral minimalists, who do not have the time and will to help and support the police. It is a social reality of crime prevention in Slovenia. The following four factors of crime prevention prevail: *Social crime prevention* (i.e. training/work with parents, organised youth work, solving social problems, friendly school climate, development of a sense of belonging to the community, the availability of more leisure activities, and competent school teachers; *Self-protective measures* (i.e. information about crime prevention and self-protection); *Formal social control measures* (i.e. reactive – repressive policing, punishment of criminals; *private security* (i.e. security guards at schools and private security services) (Meško, 2004).

In the Slovenian culture the police are still perceived to have a leading role in crime control and crime prevention. Therefore, the police should have learnt to communicate professionally with all possible partners in crime prevention and control. We emphasise that a high level of police professionalism in establishing partnerships should be developed in order to gain possible partners and not to underestimate, make hasty judgments, have too high expectations, be suspicious, cynical or prejudiced.

References

Anžič, A. (ed.) (1997). *Zasebno varovanje in detektivska dejavnost – dileme in perspektive*. Ljubljana, Visoka policijsko-varnostna šola.

Anžič, A. (1998). *Zasebno varovanje in detektivska dejavnost – novi izzivi*. Portorož, Visoka policijsko-varnostna šola.

Anžič, A. (1999). *Nove možnosti zasebnega varstva v Sloveniji*. Portorož, Fakulteta za policijsko-varnostne vede.

Bardach, E. (1998). Getting Agencies to Work Together: The Practice of Theory and Managerial Craftsmanship. Brookings Institute, Washington, D.C.

Meško, G. (1997). Zasebna varnost: filozofija, praksa in perspektive. In: Anžič, A., (ed): *Zasebno varovanje in detektivska dejavnost – dileme in perspektive*. Ljubljana, Visoka policijsko-varnostna šola, 251–262.

Meško, G. (1999). Policisti in varnostniki – sodelavci ali tekmeci? In: Anžič, A. (ed.), *Nove možnosti zasebnega varstva v Sloveniji*. Portorož, Fakulteta za policijsko-varnostne vede.

Meško (2004). Partnersko zagotavljanje varnosti v lokalni skupnosti – želje, ideali in ovire. *Revija za kriminalistiko in kriminologijo*, 55/3, Ljubljana, MNZ, 258–265.

Meško, G., Nalla, K. M., Sotlar, A. (2004). Mnenje študentov o ciljih in naravi zasebnega varovanja v Sloveniji. *Varstvoslovje*, 6/2, Ljubljana, Fakulteta za policijsko-varnostne vede, 216–224.

Meško, G., Pagon, M. Dobovšek, B. (eds.) (2004). *Policing in Central and Eastern Europe – Dilemmas of Contemporary Criminal Justice*. Ljubljana, Faculty of Criminal Justice.

Nalla, M. K., Heraux, C. G. (2003). Assessing goals and functions of private police. *Journal of Criminal Justice*, 31, 237–247.

Nalla, M. K., Hummer, D. (1999a). Relations between Police Officers and Security Professionals: A Study of Perceptions. *Security Journal*, 12, 31–40.

Nalla, M. K., Hummer D. (1999b). Assessing Strategies for Improving Law Enforcement/Security Relationships: Implications for Community Policing. *International Journal of Comparative and Applied Criminal Justice* 23/2, 227–239.

Nalla, M., Newman, G. (1990). *A Primer in Private Security*. Albany, New York, Harrow and Heston.

Pagon, M. (ed.) (1996). *Policing in Central and Eastern Europe – Comparing Firsthand Knowledge from the West*. Ljubljana, College of Police and Security Studies.

Pagon, M. (ed.) (1998). *Policing in Central and Eastern Europe – Organizational, Managerial, and Human Resource Aspects of Policing.* Ljubljana, College of Police and Security Studies.

Pagon, M. (1998). Organizational, Managerial, and Human Resource Aspects of Policing at the Turn of the Century. In: Pagon, M. (ed.) *Policing in Central and Eastern Europe: Organizational, Managerial, and Human Resource Aspect. The Second Biennial International Conference.* College of Police and Security Studies. Ljubljana.

Pagon, M. (ed.) (2000). *Policing in Central and Eastern Europe – Ethics, Integrity and Human Rights.* Ljubljana, College of Police and Security Studies.

Pagon, M. (ed.) (2002). *Policing in Central and Eastern Europe – Deviance, Violence and Victimization.* Ljubljana, College of Police and Security Studies.

Sarre, R. and Prenzler, T. (2000). »The Relationship between Police and Private Security: Models and Future Directions.« *International Journal of Comparative and Applied Criminal Justice* 24:91–113.

Shearing, C. D. (1992). The Relation between Public and Private Policing. In: Tonry, M., Morris, N. (eds.): *Crime and Justice: An Annual Review of Research,* Vol.17, Chicago, University of Chicago, 399–434.

Shearing, C. D., Stenning, P. C. (1983). Private Security: Implications for Social Control. *Social Problems,* 30: 493–506.

The Slovene Police (2003). http://www.policija.si (Accessed May 25, 2005)

Teisman, G.R. and Klijn. E. (2002) »Partnership arrangements: Governmental Rhetoric or Governance Scheme?« *Public Administration Review* 62:197–205.

Harold K. Becker
Department of Criminal Justice,
California State University, Long Beach, USA

Impact Analysis for Crime Evaluation

Impact Assumptions

The major components of crime prevention are: micro and macro legislative and public policy making bodies, lower and higher courts and judges, local and national police organizations, and ancillary organizations of probation and parole plus numerous private and religious organizations. All of these components fit into a diverse mixture of social, political, and cultural inputs.

If we were to place all of the above variables into a very large Venn Diagram there would emerge a common characteristic of *crime control* that would naturally generate a question dealing with the following issue – do the individual components of crime prevention produce the impact on crime they were intended to make?

A majority of all competitive business organizations face a similar dilemma when analyzing impact on a product or service in the market place. Impact analysis for crime evaluation can borrow many techniques from private business.

Impact Analysis

Emile Durkheim published *The Rules of Sociological Method* in 1895, which discussed rules for the explanation of social facts.[83] In modern research the concept of impact analysis places the evaluation focus on outcomes rather than process, delivery, or implementation.[84] Outcomes

---

[83] Emile Durkheim, *The Rules of Sociological Method and Selected Texts on Sociology and its Method*, edited with an introduction by Steven Lukes and Translated by W. D. Halls, Macmillan Publishing Co., New York, 1982, pp. 119-146.

[84] Michael Scriven, *Evaluation Thesaurus*, 4th ed. Sage Publications, Newbury Park, 1991, p. 190.

are usually the post-treatment effects that were the goals and objectives of the legislation, court, police or other organizational needs – did a change take place as pre-determined by the effort? The impact, if there is one, is most often measured within the framework of quasi-experimental characteristics.

There is debate between quasi-experimental evaluation (QEE) and the more prestigious experimental evaluation (EE). The primary difference between QEE rules and EE rules is that QEE is a type of research design that conducts studies in the field or within real-life situations where the evaluator *cannot randomly* assign subjects to be victims or suspects and where the EE has greater control under laboratory conditions and subjects are *randomly* assigned to control or experimental groups. The introduction of random assignment introduces the higher possibility of outcome validity for EE.[85]

Impact analysis is not complex but it is not simple. Like any other human activity, crime evaluation has its own rules (definitions), process (how to do), and vocabulary (what does it mean statistically). As already identified, under QEE, the evaluator must deal with conditions that are not easily manipulated in the field – what you see is what you get.

Impact analysis will test for the successful introduction of a pre-designed condition, e.g. selected or general crime reduction via police arrest (apprehension) or neighborhood safety program (prevention) or juvenile anti-drug program (intervention). The goal is a reduction in crime with a specific objective to arrest by apprehension, prevent by introducing neighborhood safety techniques, or intervene by anti-drug education-counseling program(s). As can be imagined, there are many ways that any one of the above approaches can fail. Many times more than one approach will be put forward to reduce crime and it will become difficult or impossible to isolate the real cause of impact. Some of these problems can be dealt with vis-à-vis better program design prior to evaluation.[86]

---

[85] W. Paul Vogt, *Dictionary of Statistics & Methodology, A Nontechnical Guide for the Social Sciences,* 2nd ed. Sage Publication, Newbury Park, 1999, p. 103.
[86] Refer to Donald T. Campbell and Julian C. Stanley, *Experimental and Quasi-Experimental Designs for Research,* Rand McNally, Chicago, 1966 as well as other publications by Campbell.

Program Design

Many programs are pre-determined to be ineffective because of one or more of the conditions described in the following three examples:

(1) EXAMPLE. Administrative or political influence that has prejudged the program to be a success, e.g. a county probation department wanted to evaluate the disproportionate minority confinement of youth in a pilot program, if the program lowers the confinement rate of youth, an attitude of success prevailed! The program was highly rated by administrators and local politicians in the media but failed to reduce minority confinement.

Scenario. A county probation department was awarded a grant to develop a program to reduce the disproportionate number of ethnic minority youth in juvenile facilities. The project was to last several years and the planning was conducted by personnel of the probation department. There was a great deal of local news coverage and political statements were made concerning the value of the program and how the community would benefit by having fewer juveniles in formal custody. The probation department failed to coordinate their project with the local police and juvenile court, which made the intake of the juveniles remain constant. Attempts were made by the probation department at the lower caseworker level to make adjustments to the processing of the youth by creating an experimental pool and control pool of juveniles once they were processed through the police and court. The individual caseworker was expected to collect data on the juveniles. The probation department did not assign anyone to track the progress of the project or collect specific data that could be used for program evaluation. Therefore, what should have been a unified program took on the form of approximately five separate projects – depending on the interest or in some instances the lack of interest of the caseworker.

Approximately three months before the grant was to be terminated it was recognized that an initial grant requirement stated that an outside evaluator was to assess the project. The probation department tried to involve a local university's department of criminology to recommend a graduate student to conduct the evaluation. A faculty person (a member of the criminology department) did not consider that a student would be capable of conducting the evaluation and volunteered her services. The probation department accepted her.

Within the few months remaining in the project, the evaluator attempted to collect data, track the minority youth, and prepare a final report. The probation department administrative personnel and caseworkers interfered with the efforts of the evaluation and suggested that anecdotal opinions of caseworkers, describing success, could be used to establish positive impact of the program.

The evaluator refused to comply with these improper requests by the administrators. She prepared her report, stating the futility in attempting to measure program outcomes and the probation department's pressure to corrupt the project. The program was not refunded by the granting institution. Unfortunately for the program, the evaluator's professional ethics would not allow her to make false statements of program success.

(2) EXAMPLE. Starting a program with no plan to coordinate goals or objectives or identification of reliable data collection techniques, e.g. a community police department launched a community relations project to reduce conflict between local police and neighborhood members after a localized ethnic riot of widespread violence and property damage. The question was raised in the media – can police community participation produce positive results? Specific data from community members was unavailable to measure impact on the program that would produce positive outcomes.

Scenario. Pictures of several police persons beating a female ethnic-minority person, who was resisting arrest, sparked a riot in a large city. These pictures were displayed by local television stations and in city newspapers. Within hours ethnic-minority community members took to the streets, looting and destroying property. Local police could not contain the rioting and military personnel were called into the city. The rioting continued for several days with severe economic loss and several community members being killed.

A committee of public officials and police personnel held closed door meetings to discuss solutions to the community rioting. No members from the rioting community were asked to participate in the meetings. After several weeks a plan was formed and put into action. For police purposes the community was divided into several block areas and a team of police personnel assigned to the individual areas to act as a rapid response-group to community crime needs. The police identified this program as police community relations.

The police department had a planning and research unit that tracked this program by using regularly reported numbers of crimes and persons arrested. This internal evaluation of the program did not attempt to create a more descriptive database to measure the program and, more importantly, did not attempt to attract input in the form of ideas and suggestions from the community members. This program continued for several years until the next riot occurred in the same geographic area.

(3) EXAMPLE. The failure to identify a problem, e.g. the evaluator should be brought in at the beginning of problem discussion to help make problem identification and diagnosis more likely possible.

Scenario. A high school (grades 9 to 12) decided to coordinate with the local police department to decrease student use of violence on school property and in the community. The type of violence targeted was graffiti, physical threats against other students, and actual physical attacks between students. It was decided that the police department would assign a uniform officer, full time, to the campus to act as a counselor and teach a class on prevention of student use of drugs and violence. This type of program was widely available in many high schools with large minority student populations and was called a *school resource officer* program. The police department paid half the salary of the police person and the school paid the other half of the salary.

The police officer selected had a college degree in public administration and had never taught in a school environment. The police officer had been in the police department for five years working patrol and traffic assignments, not married, and was preparing, during off duty hours, for the next promotional sergeant's examination.

The police person was liked by the students, was a poor classroom teacher, and openly made jokes about other teachers to the students. Neither the police person nor the school administrators conducted opinion surveys of the students to determine the benefits of having a police person on campus. There was no attempt to collect data.

Important Elements to Successful Program Design
1. The evaluator should be part of the project plan team. It may be necessary to conduct a needs assessment to determine an organiza-

tional problem or community problem for improvement. Establishment of a start and ending project date.
2. After the problem has been defined, the evaluator can identify necessary data to be collected specific to the problem.
3. A before-after experimental data collection source will be identified and a control before-after group established for comparative purposes (to track validity and historical continuity).
4. It is extremely beneficial if the evaluator is someone who is outside the organization that is seeking verification of project outcomes. However, a member of the organization should be assigned to the evaluator to act as guide and sponsor within the work-a-day world of the organization. This will help open local resources that otherwise might be closed or difficult to append.

It is the responsibility of the evaluator to develop the following four concepts within the program designto have the project reach its stated goals and objectives for evaluation.[87]

- Determine the types and sources of evidence needed for evaluation
- Develop a data analysis plan
- Formulate evaluation questions
- Identify reporting procedures

Evaluation Analysis

Two of the many methods to produce impact analysis of data are: regression analysis – which is a method of explaining or predicting the changeability of a dependent variable using information about one or more independent variables to describe causal relationships or to predict outcomes. Regression is a statistical method for studying the relationship between one dependent variable (Y axis on a graph) with one or more independent variables (X axis on a graph). The concept of regression was developed by the English scientist Francis Galton (1822–1911) during his enquiry of the relationship between the heights of fathers and sons. Galton used a linear equation to describe the relationship.[88]

---

[87] Gerald J. Bayens and Cliff Roberson, *Criminal Justice Research Methods, Theory and Practice*, Copperhouse Publishing Company, Nevada, 2000, pp. 327–328.
[88] Paul D. Allison, *Multiple Regression, A Primer*, Pine Forge Press, Thousand Oaks, 1999, p. 1–4 and Vogt, op. cit., p. 239–240.

The second method for impact analysis is a comparative-change design that has the practicality of descriptive statistics and is described by Cook and Campbell in their 1979 text on *Quasi-Experimentation: Design & Analysis Issues for Field Settings*.[89] Both regression analysis and comparative-change methods can be expanded into an *interrupted time-series* design where several pretests are conducted before treatment and several posttests are conducted after treatment.[90]

Example of a Regression Analysis Design

An example of the first method using regression analysis is a simple scatter plot with a least squares regression line or trend line (see formula and diagram below) representing the number of arrests for homicide for males between 14 years of age to 24 years of age in a large urban community in 2003.

The equation for the regression line has one dependent variable and one independent variable and would have the following general formula for a line:

$$y = a + bx$$

a and b are numbers to be calculated. This entire process can be done with a computer statistical program. The vertical axis Y is the dependent variable HOMICIDE and the horizontal axis X is the independent variable AGE. As age increases, the number of arrests for homicide increase.

A more complex model of the data would be a multiple regression technique that contains one dependent variable and more than one independent variable. The formula for a multiple regression would be the following:

$$Y = a + b_1 x_1 + b_2 x_2 \ldots$$

---

[89] Thomas D. Cook and Donald T. Campbell, *Quasi-Experimentation: Design & Analysis Issues for Field Settings,* Rand McNally, Chicago, 1979.

[90] W. Paul Vogt, op. cit. p. 143.

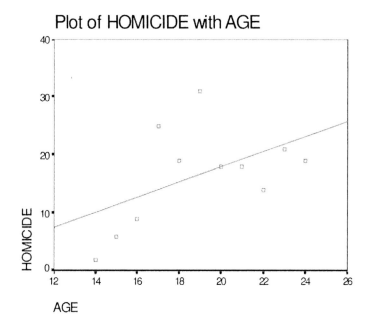

The use of regression techniques has great utility in impact analysis and should be engaged more frequently.

Example of a Comparative-Change Design
The second method is a comparative-change design that has the following expression:

$$\frac{X_E \: T \: Y_E}{X_C \: Y_C}$$

Where
X_E is the pretest of the experimental group
X_C is the pretest of the control group
T is the treatment or activity to make a change
Y_C is the posttest of the control group
Y_E is the posttest of the experimental group

Probably the comparative-change design is one of the most widely used methods in impact analysis. It is manageable and quickly understood by organizations seeking to test for change. A survey can be administered to the nonrandom members of the experimental group that will identify the characteristics that are going to be changed by some treatment (activity, training, information, situation, etc.) that relates to a change in criminal behavior. Normally the same survey will be administered again to the experimental group as a posttest after the treatment.

The same survey will also be administered to the control group during the same time periods with the experimental group, but without the treatment. The X_E and X_C pretests should portray similar results but the Y_E and Y_C results should be different if the treatment was effective. The control group also becomes an indicator of worldly events that might directly influence both groups.

The comparative-change design can be expanded into an *interrupted time-series* design where several pretests are conducted before treatment and several posttests are conducted after treatment instead of the one pretest and one posttest for experimental and control groups.

Only students who indicated that they had answered all the survey questions 100% honestly were selected for comparison. The following three tables represent control and experimental group student responses of 110 students originally surveyed in an X_C pretest to 104 students originally surveyed in a Y_C posttest and 108 students originally surveyed in an X_E pretest and 99 students originally surveyed in a Y_E posttest.

The control group students were selected from the boys and girls who were required to attend physical education classes and the experimental students, who received the treatment educational information program, were selected based on high absences from school and low grades.

Table 1: High School Students Self-Reported During Past 30 Days Drug and Behavioral Characteristics on School Property

	X_C	Y_C	X_E	Y_E
	Pretest	Posttest	Pretest	Posttest
Answered honestly	N=58*	N=51*	N=83*	N=70*
Students	Yes %	Yes %	Yes %	Yes %
During Past 30 Days				
Used marijuana on school property	5.7	8.4	9.0	4.6
Used alcohol on school property	7.0	6.9	10.0	8.3
Used cigarettes on school property	1.7	1.4	4.6	2.8
Took a gun to school	4.3	3.5	5.5	1.4
Took other weapon to school (knife or club)	10.0	12.0	10.7	6.1
At school do you feel ›unsafe‹	12.4	11.5	15.8	10.3
In your neighborhood do you feel ›unsafe‹	9.1	9.9	10.0	7.1

* Table only compares students self-reporting twice that they answered all questions honestly

Table 2: High School Students Self-Reported During Past 12 Months Drug and Behavioral Characteristics on School Property

	X_C	X_E
	Pretest	Pretest
Answered honestly	N=58*	N=83*
Students	Yes %	Yes %
During Past 12 Months		
Been offered, sold, or given drugs at school	25.9	27.8
Seen someone carrying a gun, knife, or other weapon	26.8	31.7
Been bullied at school	21.1	18.1
Been threatened or injured with a weapon at school	5.2	9.6
Been afraid of being beaten up at school	8.6	10.5
Been in a physical fight at school	22.8	20.8
Had property stolen at school	19.0	23.2
Did you damage school property	13.8	15.8
Have you changed home addresses (moved)	22.8	23.6

* Table only compares students self-reporting twice that they answered all questions honestly

Table 3: High School Students Self-Reported During Past 30 Days
Community Drug Use and Student Opinion

	X_C Pretest	Y_C Posttest	X_E Pretest	Y_E Posttest
Answered honestly	N=58*	N=71*	N=73*	N=81*
Students	Yes %	Yes %	Yes %	Yes %
During Past 30 Days				
Used alcohol	23.9	30.2	40.0	22.9
Drink alcohol until I get really drunk	5.6	3.6	8.3	4.2
Five or more alcohol drinks, within a few hours	15.6	18.5	26.6	19.7
Used marijuana	7.5	10.1	20.2	11.8
Used cigarettes	8.6	5.6	10.8	4.1
Used smokeless tobacco	3.4	2.1	5.1	-0-
Used Inhalants	2.3	4.9	9.7	3.3
Used Cocaine or Crack	4.9	7.2	7.4	1.4
Used Methamphetamine	2.2	5.8	5.6	3.2
Used Ecstasy	1.8	1.4	3.1	-0-
Used LSD or other psychedelics	1.7	1.4	1.2	-0-
Student Opinion				
Cigarettes are ›easy‹ to get	65.7	69.3	62.1	66.6
Cigarette use daily is ›harmless‹	10.6	11.4	9.7	7.8
Alcohol is ›easy‹ to get	55.2	67.1	62.7	72.8
Alcoholic use daily is ›harmless‹	18.7	15.1	27.8	63.3
Marijuana is ›easy‹ to get	47.3	51.4	58.8	72.5
Marijuana use daily is ›harmless‹	12.8	17.2	17.1	50.0
Do you belong to a gang	17.9	14.1	15.7	11.4

* Table only compares students self-reporting twice that they answered all questions honestly

Table 4: High School Students Self-Reported General Information: Gender, Grade, and Age

	X_C Pretest	Y_C Posttest	X_E Pretest	Y_E Posttest
Answered honestly	N=58*	N=71*	N=73*	N=81*
Students	Yes %	Yes %	Yes %	Yes %
Gender Boy	50.0	48.6	49.3	52.5
Girl	50.0	51.4	50.7	47.5
Grade 9th	98.2	98.6	93.2	84.0
10th	1.8		1.4	8.6
11th		1.4	4.1	4.9
12th			1.4	2.5
Age 14 and below	86.2	84.5	62.5	49.4
15	13.8	12.7	27.8	37.0
16		2.8	6.9	9.9
17 and above				3.7

* Table only compares students self-reporting twice that they answered all questions honestly

Summary

The primary focus of *impact analysis for crime evaluation* is on outcomes rather than process, delivery or implementation of a project. However, evaluations *can* look at both outcomes and process, if possible. They should look at anything that is relevant, for example, comparisons that will help explain impact.[91]

The techniques of quasi-experimental evaluation described in this paper are regression analysis, comparative-change, and the expanded use of pretests and posttests of interrupted time-series. These techniques may fall victim to the nonrandomized selection of subjects that true research experiments can maintain.

Therefore, the results of quasi-experimental impact analysis must be considered at best an *estimate* of life experiences and a work in progress. In practice, the evaluator deals with a hypothesis, not a theory – and information gained from the evaluation cannot be considered a final answer to a problem but a statistical bridge to the better understanding of a problem.[92]

---

[91] Michael Scriven, op. cit. pp. 250–251. Also refer to Delbert C. Miller, *Handbook of Research Design and Social Measurement*, 5th ed., Sage Publications, Newbury Park, 1991.
[92] Refer to Stephen W. Hawking, *A Brief History of Time*, Bantam Books, New York, pp. 9–10 for a brief explanation and definition of theory.

Jim Hilborn
Chairman of the Baltic Crime Prevention Practitioners' Association, Tallinn, Estonia

Anu Leps
Ministry of Justice, Tallinn, Estonia

Crime Prevention Policy in Estonia 1991–2005

For the past 2 decades Estonia has been observing the development of crime prevention policy in the UN, Council of Europe and different EU countries. And with the regaining of its independence in 1991, it has taken some of the words, and concepts, that were being used in these other countries and placed them into its own documents and strategies.

The Development of Crime Prevention in the UN and EU

In the early 70s a series of evaluations of the police, and corrections has demonstrated the limits of traditional criminal justices. *The Sixth United Nations Congress on the Prevention of Crime and Treatment of Offenders* in Caracas (1980) had urged that greater efforts should be made to seek new approaches and to develop better techniques for crime prevention.

The Seventh Congress (1985) in Milan adopted a Plan of Action and Guiding Principles for Crime Prevention and Criminal Justice that emphasized crime prevention as part of social policy: the relationship between development and criminality, studies on the social impact of crime, intersectoral planning, community participation in crime reduction efforts, traditional forms of social control, victim support, social marginality and injustice, periodic appraisal of criminal justice policies, unrestricted access for individuals to the legal system, scientific cooperation and cooperation among developing countries.

The *Eighth Congress in Havana* (1990) adopted a specific resolution on the prevention of urban crime.

The *Ninth Congress in Cairo* (1995) asked the Crime Commission to finalize and adopt the proposed guidelines in the field of urban crime prevention. This, the United Nations Economic and Social Council did in 1995.

The 9th UN Congress described two models of crime prevention – primary and situational. It wrote that Crime prevention strategies vary in nature, level, scope, time-frame and cost. *Primary prevention – seeking to create socio-economic conditions less conducive to crime – has the longest horizon, and its effects are not easy to assess.* Community initiatives vary in time and scale. *While situational crime prevention, aimed at reducing opportunities for crime, may be readily instituted, it should be carefully evaluated because its effect is likely to displace rather than prevent crime.* Efforts to prevent crime might include target-hardening, access control, and deflecting offenders by increasing the risks and by reducing rewards. Eliminating or restricting facilitators of crime, such as firearms, is a matter for urgent consideration and decisive action (emphasis added).

In the same year HEUNI published *Crime Prevention Strategies in Europe and North America* (Graham and Bennett) which provided an excellent overview of the field. This work made a distinction between criminality prevention, situation prevention, and community crime prevention. It also mentioned the earlier typology, based on a public health model of prevention that divided crime prevention into three groups: primary prevention, secondary prevention, and tertiary prevention. This book was translated into the Estonian language, and would help guide Estonian policy makers.

In 1998 the UK created the Crime and Disorder Act with a legal framework for a country-wide series of Crime and Disorder Partnerships. The British PM vowed to be »Hard on Crime, Hard on its Causes«. The UK experiment is ongoing, with a mixture of positive and negative outcomes. By the 10th UN Congress in Vienna, crime prevention theory had developed significantly.

The 10th UN Congress noted that policy discussions usually distinguish between just two kinds of prevention, social prevention and situational prevention, which correspond to the two main ways of preventing crime – reducing criminal motivation and reducing crime opportunities. For the purposes of the present discussion it is useful to distinguish between four different general approaches (three of which seek to reduce criminal motivation), which are distinguished by their own set of objectives and techniques. These four approaches to crime prevention are:

- CHILD DEVELOPMENT.
- COMMUNITY DEVELOPMENT.
- SOCIAL DEVELOPMENT.
- SITUATIONAL CRIME PREVENTION.

Unlike the three other forms of crime prevention, all of which seek to reduce the motivation for crime, situational prevention seeks to reduce opportunities for crime.

By 2002 the UN had completed its new guidelines with an excellent short definition of crime prevention. The UN said that »crime prevention« comprises strategies and measures that seek to reduce the risk of crimes occurring, and their potential harmful effects on individuals and society, including fear of crime, by intervening to influence their multiple causes.

It went on to say that crime prevention encompasses a wide range of approaches, including those which:

- Promote the well-being of people and encourage pro-social behaviour through social, economic, health and educational measures, with a particular emphasis on children and youth, and focus on the risk and protective factors associated with crime and victimization *(prevention through social development or social crime prevention)*;
- Change the conditions in neighbourhoods that influence offending, victimization and the insecurity that results from crime by building on the initiatives, expertise and commitment of community members *(locally based crime prevention)*;
- Prevent the occurrence of crimes by reducing opportunities, increasing risks of being apprehended and minimizing benefits, including through environmental design, and by providing assistance and information to potential and actual victims *(situational crime prevention)*;
- Prevent recidivism by assisting in the social reintegration of offenders and other preventive mechanisms *(reintegration programmes)*.

Within a few years crime prevention policy with examples of good evidence-based practice had improved dramatically. The UN *Guidelines for the Prevention of Crime* (2002) are excellent. Some of the key policy points include:

- There is clear evidence that well-planned crime prevention strategies not only prevent crime and victimization, but also promote community safety and contribute to the sustainable development of countries. Effective, responsible crime prevention enhances the quality of life of all citizens. It has long-term benefits in terms of reducing the costs associated with the formal criminal justice system, as well as other social costs that result from crime. Crime prevention offers opportunities for a humane and more cost-effective approach to the problems of crime.
- It is the responsibility of all levels of government to create, maintain and promote a context within which relevant governmental institutions and all segments of civil society, including the corporate sector, can better play their part in preventing crime.
- The present Guidelines address crime and its effects on victims and society and take into account the growing internationalization of criminal activities.
- Community involvement and cooperation/partnerships represent important elements of the concept of crime prevention set out herein. While the term »community« may be defined in different ways, its essence in this context is the involvement of civil society at the local level.
- Crime prevention considerations should be integrated into all relevant social and economic policies and programmes, including those addressing employment, education, health, housing and urban planning, poverty, social marginalization and exclusion. Particular emphasis should be placed on communities, families, children and youth at risk.
- Crime prevention requires adequate resources, including funding for structures and activities, in order to be sustained. There should be clear accountability for funding, implementation and evaluation and for the achievement of planned results.

This last point is critical if crime prevention is to be institutionalized. Of course then the EU had to come up with its own documentation.

Communication from the Commission to the Council and the European Parliament

First it provided a nice definition of crime which does help to remind everyone that crime is a social construction.

The prevention of crime in the European Union

The concept of crime

Crime includes punishable conduct by individuals and by spontaneous associations of persons. The concept, however, covers separate realities:

- *Crime in the strict sense*, i.e. offences defined as such in national criminal laws (e.g. homicide, rape, certain illegal trafficking);
- *Less serious offences* that are actually more frequent (e.g. theft, handling stolen goods, acts of violence, fraud, embezzlement);
- *Violence in various contexts* (schools, sports stadiums, public highways, domestic violence etc.);
- *Anti-social conduct* which, without necessarily being a criminal offence, can by its cumulative effect generate a climate of tension and insecurity.

The potential for expansion has proven to be a very critical point in the UK which has gone far past crime control, crime prevention or crime reduction into the promotion of community safety, and the whole issue of the quality of life in UK communities.

While the UN definition was too simple and clear the EU Commission's definition was the reverse:

Crime prevention includes all activities which contribute to halting or reducing crime as a social phenomenon, both quantitatively and qualitatively, either through permanent and structured cooperation measures or through ad hoc initiatives. These activities are undertaken by all the actors likely to play a preventive role: local representatives, enforcement services and the judicial system, social services, education system, associations in the broad sense, industry, banks and the private sector, research workers and scientists, and the general public, supported by the media.

The *Communication from the Commission to the Council and the European Parliament* went on to describe three different categories of crime prevention.

Three categories of measures can thus be distinguished according to whether they are intended to:
- reduce opportunities, making crime more difficult and riskier and reducing the profits to criminals;
- reduce the social and economic factors which encourage the development of crime;
- provide information and protection for victims and prevent victimisation.

The EU established the EUCPN (European Union Crime Prevention Network) on the 28th of May, 2001. The EUCPN covers all types of crime, but pays particular attention to juvenile, urban and drug-related crime. The core objectives of EUCPN are to contribute to developing the various aspects of crime prevention at Union level and support crime prevention activities at local and national level. Issues of structure and adequate resource allocation have always prevented the full development of the EUCPN.

The Council of Europe has also recommended to the European Parliament the need to establish a European observatory on urban security, which, at the level of Council of Europe member states, would be responsible for:
1. gathering, analysing and making available to all parties concerned information on crime and the operation of systems of justice in the different countries;
2. keeping a regularly updated register of the security practices which bring the best results;
3. organising exchanges between those in charge of security policies;
4. offering training courses for security policy agents.

Such a European observatory would be a major step in the development of crime prevention at the EU level.

There are several efforts within the EU to establish Master's level training programs in crime prevention. The EFUS is working with the University of Burgundy to start a Master's in Urban Safety. The 1st Beccaria project has been promoting quality management in crime prevention and is hoping to establish a Master's Degree program in Crime Prevention.

The Council of Europe had the project *Responses to violence in everyday life in a democratic society* (2002–2004) which resulted in a series of excellent publications. The one on *Urban crime prevention – a guide for local authorities* was translated by the Ministry of Justice and shared with local authorities, police, etc. Another important document was *Security and democracy under pressure from violence* written by Michel Marcus, who is a magistrate and the executive director of the European Forum for Urban Safety, a non-governmental organisation with a membership of 300 European local authorities. This project also developed a set of 12 principles for dealing with violence for which a wide consensus is emerging at the European level:

- Integrated approach: violence in everyday life necessitates a comprehensive and co-ordinated response applied through the thematic, horizontal, vertical and strategic integration of national prevention policy and its implementation at all levels;
- Systematic reliance on partnerships: an integrated response to everyday violence should be based on partnerships of all the people and institutions involved in reducing violence, in order to pool resources and share responsibility.
- Democratic accountability and participation of civil society: responses to violence should be accountable to citizens' democratically elected representatives at all levels and involve the active participation of civil society.
- Preventive approach: in the first place violence should be prevented before it takes place but when violence occurs, its consequences should be minimised.
- Victim-oriented approach: satisfactory support, care and protection of victims should be used as essential standards for planning, implementing and evaluating responses to violence.
- Offender-oriented prevention: rehabilitation of offenders, their eventual reintegration into society and the prevention of recidivism should be taken as serious aims in a comprehensive prevention policy.
- Developing the use of mediation: mediation as a non-violent and restorative means of preventing and solving conflicts should be pro-

moted while its scope of application, methods and ethics should be clarified.
- Giving priority to local prevention programmes: sufficient priority and resources should be given to local partnerships for the prevention of violence.
- Planning and continuous evaluation: responses to violence should be carefully planned based on situational analyses, adequately documented and continuously evaluated through evidence-based criteria.
- Sustainability: prevention programmes should be designed and resourced for sufficiently long periods of time to ensure that the targeted impact can be reached and sustained.
- Training for all partners: people working in violence prevention partnerships should receive training or guidance to match the skills required in their tasks.
- Interdisciplinary research policy: interdisciplinary research into violence should be supported in order to generate an adequate knowledge base for policy development and practice.

These basic principles could be applied to crime prevention in general and not just to violence. Indeed, crime can be seen as always involving some violence, direct or indirect, overt or covert, against the individuals and/or communities that are being negatively impacted upon by the actions of the individual crime or organized crime.

As a result of this project, the Council has continued it with a new project using these principles with an emphasis on »*Children and violence*« (2005–2007).

In many ways it would seem that Crime Prevention policy and practices are in good shape. However, the picture is more complex and unclear.

There is almost a separate and competing movement to develop EU level policy and practices to deal with the threat to the different states of organized crime. This effort could easily divert funding from the urban based model of crime prevention which has been developing for the past decade. The UNODC and the European Commission have agreed to increase mutual efforts and provide joint financing for projects aimed at preventing and controlling drug addiction, production and trafficking, as well as other forms of organized crime.

But first it is time to look at the internal efforts of Estonia in the period of 1991 to its becoming part of the EU in May, 2004. Much of its policy was derived from the Crime Prevention activities within the UN and EU.

Crime Prevention in Estonia (1991–2005)

The first few years of the restored Estonian Republic had been chaotic with a massive increase in social disorder and recorded rates of crime. To what degree there was such a real increase in crime, or just a more accurate recording of criminal events, is open to debate. What is clear is that crime was going up along with the fear of crime and a general sense of insecurity. The worst period had ended in 1994 when the murder rate peaked. To the degree that there was social policy planning, it was based on the priority to establish a strong economy based on neo-liberal economic principles, and then let the »invisible hand« of the market work to solve Estonia's social problems.

By 2000 Estonia was ready to produce its own crime prevention documents.

Description of the Crime Prevention System and Development Strategy (2000–2003)

Under this strategy the division into three crime prevention levels was very similar to existing UN and EU documents. They were

IMPLEMENTATION OF SOCIAL PREVENTATIVE MEASURES – the aim is to weaken and, if possible, to eliminate the effect of crime causation and enabling factors.

IMPLEMENTATION OF SITUATIONAL PREVENTATIVE MEASURES – the aim is to make it difficult to commit an offence and to increase the risk and hazard of »being caught« for the potential offender.

DEALING WITH THE CONSEQUENCES OF OFFENCES – the aim is to decrease the number of repeated offences by offenders.

And it was noted that

Preventative activities occur on mainly three levels:
- STATE LEVEL;
- LOCAL GOVERNMENT LEVEL;
- COMMUNITY LEVEL.

Four ministries, the Ministry of Justice (MOJ), the Ministry of the Interior, the Ministry of Education and the Ministry of Social Affairs, participate in crime prevention work through the National Crime Prevention Council (NCPC). Board crime prevention policy was worked out at the State level in the NCPC with support from the Crime Probation and Prevention Division in the Ministry of Justice. Then Parliament would vote on the proposed directives.

On the level of local municipalities, crime prevention means working out specific measures and applying them locally in order to increase the security of local people. For better co-ordination of work some of the counties and also local municipalities have established their own crime prevention councils or they have committees working with other organizations.

However crime *prevention work is not obligatory, it is voluntary at the local level*. The State makes its plans, its different Ministries work out strategies, but the delivery at the local level is not mandated. Thus the crime prevention strategy has no legal teeth.

The Estonian CP document did set out some general goals in what is very much a top-down planning document with little room for the involvement of either local government or the participation of the public.

In the strategy part, listing six goals for the creation of a functioning prevention system until the year 2003 there were the following steps to be implemented:
- 2000 – Organisation of crime preventative activities at state level.
- 2001 – Increase in the responsibility of local authorities for crime prevention.
- 2002 – Supplementation of the financing principles of crime prevention.
- 2003 – Making the population aware of the possibilities regarding crime prevention, creating the law-abidance of the population.
- 2004 – Increasing the competence of people who participate in crime prevention.
- 2005 – Systematic investigation of the reasons for and consequences of crimes and the measurement of the effectiveness of preventative means.

In terms of crime prevention planning, it is rather remarkable that the gathering of the necessary criminal intelligence is left so late in this timeline.

This development strategy was the first attempt at crime prevention planning step. It is now possible to conclude that it was too ambitious in its goals for the following years, but it did make some small changes in the state level organization work (concerning the ministries, the council, etc.) and the work done in the community level by giving out more knowledge and information about crime prevention and by supporting the start of initiatives from NGO level (Neighbourhood Watch Movement).

This strategy was soon followed by a more concrete emphasis.

State Strategy for Crime Prevention until the Year 2005

Goals of the strategy
- More efficient inclusion of the public in crime prevention
- More efficient protection of property
- Increased safety on streets and public places
- Decrease in criminal offence and crimes committed by young people
- Better availability of victim assistance
- Prevention of repeated crimes

In this strategy, tactical steps could be more or less measured. The first Crime Prevention document had had some broad principles and an unrealistic timeline. The next Crime Prevention document was focused on action.

There have been some real results
- There was a special Crime Prevention Division 2002–2003 and afterwards the structure changed and since December 2003 there has been a Criminal Policy department inside the Ministry of Justice. Crime Prevention policy and practice is one of the department's functions. It is looking at the research done in this area and promoting an evidence-based approach to criminal policy.
- There is a new victim support system with the Victim Support Act (which came into force on the 1st of February 2004). The VS volunteers are working in regions across Estonia since the beginning of 2005 and all together we have almost 40 VS volunteers.
- In 2004 the Estonian Crime Victim Survey was done (part of the International Crime Victim Survey) and it stated that the overall crime victimization rate has gone down in recent years. 33% of the

people questioned had been victims of some sort of crime at least once in 1999, whereas the figure was 32% in 2003. In terms of the number of crimes experienced per 100 respondents, 79 different offences were committed against a group of one hundred respondents in 1999, compared to 62 offences in 2003.

- Since 2004 the Ministry of Justice has had limited funds for supporting the crime preventive initiatives implemented at community level, among NGOs and local authorities.
- A State Legal Aid Act was passed on 28 June 2004 and the purpose of this Act is to ensure the timely and sufficient availability of competent and reliable legal services to all persons.
- The police are now more community-based, and focused on targeted crime reduction. The result is that people have more trust in the police. This increase in public confidence is a really positive change.
- There has been a reduction in the number of crimes of violence against persons. The number of crimes against property has not been reduced.
- Individuals have started to take steps to protect their property themselves.
- In the Planning Act (came into force 1st January 2003) there is article 8 section 16 about the comprehensive plan stating that:
    - make proposals to prevent, by way of planning, the risk of criminal activity in urban areas;
    - In the Planning Act about the detailed plan there is article 9 section 15 stating that:
    - establish requirements and conditions to prevent the risk of criminal activity. The European Standard has been translated and changed concerning the Estonian system into Estonian Standard No. 809 – 1:2002. Prevention of Crime – Urban Planning and Building Design. Part 1: Urban Planning.
- There is a new Penal Code (in force since 1st Sept. 2002) gives possibility to use community service as an alternative punishment and concerning the juveniles' special treatment in criminal proceedings is getting more attention and there are already special judges, prosecutors, probation officers for dealing with juvenile cases.
- There is a new Code of Criminal Procedure (it came into force 1ST July 2004), which gives the leading role to the prosecutors in pre-trial criminal procedure.

- The old Soviet camp system is starting to be replaced by new single cell design prisons in accordance with EU standards but also giving better control over the prison population.

These are real accomplishments. However a lot of them involve the improvement of the criminal justice system. Crime Prevention is seen as a function within the CJS and not as a significant innovation.

One of the real successes of crime prevention in Estonia has been the active participation of civil society organizations, or NGOS. The third sector is actively involved in crime prevention, mainly through social work, youth work, drug prevention and the Neighbourhood Watch movement. The NGO Estonian Neighbourhood Watch Association was identified by the ICPC in 2005 as an example of best practices in crime prevention work with youth in the urban context.

The Ministry of Justice has several different good cooperation partners from the NGOs: for example Estonian Neighbourhood Watch Association, Caritas Estonia, Convictus Estonia, Estonian Union for Child Welfare, Tallinn Children Support Centre, etc.

On the international level, Estonia is a member of the European Crime Prevention Network (EUCPN), it currently has 2 bilateral cooperation projects (COPS, BECCARIA) with different European Countries. The leading partners are the UK and Germany. Both the UK and Germany have provided major inputs into the development of probation and policing in Estonia as well as crime prevention. The Netherlands and Sweden have also contributed to the development of Victim Services, and in cooperation with Sweden after the cooperation project in 2002 there was a book produced on local level crime prevention that has been translated into both the Estonian and the Russian languages.

From Urban Crime Prevention to State Security

The recent acceptance by the Parliament in 2003 of the document »Criminal Policy Development Strategy until the year 2010« is a positive moment. It includes an excellent review of the policy issues and the best evidence available on what works in the area of crime prevention. This document provides guidelines for the work of the different Ministries responsible for integrating crime prevention into their everyday work and also to the local authorities.

The analysis in the document is quite critical of the present situation in Estonia, and also makes clear that despite the body of knowledge that has been built up over the past few decades, the institutionalization of crime prevention is still not working as well as it had been planned to work in Estonia just as it has been in much of the EU (Van Dijk, 2004).

Estonia is basically still depending upon the repression of crime through the use of traditional practices of the criminal justice system, and it has the highest rate of incarceration in the EU despite the establishment of a probation service in 1998, which might have helped to reduce the size of the prison population. Instead of a reduction, there has been a doubling of the total population that is under some form of state supervision.

Estonia is like a hungry man who is looking at a buffet of crime prevention strategies, and choosing to stay hungry. Estonia is not yet ready to really move into a state level system of crime prevention activities since that would require both the political will to create the necessary legal framework, and also the allocation of significant resources over a long period of time. Anyhow we do a lot of work every day for achieving an adequate state level crime prevention system.

Estonia looks at the UK which is an example of a country that has created the necessary legal framework and allocated massive amounts of resources to the implementation of its crime and disorder reduction partnerships with resultant real gains but which is still experiencing significant problems. So crime prevention as a laudable idea is to be commended but Estonia has other priorities.

The UN system has always had a tension between two models of crime prevention. The International Centre for the Prevention of Crime in Montreal has advocated crime prevention at the level of the city, and an emphasis on crime prevention through social development. The European Forum on Urban Safety also focuses on the level of the city. Both organizations have been supported by Canada and France who have supported the CPSD (crime prevention through social development) model.

In the UK and in the USA, CPSP/OR (crime prevention through situational prevention or opportunity reduction) has had far more policy influence. Indeed the Jill Dando Institute of Crime Science, at University College London, makes it clear that only crime prevention through situational prevention warrants the name »crime science«. Implicitly crime prevention through social development is devalued. And it is clear that CPSP has established a body of evidence in support of this approach, especially in the work of Ron Clarke and Herman Goldstein.

The UN office in Vienna has now had a name change. The Centre for International Crime Prevention vanished. The new name, United Nations Office for Drug Control, more accurately described its emphasis on corruption, organized crime, trafficking in women, terrorism.

The 11th UN Congress: For Reasons of State

The 11th UN Congress was not just another Crime Prevention and Offender Rehabilitation Congress. Rather it was named the Crime Prevention and Criminal Justice Congress. The new name was a reflection of the way that the world has greatly changed since the 11th of September, 2001.

In the previous UN Congresses, such as the 9th (1995) and 10th UN Congress (2000), the emphasis had been on Crime Prevention and Offender Rehabilitation. Van Dijk (2004) points out that the crime prevention philosophy advocated by Bonnemaison in France in the 80s was predicated on the assumption that law breakers can and should be socially reintegrated. To a large degree the end goal of social inclusion and integration was replaced in the 11th UN Congress by exclusion and an active defence against organized crime and terrorism.

There was still a significant emphasis on CPSD with the ICPC running Workshop 3: Strategies and best practices for crime prevention, in particular in relation to urban crime and youth at risk. The ICPC also released its newest publication, Urban Crime Prevention and Youth at Risk: Compendium of Promising Strategies and Programmes from around the World. As mentioned, Eesti Naabrivalve, Estonian Neighbourhood Watch Association, is identified as an example of a promising strategy.

However it is also clear that the overall emphasis was on the protection of the State against corruption, organized crime and terrorism. Crime Prevention is clearly subordinate to Criminal Justice and the protection of the State.

The Bangkok Declaration is quite clear in its emphasis:

Greatly concerned by the expansion and dimensions of transnational organized crime, including illicit drug trafficking, money-laundering, trafficking in persons, smuggling of migrants, illegal arms trafficking and terrorism, and any existing links between them, and by the increasing sophistication and diversification of the activities of organized criminal groups,

Emphasizing that .... International cooperation, which is among the most important elements to *combat terrorism in all its forms and manifestations, and reaffirming that no terrorist act can be justified in any circumstances,*

In a spirit of common and shared responsibility, we reaffirm our readiness to seek to improve *international cooperation in the fight against crime and terrorism*, on the multilateral, regional and bilateral levels, in areas including, among others, extradition and mutual legal assistance. We seek to ensure our national capacity and, where appropriate, the coherence of our international capacity, through the United Nations and other relevant global and regional organizations, *to engage in international cooperation, in particular in the prevention, investigation, prosecution and adjudication of transnational organized crime and terrorism and in discovering any existing links between them.*

We call upon donor States and financial institutions to continue to make adequate voluntary contributions on a regular basis for the provision of technical assistance to developing countries and to countries with economies in transition, in order to help build their capacity to prevent and tackle crime in all its forms and apply the United Nations standards and norms in crime prevention and criminal justice and, in particular, to facilitate their becoming parties to and implementing *the international instruments against terrorism and the relevant international instruments against crime, such as the United Nations Convention against Transnational Organized Crime and the Protocols thereto, the United Nations Convention against Corruption and the international drug control conventions.*

The »War on Drugs«, the »War on Terrorism«, the »War on Corruption« are all merged into one thing, the protection of the State. The State will wage *war* against its enemies, whether they are external or internal.

Human Rights Concerns and the New Crime Prevention

And there is a real danger that the »ends« will subvert the »means«. It is no accident that the recent efforts by the UK government to extend the Anti-Social Behavior Orders has drawn criticism because of human rights concerns in the same way as its stands accused of flouting international human rights law over its treatment of foreign terror suspects rounded up after the September 11 attacks in America.

The response by Louise Casey, director of the Home Office antisocial behaviour unit, was that these critics including »youth workers, social workers and the liberal intelligentsia« should accept there is strong public support for the sanctions in addressing »a culture of intimidation«. And these critics are »not living in the real world«.

The Council of Europe's Commissioner for Human Rights, Alvaro Gil-Robles, who had expressed concern about the use of Asbos, and the members of Asbo Concern which include organizations such as

- National Association of Probation Officers
- Community and Youth Workers Union
- British Association of Social Workers
- Mind
- Children's Rights Alliance
- National Autistic Society
- Developmental Adult Neuro-Diversity Association
- Forum on Prisoner Education
- British Section of the European Group for the Study of Deviance and Social Control
- Staff group of Manchester Law Centre

as well as a diverse group of sex worker associations, were all organizations that were not living in the real world.

It is very similar to the way that President Bush dismissed the concerns of Amnesty International about abuses in Guantánamo, Afghanistan and other detention camps around the world. The issue is not dealt with, the messenger is devalued.

Where now, Estonia?

If the recent document on »Criminal Policy Development Strategy until the year 2010« was strong on analysis but weak on implementation at the local level, there is another key document that may be more critical for the future of crime prevention in Estonia.

This document is the *National Security Concept of the Republic of Estonia* (2004). It presents the goal and guidelines of Estonia's National Security Policy and a general evaluation of the existing security environment. This document was drawn up and adopted on the basis of the Peacetime National Defence Act.

The document includes sections on terrorism and organized crime side by side. The potential linkage is made very clear.

Threat of international terrorism

Although the likelihood of a direct military threat is decreasing, non-conventional threats, primarily the global nature of international terrorism, and the possibility of the uncontrolled proliferation of chemical, biological, and radioactive or nuclear weapons are presenting international cooperation with serious new tasks.

International terrorism and organised crime, the latter providing a hotbed for the former, are spreading in areas where national security, law and order, as well as rule of law are failing. The elimination of the threat of terrorism requires quick and effective international cooperation, in which Estonia participates within the scope of its commitments and capabilities. In addition to international cooperation, Estonia also implements domestic counter-terrorism measures.

Threat deriving from organized crime

International organised crime could often be extensively intertwined with the activities of terrorist organisations and be connected with the proliferation of weapons of mass destruction. It is therefore a significant threat factor to international stability and Estonia's national security.

A noticeable threat to the functioning of the rule of law in Estonia, and thereby, to national security, is the possible increase in the influence of international organised crime within society and the accompanying corruption as well as its penetration into politics, the civil service, and the economy.

After a section on environmental threats, especially from the older type nuclear power plants (in Russia) there is a section on threats of a social origin.

Threats of a social origin

Drug addiction, alcoholism, and the spread of HIV/AIDS, along with other dangerous contagious diseases, pose a threat to Estonia's economic welfare as well as the nation's social and political stability. Emergencies in Estonia's vicinity could be accompanied by a large flow of refugees and extensive migration.

In another section the issue of the danger of organized crime to national security reappears.

Maintaining law and order

The central government agency in the fight against organized crime is the Central Criminal Police *(Keskkriminaalpolitsei)*. In this sphere, the Central Criminal Police cooperates closely with other police agencies, the Security Police Board, the Board of Border Guard *(Piirivalveamet)*, the Tax and Customs Board *(Maksu- ja Tolliamet)*, and the Prosecutor's Office *(Prokuratuur)*. The systematic fight against organized crime must concentrate upon the avoidance and prevention of crimes providing large illegal profits.

Greater emphasis is being put upon making more efficient use of various opportunities offered by Interpol and Europol as well as upon cooperation with neighbouring states. It is also necessary to establish a witness protection system, in order to participate in international witness protection programs.

The report is a mixture of internal and external concerns, of hard and soft security issues. At the end the issue of HIV appears again.

Enhancing social safety

To enhance the nation's social safety, it is essential to solve labour market problems, establish a sustainable social security system that covers risk groups, and educate and train a sufficiently large qualified work force to ensure the continuation of economic growth.

In the case of public health emergencies, there could be large numbers of people requiring medical care due to the outbreak of contagious diseases, poisonings, or exposure to radiation. Estonia is establishing its national preparedness for public health emergencies, basing it upon close cooperation with other EU Member States.

Fighting contagious diseases, including the spread of HIV/AIDS and tuberculosis, is the state's responsibility. In Estonia, measures for preventing the spread of particularly dangerous contagious diseases are implemented in accordance with international medical regulations. National programs are being implemented to reduce drug addiction, to limit the spread of HIV/AIDS and tuberculosis (all emphasis added, pp. 19–20).

When read in combination with the Bangkok Declaration it is quite clear that Estonia could easily go in a direction where concerns about human rights and harm reduction are subordinate to issues of State security. Indeed it is a direction that can be seen across most of the EU.

Possible futures

In his presentation at the Opening Plenary of the Conference on Sustainable Prevention Policies and Practices: Present and Future Challenges December, 1, 2004, Paris ICPC 10th Anniversary Colloquium, which was entitled *Crime prevention in a globalized world: foundations, setbacks and challenges*. Prof. JAN VAN DIJK Deputy director, United Nations Interregional Crime and Justice Research Institute (UNICRI) Turin, Italy made it quite clear that crime prevention had not gone the way that he had hoped.

He told the audience how fifteen years ago, he had identified the advance of crime prevention, alternative sanctions and victim assistance in Europe and the USA in the eighties as manifestations of a further stage in the ›civilizing process‹, replacing imprisonment by less inhumane, preventive and reintegrative responses to problems of crime (Van Dijk, 1989). Now the current stagnation or rollback of many social and penal reforms introduced in the final decades of the last century seemed to fly in the face of such optimistic notions. He put it rather bluntly:

There is little point in denying that for crime prevention the political winds seem to be blowing in the wrong direction.

However, he also thought that the present setbacks may also include the potential for future gains. He used the example of the earlier cholera epidemics where repressive steps had been followed by proactive and inclusive public health measures. He had the following argument:

I will sketch how the HIV epidemic may start to influence drugs and other social policies in the West in unexpected ways.

For a few years the world has been confronted with a second HIV epidemic, largely transmitted through drug injection, commercial sex and prison communities. The epidemic is most concentrated in Asia and in the countries of the former Soviet-Union. The overlapping populations of injecting drug users, prisoners and exploited sex workers comprise over fifty million people worldwide. If current regional trends in drug injection, imprisonment and migrant sex work prevail, the group will become gradually larger in the coming years. At the same time, if current trends can be extrapolated, larger and larger segments of it may carry the HIV virus. They will increasingly also reside in Western Europe and North America.

The main actual and potential carriers of the new HIV epidemic, then, is comprised of an expanding underclass of injecting drug users, prisoners, ex prisoners and exploited sex workers, all pursuing an increasingly transnational lifestyle. The main cities of the nineteenth century were confronted with streams of poor immigrants from rural areas seeking employment in the new urban industries. They constituted for some time a problematic group and were called the ›criminal underclass‹. In the framework of globalization, developed countries are now similarly confronted with an emerging group of loosely integrated immigrants. They constitute a transnational underclass drifting to the powerhouses of the globalizing economy.

The emergence of drug-related HIV epidemics within the ranks of this transnational underclass will raise the stakes of policies regarding their presence. As was the case with cholera and many other contagious diseases, those living in poor physical, economic and social conditions are especially at risk to be infected by HIV. From these vulnerable groups the virus will spread out to the general public, through the commercial sex industries or otherwise. The inhumane living conditions of those constituting the new urban underclass can no longer be neglected.

As has happened with epidemics in the nineteenth century, the initial dominant response has been to blame the drug- and crime-related HIV problems on the carriers of the virus themselves. A policy of repression and exclusion carried favour with public opinion so far. Such policies of exclusion are known to be counterproductive and will soon be *seen* to fail. The risk groups may be driven further underground but the transmission of the epidemic will continue from there unabated. Subsequently policies advocating a more practical, public health approach which shows results, will increasingly find support from a public confronted with the impact of the epidemic on their own communities. In the coming years the drug-related HIV epidemic is likely to propel more and more governments towards the development of new institutional arrangements for adequate health care for injecting drug users, reaching out to marginalized groups, including prisoners, regardless of their nationality or residential status.

The international community has still a long way to go before real progress can be made in the prevention of the drug- and crime-related HIV epidemic. The world's public opinion resembles that of Europe and the USA during the first cholera epidemic of 1832. The infected drug users, like before the patients of cholera, are made the scapegoats of their own, environmentally induced misery. Majority support is not yet available for an evidence-based, public health approach to the problem, reaching out with adequate medical and social care to the groups most at risk, rather than discriminating against them. However, when awareness will grow of the seriousness of the current epidemic in Asia and Eastern Europe in particular, and of the subsequent danger of spreads of the virus among the middle classes in the West, a shift in public opinion is likely to occur. *More and more opinion leaders will then speak out in favour of politically controversial but much more cost-effective approaches than the current model.* A radical shift in public opinion took place in all major Western countries with the arrival of the second cholera epidemic of 1849. *The first signs of a drug-related HIV epidemic in Western Europe imported from the East, might well trigger a similar, fear-induced but eminently sensible response now.*

Many beautiful words have been written about the need for global governance to give globalization a social dimension (ILO, 2004). If the scenario suggested above becomes reality, not those high-minded proposals but fear of HIV and related contagious diseases will act as catalyst of institutional arrangements of care for some of the most marginalized and disenfranchised groups in our times. The dreadful HIV epidemic, or other epidemics such as avian flu, may so, surprisingly and paradoxically, become once again the driving force behind new policies of social inclusion. Countries may soon be forced to accept legal harmonization and global solidarity to an extent unimaginable in the current political climate, not because of interdependencies in international trade but because of the transmission of dangerous viruses among the very poor.

In conclusion, globalization processes have eroded political support for policies of social inclusion, notwithstanding its proven effectiveness in reducing crime. Globalization processes are creating interdependencies in the security domain, including the transnational transmission of HIV and other blood-borne or air-borne diseases. *The world may soon witness a renaissance of crime prevention approaches driven by concerns about HIV and other global security concerns.* The knowledge base on what works in crime prevention may soon be very much in demand. ICPC as the United Nations specialized agency on crime prevention is well-placed to play a catalyzing role in its worldwide promotion (all emphasis added).

His analysis would seem more accurate in its description of the present trend toward repression, and the potential for real change. Given that Estonia is now facing the very HIV pandemic that he is using as an example, his analysis gains even more force.

Estonia will probably continue to move toward more repression since it is the direction implicitly outlined in its National Security Plan and explicitly in the Bangkok declaration. While it is not likely that any Estonian political party is ready to promote crime prevention beyond vague slogans, the stated priorities of the latest Minister of Justice are alternative punishment and crime prevention measures. And today the crisis that Van Dijk mentions is upon Estonia.

Perhaps Estonia will be one of the first of the EU countries to move to providing the crime prevention resources that are necessary for the real institutionalization. It is clear that Jan Van Dijk and the UN Guidelines of 2002 argue that a political will is necessary for real deeds and not just words.

Today crime prevention is like the weather in Estonia, which is often overcast and cool. However, Estonia also has its own brief summer, so we can hope that it will be a leader in the realization of the promise of urban crime prevention and social inclusion. Only time, and our efforts to create the future we wish, will tell whether or not Van Dijk has valid reasons for hope.

Radim Bureš

Crime Prevention Department, Ministry of the Interior of the Czech Republic, Prague

Crime Prevention System and Activities in the Czech Republic

1 Background

In the years 1990 to 1992, the number of crimes committed in Czechoslovakia tripled of the incidence of crime in 1989. The dramatic rise in the crime related figures in the years of the young Czechoslovak democracy triggered a wide discussion about the capacity, limitations, and efficiency of the government enforcement of the criminal law. The government started laying grounds for a prevention-based policy to analyse causes of the rising crime and to limit possibilities and motivations to commit crime. In 1996, the government, for the first time, decided to allocate money from the state budget to support a program intended solely to reduce crime by means of introducing prevention measures. Next to reducing crime, the program had been designed to increase the feeling of public security and public reliance on the state administration and the law enforcement and also to support victims.

2 Management of Crime Prevention in the Czech Republic

The strategy has been built on three main pillars – departmental crime prevention, community-based crime prevention and nationwide information strategy. The overall co-ordination is provided by the National Crime Prevention Committee. The national policy is set up in Crime Prevention Strategies, which are adopted by the government resolution for three-year periods. The crime prevention activities in the Czech Republic are supported by the government. Subsidies from the national budget are used to support local crime prevention projects submitted by municipalities. The crime prevention budget is about 80 million Czech crowns a year (aprox. 207 mil EUR). An important part of the crime prevention system in the Czech Republic is training of all crime prevention agents. There is neither a separate course in crime prevention at Czech higher education institutions nor in criminology. The only way how to learn on crime prevention are on-the-job training provided by the Ministry of the Interior (and some other central administrative bodies) for municipal crime prevention managers and other field workers.

The *National Crime Prevention Committee* was established as an interdepartmental advisory body in order to help to create and coordinate the crime prevention policy. Membership of the Committee was composed of representatives of the Ministry of the Interior, Ministry of Justice, Ministry of Labour and Social Affairs, Ministry of Defence, Ministry of Health Care, Ministry of Finance, Ministry of Education, Youth and Sports, Prison Service, Probation Service, Supreme State Prosecutor Office and a representative of the Inter-Agency Anti-Drug Committee and of the Czech Government Council for the Roma Minority Issues.

In 1997, the first National Strategy in Crime Prevention was compiled and adopted by a Government resolution. Since then National Crime Prevention Strategies are prepared every three years. In addition, each year a report is written on the implementation of the Strategy and on next year's priorities.

3 Community-Based Crime Prevention

Due to the fact that crime is mostly a problem of larger municipalities, the National Crime Prevention Committee decided that the government subsidy provided via the so-called *Comprehensive Coordinated Crime Prevention Program on the Local Level* shall be offered to municipalities of a minimum of 30 thousand inhabitants troubled not only by a high incidence of crime, but also by other crime-related problems such as unemployment, a high number of people long-term dependent on welfare, a high number of divorced or single-parent families with small children, a high concentration of socially deprived communities, etc. As far as types of crime were concerned, the Committee decided to pay special attention to those most troublesome and, at the same time, feared. These are *violent crimes and crimes against property* (pick-pocketing, car theft, breaking into cars, bike theft, house and general burglary, theft of items from apartments, homes, shops, summer residences, attics, cellars, pram storage facilities, etc.). Municipalities seeking subsidies were required to draft their own prevention program and have it approved by the city council, to provide management support of the program, and to secure co-financing of the program by the municipality. Crime prevention programs of all municipalities seeking subsidies were required to be based on an analysis of the security risks, a sociological survey of public perception of safety, a social and demographic analysis of the given municipality and an audit of all institutions and bodies in charge both of crime prevention and repression.

Municipal crime prevention policies initially focused on pooling together all the bodies concerned with prevention (Police of the Czech Republic, Municipal Police, municipal bodies, NGOs, religious groups and organisations, and members of the public). The element of coordination later became one of the prerequisites of crime prevention on the municipal level. In 1996, the National Crime Prevention Committee approved the methodology of the Comprehensive Coordinated Crime Prevention Program on the Local Level. The main principles of the methodology have remained valid so far. Initially, there had been 18 municipalities participating in the first wave of the Comprehensive Coordinated Crime Prevention Program on the Local Level supported by a government subsidy. In the year 1998, the project got extended to municipalities with 10 thousand plus inhabitants and the number of participating entities rose to 43; in 1999 it was as many as 66 municipalities. In the year 2000, the government approved the *Strategy of Crime Prevention on the Local Level for the years 2001-2003* and the current system is commonly referred to as the *Program of Crime Prevention on the Local Level,* in the following text simply referred to as the *Program.*

In between 1996 and 2002, the government released *CZK 508 251 000* for municipal crime prevention programs. *There have been altogether 2737 projects* of social and situational prevention, public access to information and training of prevention program managers. The number of municipalities registered with the Program in 2002 is 93.

The current crime prevention system on the local level was intended to support municipalities of over 10 thousand inhabitants. The increasing juvenile crime in small municipalities and in the rural areas has been calling for extended prevention programs to cover smaller municipalities and micro-regions. The Ministry of the Interior in co-operation with the regional police headquarters proposed a new programme called »Partnership«. This programme started as pilot project in 2003 and fully replaced the previous program in 2005. Its objective is to support preventive projects in smaller municipalities. In bigger cities the program is open for small, well defined communities. The police are responsible for indication of most urgent crime problems and for initiation of common solutions. This way the police are more involved in searching for solutions of local crime problems.

Summary

- The government is responsible for supporting crime prevention on the local level
- The municipality should participate, both in human resources and financially
- Only most needy municipalities are eligible for funding
- The system for granting subsidies should be mostly transparent and open
- Conditions for becoming eligible for grants are as follows:
    - High crime rate,
    - High rate of other social pathology (number of people dependent on social benefits, unemployment rate),
    - Willingness to participate in the program (city council decision),
    - Pay at least 10% of project cost,
    - Appoint crime prevention manager,
    - Participate in training;
- When offered participation in the Program the municipalities should:
    - Make crime audit,
    - Prepare projects in cooperation with other local agents,
- Presented projects are pre-screened by crime prevention department for meeting criteria and clarity
- Actual selection is done by selection committee composed by experts appointed by relevant ministries (Education, Labor and Social Affairs etc.),

- Selected projects are endorsed by the National Crime Prevention Committee,
- Ministry of Finance provides approved funds to municipalities, which provide direct payment for projects.

Outline of subsidies allocated to projects in 2001–2003

Type of Project	Number of Projects Subsidized	Total Subsidy
social prevention	787	49 268 500
situational prevention	179	74 106 000
public information	86	5 713 500
mandatory issues	146	3 133 000
TOTAL	1198	132 221 000

4 Crime Prevention Programmes under the Auspices of Different Ministries

Specific targeted prevention programs are also drafted *on the level of individual ministries* and they reflect the responsibilities of the individual ministry. There are programs for prevention at schools, prevention within army forces, specific preventive programmes for social services or probation service.

Prevention and Police Work

All county Police Headquarters have established so-called *Prevention and Information Groups of the Police of the Czech Republic*. Members of the police in charge of prevention focus primarily on coordination with the government administration and local self-government (planning and implementation of preventive measures – community policing), support of the public, prevention and information activities focused on the youth, and on drafting and distribution of information fliers and other preventive printed matter. The Prevention and Information Groups not only advise people on how to protect their apartments and homes from burglars and cars from being stolen, but they also organize debates at schools and police promotion activities (contact days, police days, promotion days – showing rapid reaction forces, canine squads, etc.). Sixteen municipalities have included in their Prevention and Information Groups of the Police of the Czech Republic so-called Advice Points, offices equipped by security devices, which provide a wide range of prevention-related services to the public.

Annually, the Ministry of the Interior prevention program draws from the Ministry a budget of about CZK 3,900,000 to finance establishing and equipping *Prevention and Information Groups* and contact points and to support police activities vis-à-vis children and the youth (e.g. school debates). The program is also open to support some prevention-related research and to support innovative pilot projects.

THE MINISTRY OF EDUCATION, YOUTH, AND SPORTS has established the so-called Basic Prevention Program, which serves as a basic tool of prevention of socially pathological behaviour at schools. The program is binding for all schools and other institutions of learning and is monitored by the Czech School Inspection. At each school the Ministry appointed a prevention manager and has paid increased attention to the new forms of behavioural counselling (e.g. children with behavioural problems may be seen by newly established counselling centres).

MINISTRY OF LABOUR AND SOCIAL AFFAIRS focused on developing different types of social work, including streetwork, new types of facilities (e.g. new halfway houses for young people raised at institutions), and jobs for fresh graduates and hard-to-employ people.

The authorities also considered alternative punishment in the form of a community sentence. *The Act on Probation and Mediation Service* has given rise to 74 centres (since 2001) in charge of administering alternative proceedings and punishment and, especially in the context of juvenile crime, mediation. The Ministry of Justice busied itself with the amended bill on juvenile justice (Act No. 218/2003 Coll., adopted on June 25, 2003, in force as of January 1, 2004).

5 Preventive Measures

Situational Crime Prevention

By means of implementing technical, material, and logistical measures, *situational prevention* strives to minimize crime-increasing factors, to remove motives to commit crime or to make crime more complicated, to deflect the offender from the crime, to reduce proceeds or gains from crime, and to facilitate detection of crime. Examples of situational prevention are municipal CCTV systems, centralized crime protection desks, streetlights, connecting, computer, and other technological equipment, etc. Altogether, the program has supported *425 projects of situational prevention by the total sum of CZK 259 673 000*, 196 of the projects were municipal CCTV systems (CKK 213 586 000, i.e. 82.2 per cent).

The projects of municipal CCTV systems have most often been implemented by the local authorities in close cooperation with the municipal police (93 per cent of the projects), the rest falls under the Police of the Czech Republic.

Social Crime Prevention

Social prevention focuses on potential offenders by introducing changes in their social environment (family, school, community, etc.). It focuses primarily on juvenile risk groups, members of which either have a criminal record or cause problems at school, come from socially deprived background or have no social background at all (e.g. young people at age 18 leaving orphanages or correctional facilities), juveniles experimenting with drugs, socially deprived groups such as the homeless, drug addicts, prostitutes, people released from prisons, etc., but also victims of crime, people living in socially deprived areas, people who have fallen victim of inter-racial conflicts, etc. The social prevention programs include projects of sports activities (playgrounds, skate and in-line facilities, sporting equipment), hobbies and educational activities (arts, technical hobbies, various residential and non-residential activities (contact facilities, asylum facilities, hotlines, streetwork, etc.) as well as educational and promotional activities, mostly at schools. *The 1753 social prevention projects supported by Program in 1996–2002 cost in total CZK 204 060 500.*

The social prevention projects are most often implemented by NGOs (34.3 per cent of the subsidized projects) and the self-administration (30 per cent), followed by schools (12.9 per cent), religious organizations (7.1 per cent), local government (4.7 per cent), and the Children and Youth Centres – DDM (4.2 per cent).

6 Nationwide Information Policy

One of the most important elements of prevention is *spreading information to the public*. The public is informed by the media, by means of public debates and presentations, fliers, or via contact points. People may seek information concerning protection from crime, but also available welfare and other social services, relevant legislation, incidence of crime and trends, or activities of the Police of the Czech Republic and the Municipal Police. *The 254 public information projects supported by the program in 1996–2002 cost in total CZK 18 167 700.* Most of the public information activities and campaigns have been organized by the municipal self-administration in co-operation with the Municipal Police (68 % of the public information projects), Police of the Czech Republic (20%), and NGOs (8).

Some of the information is provided centrally by the Ministry of the Interior. Advice has been developed on patterns of safe behaviour and on security protection measures (or safety tips) in various life situations. They are known as the so-called »ten points«. These tips are distributed by leaflets and fliers and on Ministry of the Interior's web site. There is a long list of these »ten points«, starting from advice how to secure your home, your company seat, your car, your second (summer) home up to safe behaviour in public transport, safe behaviour for women and girls and senior citizens. Extensive information is provided for crime victims. In addition to the short »ten point« tips, also more elaborate information material is provided. Brochures on protection of homes e.g. list up certified security devices (alarms, locks, bars, glass follies) or contain construction tips and advice.

The public is regularly advised by the Ministry on new security devices, either on its web page or through the media. The crime prevention department also publishes a bimonthly (formerly monthly) »*Information bulletin*«. This bulletin brings to crime prevention practitioners and related experts (social services, probation services, police) information about crime prevention theory and practice, including best practice project information from abroad (also the Beccaria conference in January 2005 has been reported!!). The bulletin is distributed mainly in its electronic version, simple printed »hard copies« are distributed only to some target groups (e.g. municipality mayors). Part of the bulletin is devoted to a digest of crime prevention related articles from various newspapers and academic journals.

Close cooperation with the media resulted in a number of incidents of media (TV, radio broadcasting) appearances of crime prevention department staff discussing safety and security tips and advice. These programs are focused mainly on senior citizens and housewives and there is a good customers feedback.

7 Evaluation Results

There is limited evaluation of single projects and almost no academic, independent type of evaluation. This is mainly due to the lack of criminological expertise in the country. The feedback for the crime prevention program is obtained mainly by public opinion polls and the development of crime statistics. The public feeling of safety and reliance on the self-administration and the police have been increasing. The national crime statistics are indicating that in the past three years the incidence of crime has been declining by, on average, 5.4 per cent a year. In municipalities involved in the subsidy program and implementing prevention programs for over three years, the figure is – 7.9 per cent (!!!). When interpreting the statistics it is important to underline that the municipal data is included and reflected under the national data. The figures will please all advocates of prevention since they statistically prove that prevention makes sense and is worthwhile.

However, it is important to underline that without the support of the government and without its subsidies it would have never been possible to promote the local level crime prevention scheme in such a short period of time.

8 Prevention Strategy for the Years 2004 to 2007 – Objectives and Priorities

Local level prevention programmes
- The Ministry of the Interior shall primarily support prevention of the following types of crime:
  - acquisition crime,
  - violent crime,
  - racially motivated crime, crime committed by extremists, or motivated by xenophobia,
  - plus projects to improve traffic safety.
- The Ministry of the Interior shall give priority to programs focused on the following groups:

- children and the youth
- primary prevention projects (after-school activities and education) basic prevention programmes for schools and other institutions of learning may receive support from more government agencies but the Ministry of the Interior,
- secondary prevention projects (SVI) and follow-up projects for juvenile offenders, children's homes may receive subsidy more government agencies but the Ministry of the Interior,
- socially excluded groups and communities,
- victims of crime, including victims of domestic violence.

These programmes are intended to help protect local communities from crime, increase public perception of safety, facilitate cooperation of all local bodies and institutions active in the field of prevention, and integrate the Police of the Czech Republic in the local level prevention activities.

Centrally managed programmes targeted at specific problems
- Prevention of trafficking in human beings for the purpose of sexual exploitation,
- Prevention of violence against women and children, including the launch of the EU project Daphne II,
- Support of victims of crime, prevention of repeated victimization
- Prevention of domestic violence,
- Prevention of football spectator violence,
- Prevention of corruption.

The above programs are structured to flexibly react to current trends in crime and possible negative development of individual types of crime, which require an interdisciplinary approach and may not be solved on the local level. In this respect, it is necessary to create a unified methodology of projects, professional training of the staff involved, and a system of financing from public sources.

Development of the system of crime prevention in the Czech Republic
- Analyses, concepts, and guidelines in the context of crime prevention ,
- Scientific research in support of crime prevention and crime-relat-

ed phenomena (focused on evaluation of risks and effectiveness of individual types of projects in both situational and social prevention),
- Drafting of standards which help evaluate and analyse individual types of projects; creation of pilot projects,
- Training of prevention experts,
- Coordination and building of information networks to connect individual players responsible for prevention (interagency cooperation and cooperation with regional governments, regional police headquarters, municipalities, and other bodies and institutions involved),
- International cooperation in the field of crime prevention; cooperation within the European crime prevention network (EUCPN),
- Media policy in the field of prevention,
- Financing of the prevention system
  - government budget financing of the development of prevention programmes and projects,
  - handling necessary paperwork and managing the process of applying for financing from the EU structural funds.

The objective is to improve the system of crime prevention, in particular its analytical processes, evaluation, HR, information flows, and guidelines and to make the Czech Republic crime prevention system a valid partner to the already existing prevention systems in the democratic countries.

9 Best Practice Examples: An Early Intervention System

Context
High levels of juvenile crime have been a problem in large urban and industrial areas of the Czech Republic in recent years. Often those involved were minors under the age of criminal responsibility and thus could not be dealt with through the justice system. Another problem was that while a number of institutions that deal with delinquency existed, they did not co-operate well with each other and their reactions were slow. Different institutions and bodies tended to deal with cases in isolation from each other, did not know about each other, and often intervened too late.

Goals
- Establish a network between all relevant bodies working with juveniles
- Establish an early intervention strategy for juvenile delinquents
- Establish diversion programs
- Create a comprehensive city database related to juvenile crime

Project Details

The project was first launched in February 2000 in the city of Ostrava, and is currently being extended to the city of Svitavy. The initiative is funded primarily by a national government subsidy (c. 250,000 USD) with a contribution by the municipal council. The project involves the establishment of a centre with a core team, trained by the Ministry of Labour and Social Affairs, to create a comprehensive information system on juvenile delinquency, and more recently, on possible child abuse cases. Data is entered by police as well as medical facilities on a daily basis, and is forwarded to social workers. It includes information on offence (type, location, when it occurred etc.) and on the background of the young person (age, family circumstances etc.) to facilitate the development of individualized intervention and rehabilitation plans.

Using this comprehensive information, social workers can begin drafting social intervention plans for individual children and youths. Probation officers are also able to access the data base to plan sentence recommendations to the courts.

The centre helps to build links between all those who are involved in child and youth cases, including the police, social services, child protection services, schools, NGOs, medical services, probation, prosecutors, and youth courts, in order to co-ordinate activities more effectively and efficiently. It focuses on early social intervention, promoting the use of diversion programmes to divert young people from the criminal justice system, from re-offending and the stigma of a record, and a possible criminal career. Diversion from the youth justice system is used only if the young person (and his or her family) actively participates in the development of the correctional plan.

Outcomes/Evaluation

In 2002, the project was evaluated by the Ministry of the Interior's

Crime Prevention Department, as part of a follow-up report on juvenile delinquency. Current assessment demonstrates increasing use of the database by all those involved in child and youth cases in the city. Information increased from 7,654 entries relating to 3,366 young people between 2000 and 2002, and currently stands at 13,542 entries for 5,699 young people. In addition, plans for intervention were initiated without delays, and there is much greater co-operation between the different sectors of the system dealing with children and youth.

Partners
Ministry of the Interior, City, police, judicial authorities, social workers, probation services and NGOs.

Prevention of Human Trafficking

Context
After political changes and the opening of borders in the early 1990s, the Czech Republic quickly became a target country for human trafficking and traffickers. The country has since transformed from a country of origin into a transit country and, increasingly, a country of destination. Steps have been taken in both the legislative and criminal justice areas to fight this, yet they have only provided partial solutions. For anti-trafficking strategies to be effective, they need to include both prevention and victim support as well.

Goals
- Prevent trafficking of Czech citizens abroad
- Provide fast and effective support to both foreign and resident victims of human trafficking in the Czech Republic
- Encourage victims of human trafficking to testify against traffickers
- Create informal networks in the fight against human trafficking
- Support local agents in the identification of victims and ensure proper referral to supporting organizations

Project Details
Three major steps have been taken since 1999 towards preventing human trafficking. A major information campaign was launched in 1999 with financial support from the American government. It was imple-

mented by the International Organization for Migration (IOM), with the support of the Czech government, and a number of NGOs, including La Strada, which has been working to prevent human trafficking since 1995. Another major UN funded and managed anti-trafficking project was implemented between November 2002 and May 2004. Within the framework of this project, the *National Strategy Against Human Trafficking* was drafted and approved by the government. The Victim/Witness Assistance Program has also been developed and implemented.

The Ministry of the Interior, along with specialised police units and NGOs work closely together in identifying victims of human trafficking. Both district and regional local authorities have also been mobilised to provide guidance and support to regionally based NGOs and other civil society members that aid in the identification of victims. They then ensure that once victims have been identified, they are referred to the proper services. The government contributes funds which are used to aid in the identification of victims and assistance, protection and voluntary return and reintegration in their home countries.

Awareness-raising seminars have been organised for both the local public administration and civil society, and a special information and awareness-raising campaign, focused on reduction of demand for sexual services, has been prepared in order to inform clients about the phenomenon of human trafficking, and also to motivate them to notify the proper organizations about suspected trafficking cases.

Furthermore, several resources are now available because of this initiative: an information leaflet for potential victims has been developed and other materials are being developed for different actors in order to guide them on how to deal with victims of trafficking. Training schemes for specific police units, with special attention to alien and border police, have also been developed and implemented. Finally, telephone hot-lines run by NGOs have been established.

Outcomes/Evaluation
The project has long-term goals and as such, it has not been evaluated yet. The preparatory UN project has already been independently evaluated with preliminarily positive results. Another project funded by the European Union's PHARE programme is underway to, inter alia, further develop and enhance anti-trafficking activities.

Partners
Government, the police, NGOs, local public administration, and local civil society.

Safe Community

Context
Property crime is a long term serious problem in the Czech Republic and its level increases the feeling of insecurity among citizens. Both safety and a feeling of security may be easily increased by using appropriate protective technical devices (defense and paralyzing sprays, alarms, etc.) and allying rules of safe behavior. The information about appropriate technical devices and patterns of safe behavior is not always well known by the broad public and local communities. Providing appropriate knowledge and information to citizens and communities is the way to considerable reduction of property crime.

The role of property crime in the overall crime situation in the Czech Republic can be highlighted by the following statistic on the type of offence for 2003:

Property Crime	70.8%
Economic Crime	8.8%
Violent Crime	6.3%
Sex. Crime	0.5%
Other	13.6%

These numbers demonstrate unambiguously that property crime is the most common type of offence.

Goal
The goal of the program is to minimize the conditions for committing crime by accessible organizational, building and technical means and by other measures (situational prevention).

Project Details
The Safe Community Program has been launched by the Ministry of the Interior and the Police of the Czech Republic with private partners. The program was discussed and adopted at the session of the Advisory Board for the Situational Prevention of Crime of the Ministry of the Interior in September 2001.

The program has the form of a nationwide long-term prevention scheme aimed at the protection of property and persons. The program is based on supporting citizens' initiative and their resolution to defend themselves against property crime. Both general information and specific business proposals are delivered to those who apply for participation in the program. The program is widely publicized in order to attract more citizens and communities (the typical applicant is an inhabitant of a high rise building).

The program offers to citizens and organizations interested
1. basic information on safeguarding of property, rules of the safe behavior and contacts to police advisory service for prevention
2. information on certificated technical means and companies' services tailored to local situation
3. optimal insurance companies' products.

The program is nationwide but proposals provided to applicants are tailored to local situation, need, requests and available funds of the applicant. Citizens or local communities send their application to the Ministry of the Interior. Applications are distributed to local police prevention services who provide the applicant with a prevention information kit, including contacts to the local police prevention service and police advisory offices. A copy of the application is directed to the Association of Technical Security Services – Gremium Alarm which contacts the applicant. After analyzing the local situation and the applicants' needs and means, a tailored prevention plan is offered, often in different options. It is up to the citizen decision to buy some of the offered products. When the product is purchased, the applicant is offered special insurance bonuses.

The pilot project was financed by the Generali Insurance Company (200,000 CZK). Particular applications are financed by cooperative building societies and persons concerned.

Outcomes/Evaluation
The whole Safe Locality program has been composed of 26 applications (projects). From them the pilot project Safe House has been evaluated only. Inhabitants of three Prague high-rise houses have evaluated the influence of the program. The form of the questionnaire survey has been used.

Partners

The Ministry of the Interior of the Czech Republic, the Police of the Czech Republic, the Prague Municipal Police, the Association of Technical Security Services – Gremium Alarm, the Czech Association of Insurance Companies, the Association of Private Security Services, Bank Association, the White Circle of Safety, certification authorities and testing facilities.

- Ministry of the Interior and Police – expert supervision and registration.
- The Czech Association of Insurance Companies – offer special program for »clients« included in Safe Community Program.
- Association of Technical Security Services – guarantee of product quality and technical certification of products, etc.

Jörg Bässmann
Federal Criminal Police Office, Wiesbaden, Germany
Evaluation as an Element of Systematic Crime Prevention in Germany

– A brief outline of the problems –

The 2004 annual report by the German Forum for Crime Prevention (Deutsches Forum für Kriminalprävention) states that »- in contrast to English-speaking countries – evaluation of prevention projects is still not the rule in Germany«[93]. This statement is true even though the issue of evaluation has been given extensive attention in Germany since publication of the First Periodical Report on Crime and Crime Control in Germany (Erster Periodischer Sicherheitsbericht). The following examples support this observation:

- The general police concept on evaluation (Rahmenkonzept Evaluation) of 17 October 2002 and the police evaluation guide (Arbeitshilfe für die Evaluation) published in 2003, which provides a model strategy that police officers can follow to help ensure that the prevention projects they conceive and design can be evaluated.
- The Baden-Württemberg initiative for promoting youth crime prevention (Förderinitiative Jugendkriminalprävention), which in 2004/2005 is providing one million euros of support to a total of 108 prevention projects. Projects are eligible for grants if they not only work systematically as described in the police evaluation guide, but also document their project work in the PrävIS database[94].
- The creation of a German award for the promotion of crime prevention (Deutscher Förderpreis Kriminalprävention) with a EUR 50,000 purse and a ten-year timescale under the auspices of the Federal Min-

---
[93] Deutsches Forum für Kriminalprävention (ed.): Jahresbericht 2004 (2004 annual report), Bonn, January 2005, p. 21.
[94] http://www.praevis.de; a database for the documentation of prevention-related projects, campaigns, bodies etc.

ister of Justice and president of the board of trustees of the German Forum for Crime Prevention foundation, Ms Zypries. The incentives related to this prize, which was awarded for the first time in 2004, are meant to engender a lasting motivation for crime prevention players to work systematically, and to produce and evaluate projects and results that can be used as benchmarks for future projects.

- The local crime prevention manual (Leitfaden Kommunale Kriminalprävention) published in 2004 by the North Rhine-Westphalian Prevention Council (Landespräventionsrat), which aims at supporting the planning, implementation and evaluation of crime prevention projects. At the same time, the North Rhine-Westphalian police have established a central evaluation unit (Zentralstelle Evaluation – ZEVA) at the state criminal police office. This unit is to provide advice and support to police authorities in evaluation matters, establish contact between police services and universities, develop evaluation criteria further and contribute to basic and advanced evaluation-related training. In January 2005, ZEVA – with the participation of scientists – conducted a workshop on developing standards both for choosing evaluators and for evaluating the impact of prevention measures.

- The AGIS-funded Beccaria Project of the Lower Saxony Prevention Council (Landespräventionsrat), which – in co-operation with partners from Belgium, France, Denmark, the Czech Republic and Estonia – not only focuses on defining evaluation standards and creating the framework for a glossary of evaluation-related terms, but in particular also takes into account the need to provide persons involved in crime prevention with special qualifications by developing an evaluation-related training programme and a part-time master's degree course.

- The »Düsseldorf expertise« (Düsseldorfer Gutachten) prepared for the city of Düsseldorf, a secondary analysis of national and international research on the impact of crime prevention endeavours, which is to guarantee that in the future the limited funds available for crime prevention will be assigned only to those prevention projects and measures that have a measurable impact on crime.

- A project by the German Forum for Crime Prevention in co-operation with Prof. Lösel, Erlangen-Nuremberg University, provides German stakeholders with international meta-evaluation studies by the

Campbell Collaboration on Crime and Justice in order to improve the knowledge base for effective crime prevention work. By now, summaries in German are available on the issues of video surveillance and social competence training for children. Another six synopses are planned for 2005.

However, referring to the efforts made in Germany as a substantial progress towards evidence-based systematic crime prevention would be an exaggeration. There are still hardly any mechanisms for ensuring that effective and innovative prevention approaches are systematically identified, tested in practice and then introduced in a professional manner. It might be assumed that the aforementioned examples prove the contrary. However, they do not, as will be demonstrated by the examples below.

Since there is a lack of evaluation studies from German-speaking countries, planning stages of projects usually also rely on data from abroad. Although it is important that such information is at hand in sources such as the »Düsseldorf expertise«, summaries of Campbell meta-evaluations or the »Infopool Prevention«[95], in many cases the general summaries available in German only provide the apparently most important research findings, which would also often require assessment as to whether they are applicable in a specific German context. They cannot replace high-quality evaluations in Germany. Thus, there is a lack of reliable data on which crime prevention planning in Germany could be based.

In addition, for the most part Germany also lacks efficient mechanisms for crime prevention management. An exception to this is the aforementioned Baden-Württemberg initiative on the promotion of youth crime prevention. Only those projects are eligible for grants that structure their work in accordance with a predetermined strategic model and furthermore document the project in the PrävIS database, which is available nationwide. In contrast to the otherwise common steering strategy, where at least the ministries of the interior usually rely on the effectiveness of requirements established at state level (e.g. in the form

---

[95] »Infopool Prävention«, a collection of information on crime prevention projects in Germany and other countries.

of decrees), this initiative offers financial incentives to the potential local project partners to work on a specific subject in accordance with predefined standards – a method that is common practice in the UK or US. However, such methods should also be evaluated under process aspects.

The list of weaknesses continues with the implementation stages. In this field, the typical German method, at least under the jurisdiction of the ministries of the interior, is to order (through provisions, decrees etc.) that certain targets, such as the introduction and work of local prevention bodies, be met and to trust in principle that this will actually be done. Such a method is at most less than ideal since some of the preconditions necessary for successful prevention are lacking at the implementation level. An example of this is the police evaluation guide, which provides the police with theoretical information about how to conceive, implement and also evaluate quality-oriented prevention projects. These guidelines, however, are not always self-explanatory, i.e. in order to apply them, practical help as well as basic and advanced training are required. Currently, there appears to be only limited assistance and training. The aforementioned Baden-Württemberg initiative for the promotion of youth crime prevention, for instance, included training measures. The North Rhine-Westphalian police also rely on training through their central evaluation unit. The British authorities have gone one step further. When they obliged local crime and disorder reduction partnerships by law to develop three-year strategies for reducing crime and disorder, the Home Office also provided the instruments required for fulfilling the tasks. One of the measures was to have external service providers[96] supply the expertise the partnerships themselves were lacking, for instance for auditing or development of strategies.

In addition to the weaknesses in crime prevention planning and implementation, the literature on this subject has frequently highlighted the weaknesses in the evaluation process itself. When looking closely at the issue it is almost impossible to avoid the impression that both federal and state governments still seem to believe evaluation in the field of crime prevention can be carried out at no cost at all. They com-

---

[96] These include the Home Office and, above all, Crime Concern and NACRO.

pletely fail to realise that the cost of high-quality scientific evaluation is worthwhile since it is the only way to obtain valid assessments of processes and impacts. Thus, for some time German crime prevention has nearly ignored the trend in English-speaking countries towards using high-quality evaluations to carry out cost-benefit analyses.[97] However, precisely such studies[98] would be able to convince national and local treasurers that investment in crime prevention measures can in fact pay off, even in financial terms. Such studies furthermore supply planning bodies with additional information that may help them choose the appropriate option for action. A current international example for this is the British »Crime Reduction Programme« started in 1999. It was initiated following a national spending review, and 10 per cent of the originally assigned programme budget of 250 million pounds was designated for evaluation purposes. The objective of this so-called evidence based policy programme (EBPP) was to generate knowledge about innovative approaches to crime reduction with a sustained impact in order to make crime control more effective in the future, even from a costs-and-benefits perspective. In the meantime, numerous interesting case studies and overall reviews of the programme[99] have been published. These studies not only highlight cost-benefit effects[100], but are also an important point of reference for future planning and implementation of crime prevention interventions by state and federal bodies in Germany.

---

[97] However, the Federal Criminal Police Office (BKA) has been co-operating for some time with Darmstadt Technical University (Prof. Entorf/Mr Spengler) on the issue of »costs of crime in Germany«.

[98] As an example cf. »Costs and Benefits of Preventing Crime« by Welsh, Farrington and Sherman (ed.), Westview Press 2001.

[99] Cf. Homel, Peter; Nutley, Sandra; Webb, Barry; Tilley, Nick: Investing to deliver: reviewing the implementation of the UK Crime Reduction Programme. Home Office Research Study 281. London, December 2004, and Homel, Peter; Nutley, Sandra; Webb, Barry; Tilley, Nick (Homel et al. [b]): Making it happen from the centre: managing for the regional delivery of local crime reduction outcomes. Home Office Online Report 54/04. London 2005.

[100] On this issue particularly cf. Bowles, Roger/Pradiptyo, Rimawan: Reducing Burglary Initiative: an analysis of costs, benefits and cost effectiveness. Home Office Online Report 43/04. London 2004.

Anja Meyer, Volkhard Schindler, Jörg Bässmann, Erich Marks and Ruth Linssen

The Beccaria Standards for Ensuring Quality in Crime Prevention Projects

In the long term, a common European approach to planning, implementing and evaluating crime prevention projects is needed. The European Commission believes this is necessary, in order to improve the quality of crime prevention projects and to make a standardized comparison between states possible[101]. A common European approach is dependent on a common conceptual framework and therefore a common basic understanding of what is meant by an orientation towards more quality in crime prevention. Furthermore, in an international context, questions concerning the transferability of projects to other societies with a different cultural background, different social structures and different institutions have not been sufficiently clarified yet. A common obligatory standard is the only way to create a basis for a systematic exchange of knowledge and experiences in crime prevention.

Such standards make it possible to combine general experience with the results of individual projects as well as to analyse outcomes and therefore to identify cases of best practice. We need a common, mandatory standard for practical crime prevention work. This will help make it possible to determine how crime prevention projects have to be laid down and implemented and which central aspects and working phases have to be taken into account.

---

[101] Please see: Kommission der Europäischen Gemeinschaften: Mitteilung der Kommission an den Rat und das Europäische Parlament. Kriminalprävention in der Europäischen Union, Brüssel, den 12.03.2004, p. 17, also see: United Nations Guidelines for the Prevention of Crime – 2002; at www.prevention.gc.ca/en/about us/guidelines

Such standards will help to further develop crime prevention, to increase its effects as well as to secure its efficient use. In order to assure the correct application of such standards, some corresponding preconditions have to be created, for example in terms of the availability of advice for crime prevention practitioners. In Germany as well as throughout Europe, we are still far away from a common approach, from a commonly accepted and applied standard in planning, implementing and evaluating crime prevention projects. The Beccaria standards for quality safety in crime prevention therefore have two objectives:

First of all, the standards are a contribution towards achieving an increased orientation towards quality in crime prevention in Germany. In this context, the application of the Beccaria standards has to be strongly promoted among crime prevention practitioners. However, the standards should not be considered complete yet. They will be continuously developed according to the experiences had in applying the standard during practical work. Another objective is to make the Beccaria standards part of the European discussion on quality safety in crime prevention. An appropriate circle for this discussion on the European level would be the European Crime Prevention Network (ECPN) or the European Forum for Urban Safety (EFUS). The Beccaria standards are also meant to become part of a common European conceptual framework for knowledge-based and quality-oriented crime prevention.

The Beccaria standards include measures and requirements for quality planning, execution and assessment of crime prevention programmes and projects[102]. They apply to the following seven key steps of a project:

1. Description of the problem
2. Analysis of the conditions leading to the emergence of the problem
3. Determination of prevention targets, project targets and targeted groups
4. Determination of the interventions intended to achieve the targets

---

[102] In the following, only projects are referred to, similarly, the programmes are enclosed.

5. Design and execution of the project
6. Review of the project's implementation and achievement of objectives (evaluation)
7. Conclusion and documentation.

The Beccaria standards offer a manual for developers, players in the field and other people with responsibility in crime prevention to ensure the quality of their crime prevention work. Whoever is responsible should ensure that

- they align the planning, implementation and review of crime prevention projects with the quality criteria outlined in science and literature.[103]
- projects are designed in such a way that they can be evaluated.
- scientific experts, advisors, contracting bodies and sponsors are at hand to provide a technical basis for judging the project's targeting of objectives and quality.

The Beccaria standards describe an overall programme of requirements to ensure quality. A satisfactory guarantee for the quality of a project can only be achieved by complying with the overall programme. The individual requirements are always in step with each other. Selective attention or inattention to particular steps of the Beccaria standards would be detrimental to the level of quality.

The following points are to be considered and implemented along with the Beccaria standards:

---

[103] The main contributors to this are:
Ron Clarke: 7 Principles of Quality Crime Prevention, p. 85ff.
Paul Ekblom: The 5 I's framework: Sharing Good Practice in Crime Prevention, p. 55ff.
SARA: Scanning, Analysis, Response, Assessment, at www.crimereduction.gov.uk/skills04.htm.
Siegfried Preiser, Ulrich Wagner: Sektion Politische Psychologie im Berufsverband Deutscher Psychologen und Psychologinnen: Gewaltprävention und Gewaltvermeidung. Qualitätskriterien für Präventions- und Interventionsprogramme, in: report psychologie, 11/12/2003, S. 660–666.
Dieter Dölling: Zur Qualität und Evaluation von Kriminalprävention, in: forum kriminalprävention, 1/2005, S. 21–24.
quint-essenz: Qualitätsentwicklung in Prävention und Gesundheitsförderung, unter: www.quint-essenz.ch.

Beccaria standard 1: Description of the problem

1.1 The existing problem is recognised and precisely described in its current state. It is thus explained:
- What exactly the problem comprises, how it manifests itself, what kind of crime it covers.
- Where the problem arises in the defined area, over what time scale and to what extent.
- Who is directly or indirectly affected by the problem (description e.g. by age, gender, social characteristics, background).
- What direct and indirect effects the problem has.
- How long the problem has existed and whether it has changed (especially recently – e.g. growth, special reasons).
- Whether the solution to the problem is being worked on in a specific place. Who is working on it at present or who should work on it in the future (youth help, teachers, police, state prosecution service)? Which methods were chosen to solve the problem and with what degree of success?

1.2 Information is provided on who the initiative for the project came from as well as what prompted the project (e.g. complaints/reports from the public, approaches from the Youth Welfare Office or the suggestion of the police).

1.3 It has been well established by research that action is needed to solve the problem.

Beccaria standard 2: Analysis of the conditions leading to the emergence of the problem

2.1 To explain the problem in question, appropriate theoretical as well as empirical findings are taken into consideration.

2.2 The variables thought to significantly influence the incidence of the problem are considered and labelled – risk factors[104] as well as protective factors[105].

---

[104] Risk factors are influences that can be detrimental to performance, for example child neglect, youth contact with delinquent peers, deterioration of neighborhoods.

[105] Protective factors can hinder the emergence of crime. For example, stable emotional bonds between youths and their parents, alarm systems in parked cars, clear lines of sight and lighting of public places which are considered trouble spots.

Beccaria standard 3: Determination of crime prevention goals, project goals, and targeted groups[106]

In determining goals, a basic distinction must be made between crime prevention and project goals. The crime prevention goals and project goals of every project must be specified clearly and precisely.

Crime prevention goals (sometimes referred to as overall goals, global goals or general goals) are always directed towards the actual crime prevention concerns of the project. These concern the (objective) containment of crime (prevention and/or avoidance of criminal acts) or the improvement of subjective security (strengthening the feeling of safety as well as reducing the fear of crime). For example, the crime prevention goal of a project could be a 30% reduction in youth assaults in the school area of city A.

Project goals, in contrast, are the direct objectives for which a project aims. The following project goals could exist for a project with the crime prevention goal of reducing youth assaults in schools: improvement of the general school atmosphere, strengthening of pupils' social skills, especially regarding fights, and a higher level of social control in school.

Project goals must have a theoretical connection with crime prevention goals: in achieving a project goal, it must be possible to work towards the existing crime prevention goal at the same time.

The project goals can be demonstrated using criminological theories as well as theory-based assumptions or experimental findings: (to stay with the same example) »improvement of the general school atmosphere«, »strengthening of pupils' social skills, especially regarding fights« as well as »a higher level of social control in school«, in each case building an applicable crime prevention approach to achieve the crime prevention goal of »reducing youth assaults in schools«.

3.1 The crime prevention goals are specified. They are developed from the description of the problem, precisely formulated, measurable, and describe the ideal situation.
3.2 The decision is made regarding any particular groups the crime prevention goals are targeting.

[106] There can be one or more crime prevention goals as well as one or more project goals and target groups in a project. When describing the Beccaria standards, only the plural form is used.

3.3 There are definitive, measurable indicators that show whether (and to what extent) the crime prevention goals will be achieved.
3.4 Strategies or crime prevention approaches are chosen which are judged appropriate to achieve the adopted crime prevention goals. The choice of strategies or crime prevention approaches is explicitly justified. Perceptions from the literature as well as practical experiences should be taken into account. The project goals are defined in concrete terms on the basis of the chosen strategies or crime prevention approaches.
3.5 The target groups, the project goals refer to, are determined. Target groups are precisely specified (e.g. by age or social characteristics).
3.6 The time frame as well as the end date (costs over time) for achieving the desired project goals should be determined.

Beccaria standard 4: Determining measures to achieve the objectives
4.1 Appropriate measures are derived and justified to achieve the project goals.
4.2 The measures are considered appropriate for reaching the determined target groups of the project goals (e.g. can this be assured through the participation of the target group?).
4.3 The availability of important time, human, expert, financial and physical resources for implementing the measures is realistically set out.
4.4 Particular indicators are determined that show whether (and to what extent) the project goals have been achieved.
4.5 Particular indicators can be validated that show whether (and to what extent) the target groups can be reached.

Beccaria standard 5: Project design and implementation
5.1 The project design is set out in written form. It covers all the relevant considerations and plans which are essential for the establishment, running and review of the project.
5.2 The likelihood of collaboration (with partner organisations) as well as synergies are clarified. The networking is target-oriented, sustainable and well invested.
5.3 A resource plan is prepared which sets forth which time, human, professional, financial and physical resources are likely to be needed to implement the measures.

5.4 The term of the project is determined.

5.5 The project is appraised and checked by an external expert in the field and by a group (external or part of their own organisation).

5.6 The cost benefit of the project, how it arises from the project plan and the expected results and effects (and the targeted project goals) are checked and found to be beneficial as well as sustainable by those involved with the project and/or by some external, professional person/group. Practicable alternatives to the planned project can be appraised as an option.

5.7 Responsibilities for implementing the individual measures are determined. Agreements are put in writing between the participants (contractors, project planners, if necessary the target groups, and co-operation partners)

5.8 A project work plan is prepared with a detailed description of the individual work steps for those responsible and the time schedule.

5.9 A review of the implementation of the project (process evaluation) as well as a review of the effects of the project (evaluation of impact, if it is planned) is included from the beginning of the project planning.

- A process evaluation needs to be carried out. A plan for the review of the running of the project as well as reaching the target groups is prepared and included in the project design.
- The case is made for whether the attainability of the project goals and crime prevention goals of the project should be appraised (advance appraisal of effects). In the event that the evaluation is carried out, a plan of investigation is drawn up, and the evaluation plans are taken into account in the project design.
- The case is made for whether a self evaluation and/or an external evaluation is planned. In the case of a self evaluation, the requirement for external professional methodological advice is assessed.

5.10 The running of the project is documented from the very beginning; every step of the project is set out and justified, as are deviations from the original plan.

5.11 The structure of the project can adapt to changing conditions. Methods for improvement are determined and implemented if shortfalls appear.

Beccaria standard 6: Review of the implementation of the project and the achievement of its goals (evaluation)

6.1 The extent to which the designated target groups are reached is determined (number, proportion). Attempts are made to account for the degree to which the target groups were or were not reached

6.2 What changes occurred and to what extent they occurred is determined. How far were the targeted crime prevention goals achieved (from comparison between the actual and expected situations)? How far were the targeted project goals achieved (from comparison between the actual and expected situations)?

6.3 Whether and to what extent the observed changes can be attributed to the implemented measures is determined and reported. What can the achievement or failure to achieve the crime prevention goals be attributed to? Likewise for the project goals?

6.4 The occurrence of any unforeseen side effects is determined: If so, what effects and to what extent?

Beccaria standard 7: Conclusion and documentation of the project

7.1 A thorough project report is prepared at the end of a project. The main findings from the project are edited, conclusions are drawn, the end report is drawn up, and the project documentation as well as project results are made accessible to a professional audience.

7.2 The main project findings are brought together and edited:
- To what extent were the targeted goals achieved (project and crime prevention goals)?
- What do the results imply for the project?
- What can the achievement/failure of the project goals be attributed to?
- What difficulties emerged in the planning and implementation stages; which positive and negative lessons can be drawn?
- What other main findings could be deduced?

7.3 Conclusions are drawn from the experiences, results and findings of the project:
- Did the chosen approach prove of value? Is the approach applicable elsewhere?
- Which suggestions for improvement, recommendations for action or possible solutions for known flaws can be concluded?

- Are there particular problems which should be a.) the subject of future projects as well as b.) the subject of evaluation for future projects?
- Which project partners or other organisations could especially benefit from the results?
- Do the findings apply to an adaptation/modification of the existing project or to a further development of a possible continuation of the project?
- How could it be guaranteed that the project can be sustained for its planned lifespan (e.g. by integration in an existing set of arrangements)?
- Can the project be transferred to other target groups and social conditions?

7.4 A project report is written which outlines:
- Project design
- The implementation of the project
- Project results
- Results of evaluation
- A plan of evaluation, if necessary analysing a range and quantity of samples as well as indicators and criteria to review the achievement of the project goals.
- Conclusions.

7.5 The project documentation is accessible to others. The results of the project are published.
- At the very least, a summary of the project documentation is put in a database (for example PrävIS, a German database of prevention projects).

Appendix

PROGRAMME AGIS
Programme for the police and juridical co-operation in criminal cases

AGIS is the name of one of the five kings of Sparta. AGIS – the name is also used for the support programme for the police and judicial co-operation in EU criminal matters.

The AGIS Programme is continuing the measures of the programmes which expired in December 2002: Grotius, Oisin, Stop, Hippocrates, Falcone. It runs from 2003 to 2007.

WHAT IS THE PROGRAMME'S OBJECTIVE?
Goals are:
- To draw up, implement, and evaluate a European policy regarding police and judicial co-operation in criminal matters.
- To develop and strengthen networking, as well as collaboration and exchange; to spread information, results and best practice, to promote local and regional co-operation; to improve and adapt training, to advance academic research.

IT IS ESSENTIAL THAT
- The themes interest all the member states.
- The collaboration with new EU member states, other third countries and existing international or regional organisations is intensified.

MEASURES CAN RECEIVE FINANCIAL SUPPORT,
- Which deal with training and further education.
- Which comprise studies and research on the subject.
- Which promote collaboration and networking but also comprise conferences and seminars.

http://europa.eu.int/comm/justice_home/funding/agis/funding_agis_en.htm

Vitae of Authors

Prof. Dr. Britta Bannenberg, born in 1964, studied Social Law at Georg-August University, Göttingen; 1st university law degree in 1989; doctorate in Göttingen; dissertation on the subject of victim/perpetrator compensation: compensation in penal practice, 1993; 2nd university law degree in Hesse 1994; 1995–2001 academic assistant to Prof. Dr. Rössner at Martin-Luther University, Halle/Saale and at Philipps University, Marburg; postdoctoral lecturing qualification, December 2001. Postdoctoral lecturing qualification thesis: Corruption in Germany and its legal control, a criminological-criminal law analysis, Luchterhand 2002, BKA Bd. 18 (Police and Research Series.)

Since April 2002, she has been a professor of Criminology, Criminal Law, and Law of Criminal Proceedings at the University of Bielefeld. Research emphasis on corruption: victim – perpetrator compensation, criminal violence, crime prevention. Co-director of the German Day of Crime Prevention (www.praeventionstag.de); member of the New Criminological Society; member of the work circle of German, Austrian, and Swiss Criminal Law teachers (current project: Reform of homicide laws)

Jörg Bässmann, born in 1962, Detective Chief Superintendent
Bundeskriminalamt, KI 14-Prävention, 65173 Wiesbaden
Professional career:
  1981: Graduated from secondary school, entered Bremen police force
  1984: Began work at the Federal Criminal Police Office (Bundeskriminalamt)
  Until 1987: Training at the Federal College of Public Administration
  1987 to 1992: Explosives investigator with the BKA crime scene unit
  1992 to 1995: Work in the field of federal/state co-ordination
  Since 1995: Work in the field of crime prevention for the BKA Institute of Law Enforcement Studies and Training (Kriminalistisches Institut)
Work focuses on gathering, documenting and publishing German and international good-practice concepts for crime prevention and on further developing documentation standards in this field. Additional activities concentrated on community policing/crime control, in particular in the US, the UK and the Netherlands.

Dr. Harold K. Becker is Professor Emeritus at the Department of Criminal Justice at California State University, Long Beach. His doctorate is in criminology from the University of California, Berkeley. He holds a master's degree in public administration and a baccalaureate degree in economics from the University of Southern California.

Dr. Becker is a consultant to the U.S. National Institute of Justice, Research and Evaluation Technical Assistance; and a peer reviewer for the Bureau of Justice Assistance, Discretionary Grant Program. He is a principal consultant for evaluating high school and middle school community policing partnership programs, 2000–05; researching anti-gang measures of local law enforcement agencies within California, 2003–04; studying fifty years (1950–99) of homicide reported by the Los Angeles Police Department, 2001–02; evaluating multi-jurisdictional drug task forces in California, 1998–99; conducting a three year study to identify solutions for curtailing gangs, violence and drugs in the Los Angeles County Schools and an evaluation of socioeconomic and behavioural data on Latino street gangs in Los Angeles County, 1998–01.

Publications include »Community Policing: The U.S. Experience,« pp.157–186 in Criminal Justice Research: Inspiration, Influence and Ideation, ed. by Ian K. McKenzie and Ray Bull. Aldershot, England, Ashgate publisher, 2001; »New Wine in Old Bottles: The Time Has Come for Therapeutic Community Policing for Youth.« International Journal of Police Science and Management, Vol. 3, No 2, 2000: »A Socioeconomic Comparison of Drug Sales by Mexican-American and Mexican Immigrant Male Gang Members,« Journal of Gang Research, Vol. 4, No. 4, 1997, pp. 37–47, (co-authored); and »Female Gang Members: A growing Issue for Policy Makers,« Journal of Gang Research, Vol. 2, No. 4, 1995. Article received the Frederic M. Thrasher award from the Journal of Gang Research.

Dr. Becker has travelled extensively in Europe and Asia to participate in conferences and present papers.

Radim Bureš, Ph.D., born in Prague, Czech Republic, in 1958. Graduated in philosophy, economy and sociology at Charles University in Prague, Faculty of Philosophy. Ph.D. in 1982. Worked almost 10 years as assistant professor at this faculty, teaching social science subjects including the Philosophy of Rights, Moral and Political Philosophy. Six-month scholarship to Oxford University in 1990, study visits to US law enforcement agencies 1997. From 1991–1993 the Head of the Department of the Philosophy of Education and Deputy Director of the Comenius Institute of Education – Czech Academy of Sciences.

Entered the civil service in 1993, assigned to the Czech Government Office for Legislation and Public Administration, now at the Ministry of Interior of the Czech Republic. In the present position as a Deputy Director of Crime Prevention Department is co-responsible for preparation and management of a crime prevention strategy in the Czech Republic.

Member of the Czech delegation to the United Nations Commission for Crime Prevention and Criminal Justice since 1996.

Participated in several international projects on crime prevention, criminal justice and human rights. Participated in working parties on guidelines for responsible crime prevention in Buenos Aires (1998) and Vancouver (2002). Czech national representative to the EU Crime Prevention Network (EUCPN). Extensive participation in Council of Europe activities concerning human rights, football-related violence and police ethics.

Since 1999 in charge of the preparation of a UN project on Trafficking in Human Beings in the Czech Republic. In charge of the unit responsible for drafting a Czech

National Strategy to Combat Trafficking in Human Beings and for implementing the above-mentioned project.

Author of a number of articles on crime prevention and human rights.

PROF. RONALD V. CLARKE, PH.D., is University Professor at the School of Criminal Justice, Rutgers University, and is also Visiting Professor at the Jill Dando Institute of Crime Science, University College London. Trained as a psychologist, he holds an M.A. and Ph.D. from the University of London. Dr. Clarke was employed for fifteen years at the Home Office Research and Planning Unit, where he had a significant role in the development of situational crime prevention and the British Crime Survey. He has held faculty appointments in Criminal Justice at the State University of New York at Albany and at Temple University, Philadelphia. He has been a Visiting Fellow at the National Police Research Unit in Australia, the Norwegian Police Academy and the U.S. National Institute of Justice.

He has extensive international experience and is regularly invited to speak at conferences and symposia held abroad. During the past five years he has been an invited speaker at meetings organized by the UN, Interpol and the EU in Austria, Belgium, Italy, Portugal, Sweden and the Netherlands, and by government agencies in Argentina, Australia, China, England, Finland, Israel, Norway, Spain, Taiwan, Turkey and the U.S. Dr. Clarke is the founding editor of *Crime Prevention Studies* and is author or joint author of some 180 books, monographs and papers, including *Designing out Crime* (HMSO, 1980), *The Reasoning Criminal* (Springer-Verlag, 1986), *Situational Crime Prevention: Successful Case Studies* (Harrow and Heston, 1997) *Superhighway Robbery* (Willan Publishing, 2003) and *Become a Problem Solving Crime Analyst* (Jill Dando Institute,, 2003).

PROF. PAUL EKBLOM, PH.D., read psychology at University College London, where he also gained his Ph.D. Since then he has mainly worked as a researcher at the UK Home Office (currently in the Science and Research Group), focusing on crime prevention. He was involved throughout its rise from obscurity to widespread recognition by practitioners and policymakers in central and local government and beyond.

Prof. Ekblom initially worked on a range of individual crime prevention studies, practical demonstration projects and consultancies, including police truancy patrols, shoplifting, a feasibility study of the ›Crime-Free Car‹, drink and disorder in small towns, and crime on the London Underground. He then spent several years conceiving and orchestrating the industrial-scale evaluation of the impact and cost-effectiveness of the UK Government's Safer Cities Programme on burglary, whose results strongly shaped the subsequent national Crime Reduction Programme. Prof. Ekblom has had extensive international involvement with EU, Europol, ICPC and UN, and was Scientific Expert on a Council of Europe initiative on Partnership in Crime Prevention. His present Home Office responsibilities focus on horizon-scanning, advising on Design against Crime initiatives and supporting the development of crime prevention as a professional discipline through knowledge management based on a rigorous and systematic conceptual framework, the Conjunction of Criminal Opportunity (www.crimereduction.gov.uk/learningzone/cco.htm), and a wider, process-based schema for capturing and transferring knowledge of good practice, the 5 I's (www.crimereduction.gov.uk/learningzone/5isintro.htm). He is currently also a visiting professor at Central St Martins College of Art and Design at the University of the Arts London, and the Adelphi Research Institute for Creative Arts and Sciences at the University of Salford.

JIM HILBORN is a Canadian health criminologist living and working in Estonia since 1996. He first came to Estonia in 1993 to promote the establishment of a probation service. His Estonian wife, Helgi Hilborn, is a psychologist who teaches in a social work program. She tries to translate his lectures and articles into the Estonian language. His background is in psychology, sociology, social policy and planning. He is interested in the development of crime prevention as an evidence-based profession. He is now working on a book, Crime Prevention Planning, which is being field-tested with students in Estonia. He recently did a review of the Crime and Disorder Reduction Partnership (CDRP) in Cheltenham, UK. He is a member of the National Community Safety Network in the UK. His clinical focus for the past decade has been on cognitive-behavioural offender rehabilitation. In collaboration with Professor Robert Ross, he has just released a revision of the Reasoning and Rehabilitation program and its literature review, Time to Think Again. In addition to an interest in crime prevention and CBT with offenders, he is working on a model of neurocriminology as one of the social cognitive neurosciences. He thinks that criminology and crime prevention are at the critical stage of becoming scientifically practitioner-based in the same way as medicine started to be in the late 1890s. As the criminal justice system becomes scientific as opposed to just being reactive and moralistic, he hopes that there will be more harm reduction and promotion of social inclusion.

DR. LARS RAND JENSEN is the Chief Constable of Odense Police in Denmark and has been Chairman of the Central SSP Committee of the Crime Prevention Council in Denmark since 1980. Born in Ålborg in 1939, he completed his law degree in 1963 and his history degree in 1966 at Aarhus University. Between 1964 and 1971, Dr. Jensen was employed by the police and prosecution authorities, and afterwards as a lecturer at the Aarhus Social College up to 1975.

Following that, he worked as head of the Crime Prevention Council until 1980, when he became Chief of Esbjerg Police as well as Chairman of the SSP Committee of the Crime Prevention Council in Denmark. This committee serves the cooperation and networking of social, educational and police tasks. Furthermore, he was a visiting fellow at the Universities of Cambridge and Oxford many times in the 1960s and 80s, and in the meantime is a member of the Council of the Social Science Faculty at the University of Southern Denmark/Odense University.

In 1992 Dr. Lars Rand Jensen took on the offices of Chief Constable of Odense Police and the Regional President for Fyn. He has published diverse books and articles on the topics of criminology, crime policy, social work, alcohol and drug abuse as well as alternatives to prison.

Vitae of Authors

ANU LEPS, born in 1979, is currently working as an adviser at the Criminal Policy Department in the Ministry of Justice of Estonia. Before this, she was first a specialist and then the Head of Crime Prevention Division in Courts Department in the Ministry of Justice of Estonia. From 1997–2001, she studied social work at the Tallinn Pedagogical Seminar and she subsequently obtained her Bachelor of Arts in social work at Tallinn Pedagogical University in 2003. During her studies she already worked as a social worker at the Tallinn City Lasnamäe District Client Centre (2000–2001), and she has done volunteer work (peer education) in reproductive health and sexual education at the NGO Sexual Health Association of Estonia since 1999.

MICHEL MARCUS is a judge and the Executive Director of the EUROPEAN FORUM FOR URBAN SAFETY, a non-governmental organisation with some 300 European member cities and regional authorities. The European Forum for Urban Safety endeavours to : enhance safety policies based on the triptyque » prevention, repression and solidarity« ; consolidate the role of cities and local representatives in local safety policy partnerships ; secure the place of local safety policies within the construction of Europe. Michel Marcus is the Executive Director of the French Forum for Urban Safety, Secretary of the International Center of Montreal on Prevention of Criminality, Consultant expert to the permanent Conference of Local Powers and to the Parliamentary Assembly of the Council of Europe, Consultant of the European Commission, Counselor of the Mayor of Dakar, President of the African Forum for Urban Safety, Member of ISPAC (International Scientific and Professional Advisory Council of the United Nations – Crime Prevention and Criminal Justice Programme), lecturer at the National School of Administration, Paris and at the Institute of Criminology of the University of Liège.

GORAZD MEŠKO, PH.D., is an Associate Professor of Criminology at the Faculty of Criminal Justice and Security, University of Maribor, Slovenia. He is the author of a book on the criminal lifestyle of Slovene prisoners (in Slovene, 1997), textbooks on criminology (in Slovene, 1998), crime prevention (in Slovene, 2002) and criminology (in Bosnian, with Petrović, 2004). He has edited publications on corruption in Central and Eastern Europe (in English, with Dobovšek and Dimc, 2000), a book on Slovenian criminology (in Slovene, 2002), crime prevention in Slovenia (in Slovene, 2004), youth violence in Slovenia (in Slovene, with Anzic and Plazar, 2004), and dilemmas of contemporary criminal justice (in English, with M. Pagon and B. Dobovšek, 2004). He has also published extensively on policing, crime prevention, fear of crime and insecurity, and local safety/security issues.

PROF. MAHESH NALLA, PH.D., is a Professor of Criminal Justice, Michigan State University, East Lansing, Michigan, USA. He has written extensively on private policing and a variety of CJ issues. He is the editor-in-chief of the International Journal of Comparative and Applied Criminal Justice.

DR. VOLKHARD SCHINDLER was born in 1959 and studied sociology and political sciences at the University of Tübingen where he graduated in 1990. He then worked as a scientific assistant at the research institute »Life-worlds of disabled people« from 1990 to 1991. From 1991 until 1998 he joined the Institute for Criminology at the University of Tübingen as a scientific assistant focusing on studies on long-term-recidivism. In 1994 he also made a research visit to the State University of New York Albany (USA). He was awarded a doctorate at the Faculty of Social and Behavioural Sciences at the University of Tübingen for his dissertation about »The victim-offender-link. About the structures of correlation between victim experiences and delinquent behaviour«. Since 1999 Volkhard Schindler has worked for the Central Police Crime Prevention Unit of the German States and the German Federal Government. His work currently focuses on the implementation and further development of evaluation in crime prevention as well as the conceptual development of police crime prevention in Germany.

PROF. LAWRENCE W. SHERMAN, PH.D., is the Albert M. Greenfield Professor and Chair of the Department of Criminology at the University of Pennsylvania, where he is also Director of the Jerry Lee Center of Criminology. He has designed and directed 25 randomized controlled trials on topics including police responses to domestic violence, restorative justice for victims of violence and property crime, police raids on drug houses, and prevention of drunk driving. In 1997 he directed a US Justice Department Report to the US Congress on PREVENTING CRIME: WHAT WORKS, WHAT DOESN'T, WHAT'S PROMISING. He has been elected President of the International Society of Criminology (2000–2005), the American Society of Criminology (2001–2002), the American Academy of Political and Social Science (2001–2007), and the Academy of Experimental Criminology (1999–2001). He also serves as Director of the Justice Research Consortium of the United Kingdom, which includes New Scotland Yard, H.M. Prison Service and the National Probation Service.

ANDREJ SOTLAR is a senior lecturer on security systems at the Faculty of Criminal Justice and Security, University of Maribor, Slovenia. His research interest concerns, in addition to contemporary safety and security issues, also private policing in Europe.

THE BECCARIA TEAM consists of Erich Marks, Director of the Lower Saxony Crime Prevention Council and also project leader, as well as Dr. Anja Meyer and Dr. Ruth Linssen, the project managers. Since December 2003 they have been carrying out the AGIS Project »Beccaria – Quality Management in Crime Prevention« at the Lower Saxony Crime Prevention Council, and are organizers of the 1st European Beccaria Conference in Hanover.

ERICH MARKS is the Director of the Lower Saxony Crime Prevention Council. After studying educational theory, psychology and philosophy at the University of Bielefeld, he became the founding director of »Brücke Köln«, an association providing youth support, where he worked from 1979 to 1983. Subsequently he worked as the federal director of DBH, a professional association for social work and criminal justice policy, until 2001. Between 2001 and 2002 he acted as the founding director of the German Forum for Crime Prevention Foundation (Stiftung Deutsches Forum für Kriminalprävention – DFK), until he transferred to the Lower Saxony Ministry of Justice in 2002.

Vitae of Authors

Erich Marks holds various honorary posts, including one as founding director of the German Foundation for Crime Prevention (Deutsche Stiftung für Verbrechensverhütung und Straffälligenhilfe – DVS) since 1983 and one as managing director of the annual German Crime Prevention Congress (Deutscher Präventionstag – DPT) since 1995. He is an honorary member of the Conférence Permanente Européenne de la Probation (CEP) and member of the Executive Committee of the European Forum for Urban Safety (EFUS).Currently he is focusing on crime prevention management, training and upskilling, crime prevention strategies and policy.

Dr. Anja Meyer joined the Crime Prevention Council at the Ministry of Justice of Lower Saxony in 2002. Since 2003 she has been responsible for the »Beccaria Project – Quality in Crime Prevention«, which is also supported by the EU.

After graduating with a degree in social sciences from the University of Göttingen with a focus on criminology, she worked as a scientific assistant at the KFN/Criminological Research Institute of Lower Saxony.

In 1993 she joined the Faculty of Law at the University of Halle-Wittenberg, where she worked as a scientific assistant until 1998 and was involved in the »Hallenser Biographiestudie« on youth violence.

In 2000 she was awarded a doctorate in social sciences from the Faculty of Social Sciences at the University of Göttingen for her dissertation on »The Autobiographic Interview as a Research Method in Criminology«.

Her current research and publications cover violence in schools, youth violence, qualitative social research in criminology as well as evaluation and quality in crime prevention.

Dr. Ruth Linssen, M.A., born in 1974, graduated with a degree in sociology, psychology and German language and literature studies at the Carl-von-Ossietzky University Oldenburg. From 2000 until 2002 she did her doctorate in sociology supported by the Konrad-Adenauer-Foundation. Her thesis focused on the portrayal of youth violence in the media associated with criminological theories. She then joined Prof. Klaus Hurrelmann as a scientific assistant at the Faculty of Health Sciences of the University of Bielefeld; in the prevention and health promotion section. Here she was a co-writer of the 14th Shell Youth Study and was also involved in a research project on the evaluation of prevention and consultation.

Since 2004 Ruth Linssen has been working for the Crime Prevention Council at the Lower Saxony Ministry of Justice, where she is a project manager responsible for the Beccaria Project »Quality in Crime Prevention«.

She also works as a lecturer in Sociology, Political Sciences and Communications at the Lower Saxony University of Applied Sciences for Public Policy and Justice at the Faculty of Police Sciences. Her publications include topics on youth, delinquent behaviour, violence, project management and crime prevention.